MACDONALD
His Life and World

P.B. WAITE
MACDONALD
His Life and World

John A. Macdonald.

General Editor: W. Kaye Lamb
Picture Editor: Paul Russell

McGraw-Hill Ryerson Limited

Toronto   Montreal   New York   London

MACDONALD: HIS LIFE AND WORLD

ISBN 0-07-082301-4

1 2 3 4 5 6 7 8 9 10   BP   4 3 2 1 0 9 8 7 6 5

Printed and bound in Canada

TITLE PAGE Macdonald never petitioned the College of Heralds for a coat of arms, but in his later years he used this unofficial heraldic bookplate, bearing the motto *per mare per terras* (by sea and land).

ACKNOWLEDGMENTS

Andrews-Newton Photographers, Ottawa, and the Rideau Club, frontispiece. Bell Canada, 140. Canadian National, 28. Confederation Centre Art Gallery & Museum, Charlottetown, 61 top, 96. Eaton's of Canada Limited, 179. Geological Survey of Canada, Ottawa, 154 all. Glenbow-Alberta Institute, Calgary, 95. Massey-Ferguson Industries Limited and Feature Four, 151. Metropolitan Toronto Library Board, 31, 34, 60 both, 125, 127, 143, 147 top, 164 top, 185, 193, 205. The National Gallery of Canada, Ottawa, 41, 88 bottom, 89 both, 115 (Gift of the estate of the Hon. W. C. Edwards, Ottawa, 1928), 145, 148. Notman Photographic Archives, McCord Museum of McGill University, 35, 46, 48 both, 49, 128 top, 157, 188, 189, 198. Nova Scotia Museum, Halifax, 172 bottom. Ontario Archives, 7, 12 bottom, 45, 62, 63, 68 right, 109, 147 bottom, 166, 183, 210. Parks Canada, 15. Carol Priamo, 12 top. Provincial Archives of British Columbia, Victoria, 128 bottom, 204. Provincial Museum and Archives of Alberta, Ernest Brown Collection, 159. Public Archives of Canada, Ottawa, title page, 9, 16, 21, 25, 26, 27, 38, 40, 44, 53, 55, 56 both, 61 bottom, 64, 66 both, 68 left, 69, 70, 77, 79, 81, 82, 86, 90, 94, 100, 101, 105, 107, 110, 117, 119, 120, 124, 131 both, 134, 138, 141, 146, 156, 160, 161, 164 bottom, 165 top, 172 top, 175, 195, 203, 207, 212 all, 214. Queen's University, Douglas Library, 17. Royal Ontario Museum, Canadiana, 11, 32, 36, 88 top, 174. Vancouver Art Gallery, 87. Vancouver City Archives, 165 bottom, 169. Vancouver Public Library, 37. Winnipeg Art Gallery, 99. Excerpt from *The Collected Poems of Sir Charles G. D. Roberts* reprinted by permission of McGraw-Hill Ryerson Limited.

Contents

Preface

I WAS ASKED to write this book, but it has been a labour of love. Having always enjoyed Macdonald and his times, it was not difficult to sit down and attempt, however ineffectively, to convey that sense to others. My colleagues will, however, see at once (as it is right they should) how cavalierly I have dealt with some important topics, in order to bring the book within the compass of 45,000 words or so. While lack of space has dictated many omissions, some subjects have been left out simply because we do not yet know enough about them. There is hardly anything in this book about the music of the time. It is true one still finds around old volumes of Beethoven and Chopin from Macdonald's time; Debussy's *Clair de Lune* was published in Paris in 1890; but it is very difficult to find out much about the appreciation and reception of music in Canada, outside of Gilbert and Sullivan operas, which were enthusiastically received, and whose tunes were everywhere.

There is a little more about literature. John Thompson read and enjoyed Balzac and Zola in French, as educated Haligonians often did, and Robert Louis Stevenson's *Treasure Island* when it came out in 1883. Macdonald recommended Charles Reade's *Put Yourself in his Place* (1870) for the sentiment suggested by the title, and he was always a voracious reader of history and biography and politics. He had clearly read Horace Walpole's letters, some of the best in the language. Most people in Parliament understood and laughed at allusions to Dickens. Edward Blake, for example, was frequently compared to Pecksniff in *Martin Chuzzlewit* (1844), whom he somewhat resembled; *Grip*, the great Canadian magazine of humour and satire, was named after the raven in *Barnaby Rudge* (1841). But no one yet seems to have studied the serials that invariably appeared in the newspapers, some of them awful, others not so bad:

> She is, indeed, supremely happy. The spring time of youth and love is hers, and no deeper heresy could have been whispered to her than the warning that such a spring time resembles
> "The uncertain glory of an April day" . . . .

This was from *The Duchess of Rosemary Lane*, whatever that is, in the Halifax *Acadian Recorder* of 1877.

Altogether, I have tried to paint this canvas of Macdonald and his age without niggling too much at detail, using a big brush and a wide palette. I have tried to put in an under-structure of political narrative, but the book's main emphasis will be on Macdonald and the society in which he lived.

I have incurred some debts. Richard Huyda of the Public Archives of Canada, Picture Division, and his staff have been most helpful. Professor G. V. V. Nicholls of the Dalhousie Law School has been kind enough to correct some few pages where I deal with law. Dr. W. Kaye Lamb, the editor of this series, has gone over the manuscript with me and made valuable suggestions. I hope I have reformed it judiciously as a result.

An old photograph of Brunswick Place, now part of Brunswick Street, Glasgow. This is generally accepted as the birthplace of Sir John Macdonald, but the identification is not certain. Old directories indicate that sometime between July 1814 and July 1815 the Macdonalds moved from Ingram Street to Brunswick Place, but whether the move occurred before Macdonald was born in January is not known.

P.B.W.

Halifax, August, 1974

1
Macdonald: the Man and His Ideas

JOHN A. MACDONALD was certainly no beauty. His face was hewn on rugged Scottish principles: a wide, full mouth with tucks at the corners; a large, inelegant nose, broad as a spade at the end, designed as much for digging as sniffing; a blaze of blue eyes set below bushy, dark eyebrows; a long, deep chin; and his whole face crowned with a mass of curly black hair that now, in 1867, piled more and more at the back of his head. Charles Langelier, who sat across the House of Commons from him for four years in 1886-1890, described him: "a pleasing voice, his eyes lively and his look pleasant, a charming smile, an enormous mass of curly hair, a slim build, his walk an elegant nonchalance, and a nose that made up his whole glory. Sir John's nose gave to his character an air at once mocking and artless. . . . " Distinctive he was indeed. If you had met him, all the slender, nonchalant six feet of him, you might well have wondered what sort of mind and character it was that made so alive that unlovely face.

If introduced to him you would be struck first by his soft voice, with a touch of hoarseness in it, perhaps the result of twenty years of public speaking, and perhaps too one of the more amiable legacies of years of drinking. You would be struck by his courtesy and good manners. Macdonald always believed in the forms of social behaviour, not only for what they were in themselves — the essential civilized dress of the human animal — but because they were a medium that made easier the transmission of thoughts and feeling. Not that he preferred manners to the man; he was too shrewd for that. But he

OPPOSITE Few of the earlier photographs of Macdonald can be dated with any precision. This striking likeness, with a hint of a smile and a glint in the eye, may be as early as any. It is thought to have been taken about 1856, when Macdonald was 41.

8

9

seemed to think that it was only rare characters who could manage life without them. So he would remember your name, and when you met him again he would smile and say, "Yes, we were introduced on such-and-such an occasion."

He tended to be punctilious in answering letters, often in his own hand, and he was to retain this habit for a long time to come. There is a letter of his written in January 1891 to a little girl in Prince Edward County, Ontario. She had written him for his seventy-sixth birthday to tell him that her birthday was on the same day as his. She also had a complaint, as so many of his correspondents did. She complained that a young fellow she had written to had never replied to her. Macdonald's reply is as characteristic of his forties as it is of his seventies:

My dear little Friend,

I am glad to get your letter to know that next Sunday you and I will be of the same age [!] I hope and believe however that you will see many more birthdays than I shall, and I trust that every birthday may find you strong in health, and prosperous, and happy.

I think it *was* mean of that young fellow not to answer your letter — You see, I have been longer in the world than he, and know more than he does of what is due to young ladies.

I send you a dollar note with which pray buy some small keepsake to remember me by, and

Believe me,
Yours sincerely,
John A. Macdonald.

It is this humanity, almost tenderness, about Macdonald that was the basis of so much of his popular appeal. He knew it, of course. He knew that popularity was power. But his personal charm was nearly instinctive. It was not put on or put off as political or other purposes required. He took men, and women, as they were, enjoyed them for whatever qualities they possessed. And his sense of humour was never far away. He would not have survived without it. His quick appreciation of the foibles of human beings did not seem to make him bitter, though he could at times be cynical. "There is no gratitude to be expected from the public," he wrote George Stephen, who

in 1888 seemed to expect gratitude, "I found that out years ago." You had to take men as they were, and the public as it was. And that was not usually as you would like them to be.

He had an often frank and sometimes disconcerting way of assessing people. John Hillyard Cameron was a Conservative colleague from Toronto. His abilities, Macdonald told a friend in 1854, were confined "to a good memory and a vicious fluency of speech." He remarked to John Carling, his Post-master-General, one day when cabinet business was over, "Carling, I wonder if God Almighty ever created a man as honest as you look?" Joseph Pope, who became his private secretary in 1882, once commented that J. J. C. Abbott (who was to succeed Macdonald as Prime Minister in 1891) had an agreeable nature and sweet smile. "Yes, a sweet smile," said Macdonald reflectively, "from the teeth outwards."

He was, in other words, genuine. At least, he was as genuine as his sensitive balance between good manners and frankness allowed him to be. And when he chose, Macdonald could be very forthright. "Dear Charlie," he wrote to one of his young cabinet ministers who wanted something unreasonable, "skin your own skunks." Yet he was often willing to

Kingston, Queen and Ontario Streets, with Lake Ontario in the distance, sketched by Colonel J. P. Cockburn in 1829, the year Macdonald's schooling ended. Many of the British Army officers stationed in Canada were competent water-colour topographers, and Cockburn ranked high amongst them.

The stone mill at Glenora as it appears today. The nearer part of the building with the gambrel roof was owned for several years by Hugh Macdonald, Sir John's father, when Macdonald himself was in his teens. It housed a grist mill and Hugh Macdonald also carded wool and dressed cloth. The enterprise was never a great success and he moved back to Kingston (and to a secure if modest position as clerk in a bank there) about the time that John A. was opening his law office.

For some years after he opened his law office in Kingston in 1835, Macdonald lived with his parents and sisters in this stone house on Rideau Street. The building still exists, was renovated recently, and is now a duplex.

admit when he was wrong. Dignity he certainly had, but it was a dignity unafraid of making a handsome apology when it was called for. The same young cabinet minister — Charles Hibbert Tupper — raised a row in cabinet in 1890 over the lack of enforcement of salmon regulations on the west coast. Macdonald asked him to hold off enforcement for a while. Tupper said he couldn't do that. Macdonald lost his temper, kicked the table, and said he would see whether or not. The cabinet backed Tupper. Macdonald came up to Tupper afterward and said, "I cannot tell you yet what was moving me, but you were right and I was wrong."

Macdonald had a temper and in the earlier years he could lose it. (In later years it was much more rare.) He may have permanently alienated his former student, a young and pertinacious lawyer — Oliver Mowat — in the Canadian House of Assembly in 1861 in Quebec City. After some accusation had been made by Mowat, Macdonald was so furious that the moment the Speaker left the chair, he roared across the floor of the House and shouted at Mowat, "You damned pup! I'll slap your chops!" And he would have, too, if Sandfield Macdonald and others had not got in the way. Mowat looked, and sometimes behaved, like the bright, plump little boy with glasses who was always in the front row at school under the benign eye of the teacher, while bad little Johnny Macdonald was, so to speak, with the boys at the back who got into trouble and occasionally were strapped for it.

Macdonald was good at baiting members on the other side of the House. He would deliberately sow dissension among opponents if he could. In the Grit party, and later in the Liberal party, there was no lack of opportunity. He believed that internecine warfare in opposition benches was as much to be fostered as party loyalty was to be encouraged on his side. So however good or bad Macdonald may actually have been in his days at school — the actual truth seems to have been that he was bookish but developing an inventive turn for mischief — in his mature years his inventive turn ripened handsomely. Even in 1874, when Macdonald was nearly sixty, *Grip*, the comic weekly, would portray him, not without justice, as the bad boy down the street who would tie two cats together to see how they would fight or pelt some passer-by with snowballs. Peace-loving he was not. On the other hand, Canadian society was pretty rough-and-ready, where a boy grew to be a man by learning to take it and, when necessary, to give it. The school-yard world was preparation for the real world. There were bullies in both places.

That was the kind of world Macdonald had grown up in. He was born in Glasgow on January 10, 1815,* of an ambitious but somewhat feckless father, Hugh John Macdonald, and a steady, capable and intelligent mother, Helen Clark. Mac-donald remembered only bits of his early Glasgow childhood; his character and development, like his accent perhaps, were shaped more by his family and by Kingston whither he came with his parents in the summer of 1820. Macdonald's accent was never the heavy one of George Brown or Alexander Macken-zie; it was rather a lilt on the tongue than a rasp in the throat.

He grew up in Kingston and in the country beyond King-ston; at Hay Bay, on the Bay of Quinte; at the Stone Mills, near where the Glenora ferry still runs across the lovely reach of water between Lennox and Addington County and Prince Edward County. Each move the family made was dictated by his father's hopes and ambitions and, equally, by his father's failure to realize them. His mother's strength and will helped to hold the family together.

From about 1824, when he was nine, young Macdonald was sent to school in the winter time. His French grammar is still in existence, dated Kingston, May 23 1825, by which time he was wintering and boarding in Kingston. He learnt to read French, and probably read it well enough by the time he was in politics in the 1840s. That he ever spoke it with any fluency is doubtful. He also studied mathematics, history and Latin. His Latin in later years seemed serviceable enough, and his knowledge of history, particularly English history, rapidly ex-panded and developed.

In the long summers from 1824 to 1829, he would go back to the Stone Mills at Glenora where his family was then, and roam the countryside alone or with his sisters Margaret, two

*The official date given is January 11, and the one Macdonald cele-brated. The registry office in Scotland, however, gives Jan. 10, 1815. See J. K. Johnson, *Affectionately yours: the Letters of Sir John A. Macdonald and his family* (Toronto: Macmillan, 1969), p. 2n.

years older than he, and Louisa, three years younger. (His only surviving brother had died shortly after 1820.) Like many boys, young John Macdonald was pushing outwards in several directions at once, now immersed in a book, now walking the wooded hills. That country was beautiful; the forested hills of Glenora looked northward over the twelve-mile stretch of Glenora Reach, and eastward along Lake Ontario towards Kingston, some thirty miles away.

His boyhood ended soon enough. He left school late in 1829 at the age of fourteen, done with schooling for good. In Upper Canada there were no colleges he could have gone to; and in the rest of British North America there were only three English-speaking universities, McGill in Montreal, King's College in Windsor, Nova Scotia, and King's College in Fredericton. Dalhousie College in Halifax had been founded in 1818 but was moribund. Queen's was founded only in 1841, and King's College, Toronto, was as moribund as Dalhousie. Well-off people in Kingston, like the Cartwrights, sent their children to university in Britain. Charles Tupper in Cumberland County, Nova Scotia, did his M.D. at Edinburgh in 1843.

Bellevue House, Kingston, which Macdonald rented in 1848. Because this quaint structure, a fine example of the Italian villa style popular at the time, had been built by a well-to-do grocer, it was known locally by a variety of names, including Tea Caddy Castle and Molasses Hall. Macdonald himself called it Pekoe Pagoda in private but Bellevue in public. It was acquired by the Government of Canada in 1964 and has been restored as a period museum.

15

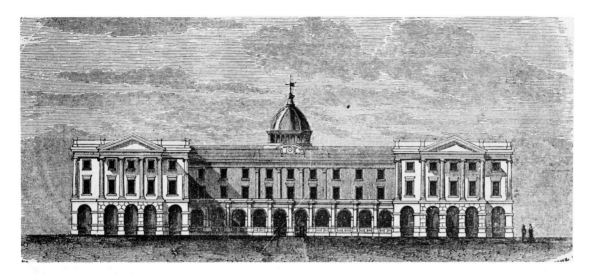

Osgoode Hall, Toronto, headquarters of the Law Society of Upper Canada, which granted Macdonald the degree of Barrister at Law in 1836. Only the east wing, to the right, had been completed at the time.

George Grant of Pictou County, Nova Scotia, later principal of Queen's, would take his divinity degree at Glasgow. But Macdonald's education was going to be quite home-grown. He sat his examinations for admission to apprenticeship to the bar at Osgoode Hall in Toronto early in 1830, and joined George Mackenzie's law office in Kingston as a young apprentice, aged fifteen.

When he went to Napanee in 1832 to take charge of a branch law office there, he was still a quiet, studious young man, with an adolescent uncertainty about himself and his place in the world. In Napanee this began to change, and the change was more marked when he took over his cousin's practice at Hallowell, near Picton in Prince Edward County. George Mackenzie having in the meantime died of cholera, Macdonald moved back to Kingston in 1835, set up practice there, and the following year, at the age of twenty-one, was admitted to the bar.

Macdonald's career after 1836 comprises a number of threads not easily separable, though in principle distinct enough. First of all, he was a lawyer and he remained one all his life. He never wholly abandoned law practice, though in later years his role became virtually nominal. His practice was a refuge when he was out of political office (and out of a salary), as he was from 1848 to 1854, 1862 to 1864, and from 1873 to 1878. Even when in office, the income from his law practice was a needed supplement to his official income. As late as 1880 he wrote his old friend, Sir Alexander T. Galt, that he wanted to secure if at all possible the Bank of Montreal solicitorship in Toronto for his firm. Although Macdonald enjoyed some professional success at the bar, it never seemed quite to engage his full energy or attract his whole interest.

That may explain the business side of Macdonald's legal career. It is an odd story. After six years of presumably profitable law practice in Kingston, he writes to Major Sadleir in Hamilton (who wants money Macdonald owes) that he is broke. "For the love of Heaven draw on me at 90 days at Quebec. I haven't got a shilling to jingle on a tomb stone." Undoubtedly Macdonald meant ready cash, that his money was all tied up. But it may also be true that Macdonald had not much of a head for business. Some of his colleagues thought so. Isaac Buchanan who had known him for years said in 1859, "I would not have supposed it possible that a man of so much intellect and versatility could on this one matter [finances] be such a child — " In this respect Macdonald may have been a bit like his father, apt to take financial matters without sufficient gravity, and on occasion even casually. His first law partner from 1843 to 1849 was Alexander Campbell. That partnership was wound up, and not without some bitterness, because Campbell was fed up with doing all the work while Macdonald was in politics, and perhaps even more by Macdonald's way of using the firm's revenues to finance current needs. After that Macdonald managed on his own for awhile. The main business of his firm then became, from 1850 into the 1880s, the legal work for a British association working in Canada, the Trust and Loan Company of Upper Canada.

By 1854, political circumstances compelled Macdonald to take on a new partner, A. J. Macdonnell. The arrangement served Macdonald well for a time, when he was in office for a decade from 1854 to 1864, but in the long run it was a financial disaster. His law partner got into financial trouble, borrowed, became fatally ill, died in 1864. As in all partnerships, then and now, each is jointly liable for the debts of both. The accounts of this firm were still in a tangle when Macdonald took another partner, James Patton, who was to last until 1878. It was only in the spring of 1869 that Macdonald discovered the full extent of the debt of the Macdonald–Macdonnell partnership. It was staggering. He owed $80,000 to the Merchants Bank and as late as 1881 the Macdonnell estate

JOHN A. MACDONALD,
ATTORNEY, &c.

HAS opened his office, in the brick building belonging to Mr. Collar, opposite the Shop of D. Prentiss, Esq., Quarry Street, where he will attend to all the duties of the profession.
Kingston, 24th August, 1835.   17ew

This modest announcement appeared in the Kingston *Chronicle & Gazette* on August 24, 1835. Macdonald was stretching a point when he described himself as an attorney, as he did not receive his degree from the Law Society of Upper Canada until February 1836, a few weeks after his 21st birthday.

still owed Macdonald $41,000. He mortgaged and sold what he could to the bank, and 1869 ended with Macdonald not worth a cent. The savings of forty years of work were wiped out. He borrowed $3,000 from David L. McPherson and started anew. This at the age of fifty-four. This in the year his second wife gave birth to a crippled child. Even a lesser man would have turned to a bit of drink.

A few years later when financial matters had eased slightly, he wrote his friend T. C. Patteson, editor of the Toronto *Mail*, who had had his own complaints about worries and debts: "Why man," said Macdonald, "do you expect to go thro' this world without trials or worries? You have been deceived it seems. . . . And as for present debts, treat them as Fakredden [*sic*] in Tancred treated his — He played with his debts, caressed them, toyed with them — What would I be without these darling debts, said he. . . . " And Macdonald repeated the advice two years later. "As to debts and troubles these come to us 'as Sparks fly upward' *Vide* Job *passim* — but they disappear like summer flies and new ones come. Take things pleasantly and when fortune empties her chamberpot on your head — Smile and say 'We are going to have a summer shower' — "[1] Macdonald had toughness. He needed it.

Macdonald was more than a lawyer; he was also something of a land speculator. This was not especially wicked; in fact it was common in days when interest rates were low, when the stock market was just getting started, and when land was about the only imaginative investment. This side of Macdonald's career has gone relatively unnoticed[2] but it was important for him. Otherwise he would have had nothing to mortgage in 1869. Macdonald had begun to buy land as early as 1842 at sheriffs' sales. Some of his purchases were wise, some not. They were not confined to the Kingston area either, but ramified all across Upper Canada. After the opening of the North-West he was still on the lookout for good land; though he personally did not buy as much, his firm did. The Trust and Loan Company gave it $500,000 in November 1881 to invest in good mortgages at six per cent. Many of these may have been in the West. In any case, Macdonald's son Hugh John moved to Winnipeg in the spring of 1882.

And he had other business interests. He had been made a

director of the Commercial Bank of Kingston in 1839, when he was only twenty-four. He was a director, and from 1864 to 1889 president, of the St. Lawrence Warehouse Dock and Wharfage Company of Quebec City. By 1888 he was president of the Manufacturers' Life Insurance Company. He was, in fact, a businessman. Altogether it points out a fundamental fact: there were precious few politicians who were not businessmen first, and last. Politicians had to live. Unless they held office in an administration, they had no salary. It becomes almost pointless to read Canadian history as if politicians had nothing else to do but politics. Politics was only part of their lives, and not always the most important part. The ordinary life of the people's representatives was business or merchandising or law or farming. Macdonald can be described not too inaccurately as a corporation lawyer, although the appellation is not usually applied to him. So can his famous French-Canadian colleague, George Etienne Cartier. Alexander Mackenzie was a stonemason, later a contractor, and after his defeat in 1878 he became head of an insurance firm. George Brown was a newspaperman; Samuel Leonard Tilley a druggist in Saint John. The list runs on, straight into the day-to-day life of ordinary people.

Macdonald's other careers were of course as administrator and politician. He was elected an alderman of Kingston in 1843 and, in the violent election of October 1844, a member of the Assembly of the Province of Canada for Kingston. He was appointed to the Conservative government of William Henry Draper in May 1847, first as Receiver General, then as Commissioner of Crown Lands. He resigned with his colleagues in March 1848 to make way for the Reform administration of Louis Lafontaine and Robert Baldwin. Macdonald continued to represent Kingston, though on opposition benches, until the return of a reinvigorated Conservative party to power in September 1854. Macdonald was then made Attorney-General West, responsible for that part of the province of Canada west of the Ottawa River — the Ontario of today.

From this time onward virtually to Confederation in 1867, with just two breaks, a week in 1858 and a year and a half between 1862 to 1864, Macdonald remained Attorney-General West. His administrative work is perhaps the most neglected side of Macdonald's life, as it is of the lives of most cabinet

OPPOSITE *Grip* published
this mock phrenological
chart of Macdonald in
April 1887, a few weeks
after he had won the
general election of that
year.

ministers. Departmental administration is a day-to-day, house-keeping routine that historians have tended to shy away from, though the records are there. There is indeed an enormous bulk of correspondence in departmental records from Macdonald that deals simply with departmental actions and business. This correspondence, being official, has survived rather better than Macdonald's private correspondence. Probably in the latter case too many people followed Macdonald's 1856 advice to Brown Chamberlin, the editor of the Montreal *Gazette*: "I hope you burn my letters. I do yours." Brown Chamberlin did not burn that one.

Macdonald was a conscientious administrator, and tough-minded in cleaning up his department where he could. He sympathized with C. H. Tupper in 1888 when the younger Tupper was to be the new broom in the Department of Marine and Fisheries. This urge for departmental house-cleaning, Macdonald told him, was natural and inevitable. Like the measles, you had to go through it. "I was," Macdonald added, "the devil of a departmental reformer when I began public life!" As Attorney-General, Macdonald was the chief law officer of the government in Canada West, and the position carried heavy responsibilities. A recommendation for commutation of a death sentence, as for executing it, had to come from the Attorney-General. In such instances Macdonald tended to follow jury recommendations to mercy, which were not uncommon in capital cases. But he tended to resist pleas for remission of terms of imprisonment. His belief was, and it was shared by most of society, that imprisonment had a sobering and chastening influence on wayward men, especially younger men. In one case, Robert Tweedy of Middlesex County had been convicted in 1853 of arson, of setting fire to a distillery. He had been sentenced to six years in the provincial penitentiary at Kingston. In July 1855, in reviewing the sentence, Macdonald reported that Tweedy had been habitually drunk, that the arson charge was clearly proved, and if he were to be released he would probably return to his evil ways. Since Tweedy was still young, Macdonald believed that "six years of compulsory labour and sobriety may wean him from his degrading habits and make him a useful member of society." In another case in October 1854, Macdonald, in recommending refusal of a petition to release a criminal, contended that the five years' imprisonment

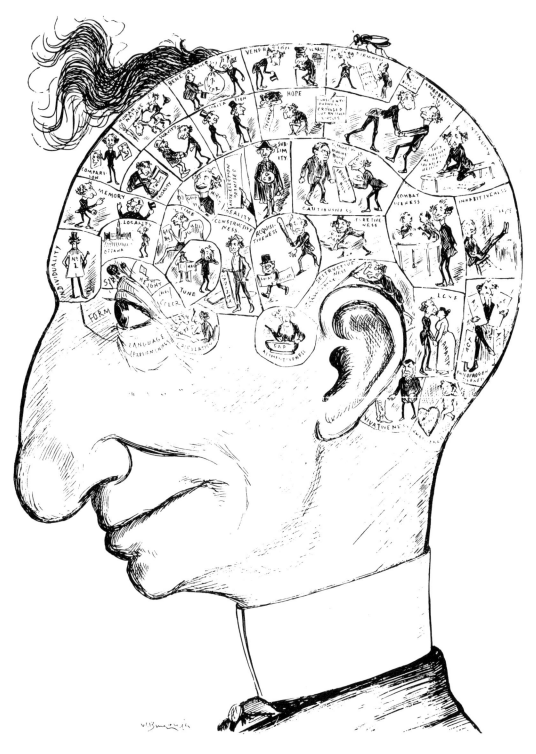

Phrenological Chart of the Head of the Country.

already served for rape (which was usually a capital offence) was an altogether inadequate sentence. Not only that, but it "would be felt so to be by the public." No law can endure without public support, nor can legal administration. It was a rough society, but it liked justice done and seen to be done. It expected crime to be punished, and by means severe enough to prevent, or at least to deter, others from doing the same. And Macdonald agreed with that.

Macdonald's best known role, however, was that of politician. When he first appeared on the political scene in 1844 he issued a statement of his position. Forget, he said, about abstract notions of what government ought to be. Concentrate on the country's development. The country needs work more than it needs motions in parliaments. In Macdonald's words, " . . . it is of more consequence to endeavor to develop its [Canada's] resources and improve its physical advantages than to waste the time of the Legislature, and the money of the people, in fruitless discussions on abstract and theoretical questions of government."[3] It is surprising how little Macdonald strayed from that basic philosophy over his long political career.

He never liked his politics narrow-minded. He never liked closed political or philosophical systems. Politics should not be conducted with strident convictions. He said in 1860 that politics required a cool head. Indeed, it required "an utter abnegation of prejudice and personal feeling." He reiterated this in years to come. A politician, he told Joseph-Adolphe Chapleau in 1885 (who positively revelled in factional infighting), can have no resentments. Forgive and forget. One of Macdonald's favourite sayings was, "It's done. There's no use crying over spilt milk."

However cool Macdonald's head, it was also fertile in suggesting arguments. He would use them almost detachedly, like a chess player making a deliberate move to forestall, or to provoke, a response. In a long letter to Sidney Smith of Port Hope just before the 1857 election, Macdonald outlined a persuasive set of arguments to counter Reform positions, and to allow the Conservative party to get both the Catholic and the Orange vote. Almost when one is about to believe Macdonald, when it appears he is brought to the point of stating a policy, he abruptly dashes it all to the ground in a five-word sentence. "These," he told Smith at the end of the letter, "are good bunkum arguments." Bunkum: something Macdonald always recognized, always used, and always distrusted, whether in speeches or in newspapers. "Mere newspaper articles," he would say, as if recognizing them for the propaganda or distortions they so often were. "We shall have a short and stormy session of the Assembly," he wrote James Gowan of Barrie in March 1861, "and we shall have little useful legislation. It is too near election time. [There was an election in early July 1861.] Experience has shown both in England and here that a moribund Parlt is a most unsafe instrument to handle. Party fidelity and all that kind of thing, gives way before the dread of the fast approaching appeal to the constituencies and the last Session is always devoted to bunkum."[4]

Notice the expression, "in England and here." Macdonald always read English politics with intelligence and interest and was frequently ready, when it suited his purpose, to cite precedents from Westminster. But that was not because he was an imperialist. He was never one before imperialism became fashionable, and he resisted it afterward. He was born a Scot but raised a Canadian. In his own way, at his own speed, with his own sense of appropriateness of timing, he was as passionate a Canadian nationalist as young Edward Blake. No, Macdonald read his English politics for its own fascination and for its bearing on Canadian parliamentary practice. He believed you could not be an effective parliamentarian without being well-read. Macdonald's complaint about John Hillyard Cameron, for example, was that however useful Cameron's legal intelligence might have been to the House, he lacked any general knowledge. He was, Macdonald said, "altogether devoid of political reading, so that he was altogether a failure as a statesman."

Cameron's other great weakness, in Macdonald's opinion, was that he was too impatient. He could not bide his time. If he had not learned it by the age of thirty-seven, he would never acquire a useful stock of what for Macdonald was that indispensable quality, patience. Patience. The world was not made in a day, or even two days. Nothing useful was ever achieved by haste, and much was done in haste that ought not to be done. Macdonald was largely unmoved by the excitement of new ideas. His mind was always seized at once with the difficulties of their practical application. He distrusted gusts of popular enthusiasm. Besides, society could not be changed that easily. Human beings could not be made into saints. You might reform this or change that, and some of these reforms and changes were desirable: but basically the human animal will work its way through or around any system. In the haste for change one might only change appearances of things, not the reality. And Macdonald was after realities. So he was patient. Alexander Campbell, his old law partner, told him half-admiringly, half-grudgingly in 1881, "You have a patience which I never saw equalled."

At its worst, of course, patience became procrastination. Distrust of popular opinion became inertia. The two combined to make Macdonald into "Old Tomorrow," a nickname he did not get for nothing. He thought the Métis in Saskatchewan in 1884 and 1885 were only after money; that whatever they managed to get from the government they would sell or drink. "No sir," he had said with conviction, "the whole thing is a farce." He was partly right, but only partly. It will not do to dismiss his opinion, but clearly other views of that agitation were possible, and it was rather typical of Macdonald at that stage of his life — he was seventy in 1885 — not to give those other views sufficient weight.

Nevertheless, his conservatism was not reaction, and in his younger years, in the 1850s, he had helped to build up the Conservative party by keeping it moving roughly with the times. He called it the Liberal-Conservative party. He even put it in one letter as "progressive Conservative."[5] He did not believe that a purely Conservative government could be created. Anyone who thought so was a fool. He was quite firm about this in 1861. Ever since 1854 he had been striving to make the party broad-minded. If once the liberal leading edge of Conservatism were abandoned, "the whole Reform party would at once re-unite and the Conservative party be [back] where they were when I took them up in 1854."

Macdonald's patience, tolerance and resilience were natural gifts; his personal life had been difficult and unhappy enough to temper and test them thoroughly. In September 1843 he married Isabella Clark. She is usually described as a cousin, but strictly speaking she was a half-second cousin; she and Macdonald had one maternal grandmother in common. Isabella is a shadowy figure. There is one portrait of her,

The only known likeness of Isabella Clark, whom Macdonald married in 1843. Within a year or two she fell victim to a somewhat mysterious recurring illness that kept her bedridden much of the time. Death threatened on many occasions, and Macdonald pursued his career under constant strain and tension. Isabella's death in 1857 finally ended what Donald Creighton has well characterized as almost a dozen years of "grey, unrelieved tragedy."

suggesting a lady of charm, intelligence and character. She was thirty-four years of age when she married Macdonald; he was only twenty-eight. After the first year of her marriage, Isabella became ill, then chronically ill, virtually confined to bed. Macdonald took her laboriously south to Georgia in 1845, travelling with painful slowness from Kingston in July and not reaching Savannah until November. In New York, on the way north in August 1847, she gave birth with the utmost difficulty — a forceps delivery — to a strong, healthy boy. She reached Kingston in June 1848. But she was not cured. She was never cured. Macdonald's marriage existed in the sickroom, with Isabella's tormented and sleepless nights, perennial opium treatments for her pain, and with her terrible lassitude.

In one of her few extant letters to her sister, she writes from her bed at Bellevue in Kingston in the summer of 1848. Her baby is asleep beside her. Her very soul is bound up with

Hugh John Macdonald, born in 1850, second son of Isabella and John A. Macdonald. This photograph was taken in 1871, when he was studying law at the University of Toronto. He had already served with the militia during the Fenian raids of 1866 and as an ensign with the Red River Expedition of 1870.

the baby. This is a sin, she knows, but she thinks it could be forgiven: "did I not purchase him dearly?" Her husband is downstairs entertaining company. He was always to be the lone host: there could be no hostess. Upstairs Isabella writes of her "weary, *weary* spirit."

The baby died quite suddenly in September 1848, cause unknown. Isabella gave birth to another boy, Hugh John, in March 1850 who did live. Sometimes her condition improved, sometimes grew worse. She came to Toronto to be with her husband briefly over the winter of 1856-57, for the Canadian Assembly met there from 1855 to 1859; but it was all a terrible struggle, and at last back in Kingston her weary spirit quite guttered out. Macdonald had managed to get there Christmas night, 1857; she died December 28th. He was left with memories of fourteen years of a luckless, sad marriage and with Hugh John, his son, almost eight years old.

The significance of Macdonald's tragic first marriage is hard to assess. Isabella's long illness drained him emotionally and financially. He had to call up his reserves of tact, forbearance, cheerfulness. Macdonald's family letters are full of "Isa," full of an almost terrifying determination to look on the best

side of things. With what pathetic care did he nurse those fragile little hopes of improvement! Macdonald's great biographer, Donald Creighton, attributes much of the worst of Macdonald's drinking habits to this inevitable quasi-bachelor life, to this lack of a vital and loving companion at home, to Macdonald's fundamental loneliness of spirit. It may well be so. But his rather happier second marriage in 1867 did not prevent him drinking, though it may indeed have ameliorated it. One tends to conclude that Macdonald drank because he liked drinking and the companionship that usually went with it. Macdonald was rather a man's man. He could be, and usually was, very gracious to women, but he seemed not to need their companionship much. If he had ever needed it, he had had to learn to manage largely without. When his first wife died in 1857 Macdonald was almost forty-three years old. When he married again in 1867, the lines of his living were too deeply carved ever to be sanded smooth. His salty, even scabrous stories, his wonderful gift for mimicry, the tremendous resources of that mind and intelligence, were to be applied to law, business and politics. And he would enjoy himself. If it was the only life he had, he was going to make the most of it.

Kingston from a lithograph by Edwin Whitefield, executed about 1852. It was one of a series portraying the five cities — Kingston, Montreal, Quebec, Toronto and Ottawa — that were at one time or another the capital of the United Province of Canada. Kingston was the seat of government from 1841 to 1844. The frequent change of location greatly complicated life for Macdonald, his fellow parliamentarians and the civil service.

The first railway in Canada, the Champlain & St. Lawrence, was not in operation until 1836, when Macdonald was 21, and he first travelled by rail in 1845. The locomotive shown here, christened *Toronto*, was built in that city in 1853 for the first railway in Upper Canada (Ontario). This was the Ontario, Simcoe & Huron, soon unkindly dubbed the "Oats, Straw and Hay Railway." It extended from Toronto northward to Allandale, near Barrie, and soon ran on to Collingwood. The *Toronto* hauled the first regular train to leave Toronto. The 1850s were the first important railway-building period in Canada. Ottawa was linked with Prescott by rail at the end of 1854, and by the end of the decade the Grand Trunk had completed a main line from Levis, opposite Quebec, to Montreal, Prescott, Kingston, Toronto and Sarnia. By 1860 the railway age could thus be said to have arrived.

2
The World of the 1860s

ONE IS TEMPTED to say that Macdonald's world was nearer to 1800 than to 1900. He grew up mainly in the 1820s, the immediate post-regency era in England, something of which was exported to British North America. Macdonald had always something of the urbanity, tolerance and sense of humour of regency England. The lack of seriousness which young Queen Victoria frequently remarked in her beloved Prime Minister, Lord Melbourne, was also to be observed in Macdonald. There were more than superficial resemblances between Melbourne and Macdonald. One rule to be observed in reading men in history is to look for the formative influences of their character in their early years. To read Macdonald in the 1860s as if he were a product of the 1860s is a profound mistake. He was not. Aware of the problems of the time he was, indeed, but his mind was furnished with habits and mores that came from a generation earlier.

Macdonald's own lifetime encompassed the first stage of the changes wrought by the industrial revolution: the railway, which Macdonald experienced for the first time taking Isabella south to Georgia in 1845; the telegraph whose cheap paper forms were a familiar part of the papers of many nineteenth-century politicians. The telephone came late to Macdonald's use, only in the 1880s, and would supersede the telegraph in a generation, worst of all, leaving no records. Gas lighting had made its appearance in the 1830s, and it was to remain the main means of illumination in streets and in public buildings until the 1880s, when electricity began to make its public appearance; but as late as 1886 it was sufficiently unusual that even in the London, Ontario, railway station, it was remarked upon.

These inventions carried in their wake profound social changes, although these took a long time to develop. The changes in manners and morals wrought by the inventions took sometimes twenty or thirty years to manifest themselves. The railway had perhaps the most immediate and far-reaching effect on the lives of people, as its nearly immediate impact on the politics of all the British North American colonies in the 1850s and 1860s was to show; but the concomitants of railways: the growth of cities, the effects on village industry and life, were still going on into the later decades of the century.

If you were to walk down the streets of a town or city in the 1860s you would be startled at the difference from the 1960s. Someone who had lived in the 1760s, on the other hand, would have recognized a world not too dissimilar. Changes much more wide-ranging and startling took place in Canada between 1860 and 1960 than between 1760 and 1860. Thus, walking down your 1860 street you would have been struck by the virtual absence of poles and wires, and the generally clean-limbed look of buildings and streets. A few telegraph wires were starting to make their appearance, but they were easily strung on the sides of buildings when needed. There were none of the great cribbings of wires and poles, necessary for electricity and telephone, that made hideous the streets of Montreal, Toronto, Winnipeg and Vancouver by the turn of the century.

The streets of the 1860s looked as clean above as they were dirty below. Asphalt paving was beginning in the United States and in Europe by the 1890s, but it was largely ignored until the automobile began to come into common use by 1910. If streets were paved, they were paved with cobblestones, and cobblestones were to last a long time. Saint John, New Brunswick, had cobblestoned streets into the late 1930s, *and* with dray carts going along them pulled by horses. Traffic is noisy now but it was not exactly quiet then, either. The iron-shod rims of those carts, plus two solid horses each with four iron shoes, on stone cobbles were not silent. Mostly, however, the streets were dirt. The mud in spring would eventually dry into dust. The dust in summer would be slaked with water, a mixture of gravel helped; and horse manure was periodically collected.

Surprisingly few streets were paved. But they did not need to be. A horse, or horses, can get a wagon through a good deal of mud. And paving with cobblestones was expensive.

Even as important a corner as Sparks and Elgin in Ottawa where the great old hostelry, the Russell House, had presided from the beginnings of Confederation until the fire of 1927, had no paving. A photograph of 1890 shows the stone crossings to enable you to get decently across the dirt, dust and horse manure of Elgin or Sparks Street. These stone street crossings were three to four feet wide and were periodically swept. In England, in Dickens' time you tipped a boy to sweep it for you. There is no evidence that anything of the kind was done here, but the principle is familiar. Similar crossings existed in Pompeii in Roman times, and the purpose was exactly the same.

By the 1890s concrete sidewalks did exist in main downtown streets, but in the 1860s plank sidewalks were almost universal. And there were not a few wood-paved roads, especially in places with easy access to timber, such as Ottawa, Quebec City, Fredericton. The Maritime delegates at the Quebec Conference of 1864 were not surprised at plank sidewalks but some did remark on the roughness of riding on wood-paved streets when the wood had rotted. Try, said a Halifax delegate, riding a caleche drawn by a lively pony and driven vigorously by a French-Canadian driver. *Bump-thump-jump:*

High water flooding the docks at Montreal about 1865. To the right is the large sidewheeler *Montreal*. She and her sister ship, the *Quebec*, in their day the finest steamers on the St. Lawrence, provided a comfortable overnight service between the two cities for many years. The famous Victoria Bridge, built to carry the Grand Trunk Railway across the river, appears in the background. It was completed in 1860. The carts in the foreground greatly resemble the Red River carts of prairie fame.

you bounced from one wooden timber to another, out of one hole into another, nearly shaken to pieces.

You had also to navigate wooden sidewalks carefully. They were slippery when wet, and positively leg-breaking if you went through a rotten plank to the dirt four to fourteen inches below. In the streets there were usually little plank bridges that took you over the drainage ditch at the side of the street and so across the dusty or muddy roadway; but not for nothing did Macdonald and his contemporaries wear what were called half-Wellingtons, a slip-on short boot that came up well over the ankles. How long, said a correspondent in the Ottawa *Citizen* in 1873, are we to have our main streets "covered with a sea of mud, through which we have to swim or wade when we want to cross?" No wonder mud scrapers were firmly fastened to veranda steps or to the stone steps at the entrance to downtown buildings.

Street lighting existed, though it was feeble enough. Gas companies had been established since the 1840s in Montreal, Toronto, Saint John and Halifax. The great fire in the Parliament Buildings in 1849 had been started, deliberately, from the gas jets. St. John's, Newfoundland, got its gas lighting in 1858. It was used for houses, too, though it was a little expensive. It need not be assumed that the gas functioned well. The Ottawa *Citizen* noted that Sunday night, October 26, 1873, in Ottawa was dark and wet and miserable and the street lamps "were in their usual condition, one tenth of the number not lighted at all and the remainder with just enough light to show where the lamp posts were situated." Such lights, the paper said, only served "to make the darkness visible."

Our interest in the look of towns and cities is a reflection of our own preoccupations as city dwellers in the 1970s, when seventy per cent of us live in communities of over 10,000 people. Only twenty per cent of British North Americans in the 1860s lived in cities or towns. The official definition of "rural" in the censuses of 1871, 1881 and 1891 meant outside of any incorporated city, town or village. Eighty per cent of Canada's population qualified as rural in 1871, and as late as 1891 the figure was still over seventy per cent. Canada was rural. Crops mattered. Alexander Mackenzie, Canada's Prime Minister from 1873 to 1878, attributed part of his defeat in the September 1878 general election to the bad harvest of that

month in Ontario and Quebec. He was equally ready to attribute the Conservative victory in the general election of June 1882 to three years of good harvests. Politicians' letters were as full of crop prospects then as they are of labour and business prospects now.

We misread our history if we take no account of rural life, or make no allowances for the slower pace of change there, or for its natural conservatism: the way, for example, that farmers' loyalties in politics tended to live on from one generation to another. One farmer did not get what he wanted, just before the election of 1891. He wrote furiously that he had always voted Conservative, his father had always voted Conservative, his sons were to have voted Conservative, but that if he did not receive satisfaction from the government, he would turn around and he and his whole family would vote Liberal until kingdom come. Elections sometimes affected people like that. Most did not change their allegiance; elections tended to turn on those that did.

It is not easy to get at the real characteristics of society, its manners, its morals, its ways of thinking and doing. It is easy to give an account of appearances. John Thompson, Macdonald's Minister of Justice, was invited to dine at Macdonald's home Earnscliffe on Monday evening, November 2, 1885. We know what it was like because he wrote his wife a description of the dinner and the people there. Lady Macdonald, he said, was very pleasant but "ugly as sin"; Lady Tilley was also there and "tried to be very pleasant and did not need to try to be ugly"; and other remarks that a man with a robust, sarcastic wit might make privately to his wife.[1] A beautiful house, and an elegant dinner.* But the nature of the talk, the manners, the atmosphere of the dinner is nearly irrecoverable. Yet unless our interests transcend the appearances of things, we remain antiquarians, not historians. In a profound sense, what Macdonald wore, the way the streets looked in his time, what Earnscliffe

*For those who would like to know, the menu was: Oysters on the half-shell / Consommé / Fish / Lamb Cutlets / Cabinet Pudding / Charlotte Russe / Lemon Ice / Fruit. The dinner would probably be preceded by sherry, which could also be served during the dinner. Claret was more commonly served than white wine, and the quality of a man's claret was sometimes taken as a general index of the cuisine as a whole.

Cutting ice on the St. Lawrence at Montreal. The large blocks were stored in insulated ice houses for use during the hot summer months. Mechanical refrigeration began to be available for the wholesale storage of meat and other food products in the later 1870s, but housewives had to get along with an ice box until long after Macdonald's day.

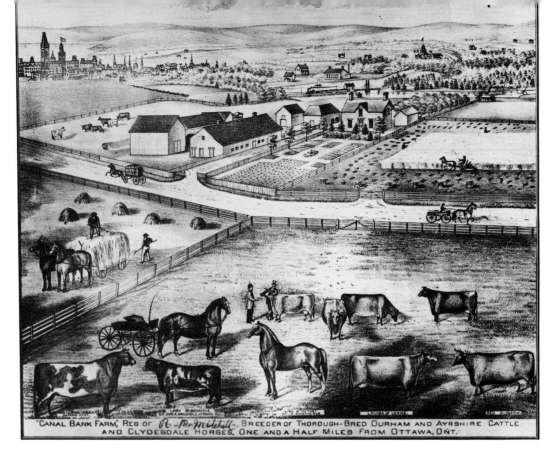

"Canal Bank Farm", Res of A. B. Mitchell, Breeder of Thorough-Bred Durham and Ayrshire Cattle and Clydesdale Horses. One and a Half Miles from Ottawa, Ont.

was like is irrelevant. It is interesting but it is superficial. What was his society and what were the ideas that made it what it was?

The answers to these questions take one straight into history. Some things can be said. One is that the word "Victorian" is wrongly used if it is meant to denote a narrow, rigorous moral code which, translated into political form, enacted sabbath laws, threw out the bars and saloons and tried to reform society by legislative means. These great reforms may or may not have been a good thing, but to associate their purpose and significance with the word "Victorian" is decidedly misleading. True, the beginnings of such movements are clearly discernible in Macdonald's time. They began because of real and palpable evils. But it was left to our Edwardian ancestors in Canada's age of reform, 1900 to 1920, to produce the effective legislation. It was, in fact, the viciousness of the saloons in the age of Macdonald, the ruthlessness of employers in the 1880s in forcing long working hours, in promoting child and female labour, the need for women to assert a political position from what had been a moral one, that produced the strong movements for

Canal Bank Farm, near Ottawa. In the 1860s and 1870s county atlases appeared that covered much of the populated area of Ontario. Each township was usually mapped in great detail, and in many instances the names of the owners of individual farms were shown. The township maps were accompanied by sketches of public buildings, private residences and perspective views of some of the larger farms. This example is from the atlas of Carleton County and shows a farm on the outskirts of Ottawa, which is visible in the distance. Various prize animals are grouped in the foreground.

35

Red River Carts on a Prairie Road by Adrian Neison (active 1877). The Red River cart was the usual freight conveyance on the prairies until the coming of the railway in the 1880s. A number of them usually travelled together, forming a train. Built entirely of wood, they were both light and strong and could carry loads of up to half a ton over rough terrain. With the wheels removed they could even serve as rafts for crossing rivers. The wooden wheels, without lubrication, squeaked and creaked unmercifully and the noise could be heard for miles across the prairies.

reform by the end of the nineteenth century. Victorian Canada in the years of Macdonald was a vigorous, lusty, hard-drinking place; the agitation for closing the saloons did not arise from nothing. The temperance movement started in New Brunswick in the 1850s, but its triumph was not complete until the end of the First World War in 1918. And what a short-lived triumph it was!

In Macdonald's time society was not used to having governments do much. Government's functions were limited because society believed that it was right that they should be. The attitude varied according to class, income and province, but overall it can be described as a wilderness of individualism with scattered and lonely shelters of charity along the way. You had to be prepared to look after yourself and yours, though the prevalence of fraternal societies is partly explained by the natural interdependence of most men upon each other. Bernard Devlin, the Liberal M.P. for Montreal Centre, supported, against his party, the idea of a protective tariff in 1876 to help the working men of Montreal and, as if that were not enough, actually went on to ask for direct government relief. He was at once rebuked by his fellow Liberal, A. G. Jones of Halifax. "It is an argument," said Jones, "I hope never to hear used in this House again; for the moment a Government are asked to take charge and feed the poor you strike a blow at their self-respect and independence that is fatal to our existence as people." That view was to be reasserted again in the 1930s. Of course, Jones was a well-to-do importer and merchant in Halifax, with a nice estate out by the North-West Arm, and to some, even then, his ideas may have seemed a little old-fashioned. But Devlin's proposal did not receive much support either.

Macdonald had already made some moves to ameliorate the conditions of workers by removing the common law restrictions against labour unions in 1872. Conservatives tended, in fact, to be a little more charitable than Reformers. The following is from the Toronto *Mail* of December 20, 1876, the Conservative standard-bearer in Toronto:

> The winter seems to be setting in with unexampled severity, and when one reflects that while the weather was still warm, and before out of door work was suspended, men who professed to be able and willing to work were begging their bread from door to door, one shudders to think of what a hard winter may bring forth. . . . Surely in such a charitable community all that is needed is concerted action and the exercise of common sense to avert what threatens to be a calamity and a disgrace to the city.

Winter poverty, what one scholar has called the "seasonal contours of colonial poverty,"[2] is another characteristic of

Wagons, not carts, were used for freighting to the mines in British Columbia. Here a wagon train is shown on its way to the Cariboo in 1868.

"Frozen to Death," from the *Canadian Illustrated News*, January 27, 1872.

Macdonald's time, especially in the years before the factory system was fully established. Winter was a time when all outside work stopped, save for the cutting of trees in the woods for next spring's drive. After harvest, farming almost stopped; farming became a kind of hibernation relieved by the continual but modest chores of looking after the animals and poultry. All construction stopped. Fishing stopped. Before the coming of the railway, transportation stopped. Even with railways, commerce slowed down in winter. Some things were too bulky to haul by rail, cordwood being one. The process of shutting down the flour mills, the lumber mills, began in November, when the freeze-up started. Winter could be a festive season for those who could feast; the bells of sleighs and cutters often made merry the winter nights; it was a season of gaiety for those whose cellars had barrels of flour, barrels of apples, sides of beef, flitches of bacon; whose jam shelves were heavy with the richness of the past summer's strawberries, raspberries, peaches and cherries; whose wine cellars were filled with good claret bought by the case. But for the poor, the improvident or the unlucky, as the case might be, dependent upon labour of some kind, in construction, in the mills, and whose prospects for winter work were meagre, winter could be a hard time. It could be a killing time.

Consider the following sequence of events. In December 1871, at Montreal, the ice "took" early in the river and in the Lachine Canal. It took before the full supply of wood for the winter had reached the city. Wood rapidly became scarce. Inevitably it became expensive. The price went up from about four dollars a cord to six or seven.* Some said the wood merchants put it up, which was true enough, though the cause was demand and supply. Early in January 1872 it was bitterly cold. On January 9, 1872, the Montreal *Gazette* reported two children frozen to death in a miserable den off Kempt Street over a bitterly cold Sunday night, January 7th. The elder was two years old, and the other three months. The mother and father were still alive. Montreal was shocked. *The Canadian Illustrated News* ran a full-page drawing of the scene, and added that a little more activity in discovering the whereabouts of such poverty "would be no discredit to the well-known, if not always wisely directed, benevolence of Montreal." The startled Corporation of Montreal purchased some hardwood and made it available to the poor families at $4.50 a cord.

As well as the hardships of poverty, the incidence of disease — smallpox, typhoid, diphtheria, measles — was heavy among such families. But all families were affected by endemic diseases. Death was no stranger anywhere, to any family. Medicine was improving but it was still rude and unscientific. If you became ill, you were better off to trust nature to pull you through. Doctoring was often of more value psychologically than medically. George Brown got a superficial flesh wound from a bullet in March 1880. He was dead of gangrene in seven weeks. Doctors could do nothing. As one doctor put it, apropos of acute appendicitis (it was called by various names and rarely diagnosed as such), "it too often happens that the first attack is, indeed, the last."

Most British North American provinces had already estab-

*See note on prices and their significance at the end of the chapter.

lished rudimentary controls for public health, brought into existence by the cholera epidemics of the 1830s and 1840s. Inoculation for smallpox was not universal, nor even commonplace, but it was available and known. The trouble was that those who needed vaccination most were often not inoculated. There was a smallpox epidemic in Montreal in 1885, and the reluctance of ordinary people to be inoculated, not surprisingly, was considerable. Worse was the forcible segregation of victims from other members of their families.

Disease was always more prevalent in cities than in the countryside, but it need not be assumed that farms and farmsteads were free of it. According to one source, the average Canadian farmhouse had still in the later 1860s and early 1870s only the most rudimentary drainage, "with a dark hole for a cellar, with a dirty hole for a well; with frozen walls in winter, wet walls in spring, and stinking walls in summer. . . ."[3] This author's most vivid recollection of old farm kitchens in summer is flies, heat and the smell of sour milk.

Ottawa's Lower Town, viewed from Parliament Hill about 1860, while the Parliament Buildings were under construction. Building materials are piled in the foreground; the Rideau Canal locks are just beyond. The Sappers' Bridge (right) spans the canal and the roadway runs down to Rideau Street, the main business thoroughfare of Lower Town. The Chateau Laurier now stands on the open space beyond the canal.

So people were born and people died. Undertakers advertised in the newspapers side by side with the grocers and the wine merchants, and with nearly the same frequency. An undertaking firm in Halifax announced that they had the largest stock of coffins in the city and were "punctual in attending to our business." Another thanked the public for the generous patronage that had been extended to him by numerous friends over the past twenty-five years, and solicited "a continuation of their favors." These notices were not intended to be amusing; they were, in fact, a rather stark statement of reality. The trappings of mourning added dimension. Official mourners, with black scarves hanging from the back of black hats; the black coach and the horses decorated with black plumes; widows wearing weeds in a splendour of mourning, modified gradually according to the lapse of time after the deaths of their husbands, though there were some who never gave them up. Even notepaper went into mourning. Lady Macdonald, a month after the death of her husband, wrote on grey paper with a full half-inch black border; six months later the paper was white with but a three-eighth-inch black border. Not all affected these ceremonies, and the death of children, particu-

The Parliament Buildings in 1866, a painting of considerable historical interest by Otto Jacobi, a German artist who had settled in Canada in 1860. It depicts Parliament Hill as seen from Lower Town, and is thus a reverse of the photograph of Lower Town taken from the Hill a few years before. (The National Gallery of Canada, Ottawa)

larly the very young, was too common an occurrence to occasion much elaboration.

When children lived, they were educated in a rather ramshackle fashion, really at the instance of their parents. When education had to be paid for, even though from an early date subsidized by colonial governments, it was at best an uncertain quantity. But even when free public education came, to Lower Canada and Upper Canada by the 1850s, Nova Scotia in 1864, New Brunswick in 1871, that was no guarantee the children would go to school. Some parents believed that children should work, not study. Some did not know or care. In any case, there was no compulsory education. That came for the first time in Ontario in 1874, when it required only that parents of children between the ages of seven and twelve have their children at school four months a year. And the law could not be enforced. In 1890, even in Ontario, a quarter of the children of school age were not enrolled in school at all, and of those on the registers only half came. Compulsory attendance was still a dead letter.

So younger children could, and did, play in the streets, and older ones could, and did, make mischief. One of the few arguments used in favour of child labour was that the children were better off in a factory than in the streets. That, of course, is debatable. The Toronto *Globe* in 1868 noticed that too many of these children were getting into trouble and suggested that corporal punishment be inflicted on the mischief makers. It was absurd, the *Globe* said, to talk of the degrading influence of corporal punishment. It was cheaper than sending children to jail. And it was better. Children sent to jail would simply "graduate in vice and lawlessness."

In the 1860s the enforcement of law was almost wholly a local matter. Police were appointed by municipalities or by counties, and that was where their responsibility rested. There were no Dominion police. The North-West Mounted Police, created by the Dominion in 1873, were specifically for service in the North-West Territories. Except for British Columbia the provinces had no provincial police. Police authority was given by the legislatures in the colonies or the provinces to the municipalities, which established their own frequently ramshackle machinery paid for out of local taxes. In Ontario and Quebec this system was primitive enough, but not ineffective.

Orlo Miller's book of 1962, *The Donnellys Must Die*, shows something of the operation, or lack of operation, of justice at Lucan, in Middlesex County, Ontario. The essential point is its localness, and it was precisely for that reason that, temporarily, vigilante justice appeared there. In Nova Scotia, New Brunswick, Prince Edward Island, and still more in Newfoundland, where municipal institutions at the county level did not in the 1860s exist, local policing was in the hands of justices of the peace, and malefactors were tried by the Court of Quarter Sessions. Even after Nova Scotia set up county municipal machinery in 1879, little local tyrannies continued to rise and fall where the justice of the peace was sometimes powerless to restrain local crime, when even his warrant could be ignored. What did one do with a local magistrate who was afraid to prosecute? Every lawless venture committed with impunity encouraged other, more flagrant violations. One answer was to appeal to the provincial attorney-general for more effective crown prosecution.

An example from Murphy's Cove, Ship Harbour, Nova Scotia, is not untypical. The local schoolteacher was able to keep excellent order among his pupils, except on stormy days, when three or four young roughnecks would visit the school, really for their own amusement, not to learn. Two or three times they disturbed the school and threatened the teacher with violence. The school trustees obligingly assured the teacher of their full support in getting him legal protection. But what legal protection was there? There was not a magistrate within six miles, and even if he were appealed to he would impose only some trifling penalty. That would merely make matters worse. Even the magistrate felt a bit timid handling those offenders, so reckless and desperate were they. The teacher was reduced to writing the Attorney-General of Nova Scotia to ask him for a short, sharp letter in an imposing official envelope that would, so the teacher believed, effectively intimidate the offenders. Really the teacher had no remedy but his own courage, his two fists and the support of the community.

Alexander Mackenzie, when Prime Minister of Canada, was appealed to by Joseph Hickson, managing director of the Grand Trunk Railway, for protection to Grand Trunk trains at Belleville, Ontario, at the time of the strike in the winter of 1876-77. Mackenzie answered quite correctly that as Prime

Minister of Canada he had no more power than Hickson had. Responsibility for the public peace in Belleville lay with the municipal authorities in Hastings County, and if they needed help, they could make an official request through the Attorney-General of Ontario for militia in aid of the civil power.

But before one can generalize effectively a great deal more work has to be done in Canada on the broad history of law and legal administration. Lawyers have not written much on Canadian history outside of constitutional issues, and Canadian historians do not, as a rule, know much law. That is a pity, for law must underlie all societies, and its character, most especially its administration, may very well determine the shape society takes.

The common law was the background of all British North American colonial law in criminal cases, and in private law too, except in Quebec. The common law of England was a vast body of legal rules and decisions going back to the eleventh century. Over this was placed statute law, as laid down by parliaments since the fourteenth century. Statute law interpreted, amended, or repealed parts of the common law. It was,

While Macdonald was in his forties the Gothic revival in architecture reached its height in Canada. He was to have close associations with two of its finest examples. LEFT The centre block of the Parliament Buildings (here shown when Queen Victoria's birthday was being celebrated in 1868) was completed in 1865. ABOVE Earnscliffe, the home in which Macdonald spent his last years, was built in 1856-57. Macdonald lived in it for a time in 1870-71, when it was owned by friends and he was recuperating from a serious illness. He did not purchase it until 1882. It was the only house he ever owned in Ottawa.

Election day in Montreal in 1860. This was in the days of "open" voting; the secret ballot was not introduced in federal elections until 1874. Voters were not infrequently intimidated or manhandled in order to influence their votes, and squads of police were needed for their protection.

if you like, the latest and newest law, and where it applied it superseded the older common law. This whole body of jurisprudence applied to the British North American colonies, although the new province of Quebec was specifically allowed by the British Parliament, in 1774, to have its own basically French law in property and civil rights. Gradually the colonial assemblies made certain statutes for their own local purposes. These were not supposed to conflict with British parliamentary law but they might, and as time went on they did, override local applications of the English common law.

So a British North American colony before Confederation had a great body of law to draw upon, and British legal precedents were commonly used in deciding local cases. So, as time went on, there were colonial precedents, and some American ones. Local statutes were used to amend or repeal certain aspects of the common law that needed clarification or change in the light of new conditions. One interesting example of this native process is the question of imprisonment for debt.

Imprisonment for debt existed in the common law. When judgment had been obtained against a man for recovery of a debt, it was enforced by a court order — an execution — against the debtor's property. If that were not sufficient to discharge the debt, an order could be issued, the writ *capias ad satisfaciendum*, for imprisonment of the debtor until the debt was paid. The basic assumption behind the principle was not so much that of implied fraud, though it was never entirely absent, but that without being able to secure the person of the debtor, a creditor had no way of bringing pressure upon him to pay his obligations. And before one gets too excited about the wickedness of imprisonment for debt, it is useful to remember that without some system for enforcing payment of debts, commerce must grind to a stop. It was already heavily founded on credit. If one were allowed to incur debts without an effective means of enforcing their collection, commerce could not work. On the other hand, it was widely recognized, both in England and in Canada, by the end of the 1860s that imprisonment for debt was really not only useless but worse than useless. Imprisonment struck directly at the root of efforts by an honest debtor to retrieve his position and pay off, if possible, his debt. It was vitally necessary, therefore, to devise a system that was not too hard on debtors, a system which could discriminate between involuntary failure to meet debts and what can be termed wilful refusal to pay; in other words, fraud.

Imprisonment for debt was abolished in England, except in special cases, in 1869. Colonial legislatures had tackled this problem earlier, and had attempted to place impediments in the way of the common law rule; the Province of Canada in 1859, New Brunswick in 1854, Prince Edward Island in 1864, Nova Scotia in 1868. But the impediments in some cases were not sufficient. A letter exists written in 1882 from the Debtors' Room of the Halifax County prison that throws into high relief some of the problems. It sounds as if taken from Dickens' *Little Dorrit*, written nearly thirty years before.

Francis Cunningham was undoubtedly in the prison because he had been put there on a writ sworn out by one of the relentless creditors against whom he inveighed, backed up and, as a rule, urged on by an unprincipled lawyer. Cunningham believed it was unjust for a court to have the power of depriving a man of liberty for nine or twelve months, and still have him

LEFT The most genteel of Victorian outdoor sports was croquet, which enjoyed great popularity. This foursome was photographed in 1864.

RIGHT Lacrosse, considered Canada's national game in Macdonald's day, has been displaced by ice hockey, which someone once described as being lacrosse being played on ice. Lacrosse originated amongst the Indians before Europeans came to Canada and it long continued to hold their interest. This photograph of the Caughnawaga Indian lacrosse team was taken about the time of Confederation.

liable for the debt at the end of it. He alleged that

at least ninety per cent of the debtors imprisoned have been labourers and mechanics out of work. Then with families of small children whom [*sic*] have had to exist as best they might while their breadgainer spends a week or ten days in prison to satiate the spite and greed of an unmerciful creditor, or a fledgling of a lawyer, who has an eye on costs, and does not care what misery he causes a family, as long as he attains his object. . . . Just think of an old man of 90 years of age [having] been imprisoned by a son in law for $2.14, and been unable to pay the debt, or fer [*sic*] a lawyer to swear him out.* Again a boy (coloured) of 18 years of been imprisoned for 50 cents debt, and $1.90 costs, without the means of paying or obtaining relief. Again a man imprisoned for $3.17 whose wife lay in bed at home on the point of death, with no one to wait on her but young children, and no one to provide for her while the husband lay in jail he could not pay $3.17, or provide or obtain credit for $5 with which to swear out. I have seen all this in this jail, in this nineteenth century and yet we boast we live in a civilized country.[4]

What Francis Cunningham had actually done to be so committed we do not know, nor do we know whether what he was saying was true. But there was enough truth in it for the

*The law provided in certain circumstances that if you swore before the magistrate that you were not possessed of the money to pay the debt for which you were imprisoned, you could be released. But this process cost $5.00.

Nova Scotia Conservative government to sponsor a bill in the Assembly in the 1882 session to end such conditions. The bill was rejected by the Liberal-dominated Legislative Council.

In this kind of society private individual charity was essential. Conscientious administrators who answered appeals of this kind, usually with letters written personally by themselves, were pearls above price. The law was not without mercy, but it was as well to keep out of its toils if you could. At the same time it has to be said that provincial societies were rough; their drinking and their playing and their amusements were not gentle. In 1869 a cockfight, doubtless one of many, was held west of Toronto, and for heavy stakes.

" . . . they were a motley crew. For the most part they were rowdies of the purest breed – Toronto, London, Buffalo and Detroit were all represented by as scoundrelly a looking gang as it was possible to produce anywhere. . . . 'Five – ten – fifteen – twenty dollars that the London bird wins,' shouted a miserable ragamuffin who did not look as if he was worth five cents. 'Make it a hundred and I take you,' was the reply of a highly adorned young gentleman. 'Done,' said the ragamuffin,

The skating party held at the Victoria Skating Rink in Montreal in 1870 in honour of H.R.H. Prince Arthur, later Duke of Connaught and Governor General of Canada. This is an example of the remarkable composite photographs prepared by William Notman, the leading Canadian photographer of Macdonald's time. Hundreds of socially prominent people were photographed individually, and the prints were then assembled and mounted against an appropriate background. The whole was then coloured by hand.

49

and he pulled from the pocket of his ragged trousers a bundle of bills amounting to several hundred and the bet was made. 'Twenty-five cents on the Toronto bird,' cried a miserable looking little old man; but the idea was altogether so low that down came a hand on the crown of his hat, and he was instantaneously extinguished." The *Globe* thought that the affair was a "disgrace to the civilization of our times."

There were worse disgraces than that, but it is difficult to get evidence. The whole history of the demi-monde in Canada is extraordinarily obscure. Ample suspicions, but little evidence. Of course at such levels the high and the low in society met, as the hundred-dollar wager above illustrates. James Gray tells something of it in *The Boy From Winnipeg* and *Red Lights on the Prairies*, but that is in Laurier's time. Macdonald once, in a humorous aside, offered protection to the demi-monde of Canada's West. There had been a scheme of assisted female immigration to provide wives for prairie settlers, not unlike *les filles du roi* in Talon's time in the 1670s. As then, too many were disreputable, and in 1882 the cabinet decided to stop it. One M.P. who had been a strong supporter of the policy waited for the news, and was visibly disappointed when Macdonald told him of the cabinet decision. Seeing his chagrin, Macdonald put a friendly hand on the M.P.'s shoulder and said, "You know, Angus, we must *protect* the Canadian whores."[5] That the demi-monde existed and flourished in the 1860s and 1870s is undeniable. There were streets below Citadel Hill in Halifax (not more than a block or two from the new high school) where you could have any entertainment you wanted. It was the same in Quebec, at least before, probably after, the British Army moved out in 1871. Montreal by gaslight was said to have been positively luxurious.

Young Hugh John Macdonald was studying law in Toronto in 1871 (and thought it of mind-shattering dullness); he could have said something of the demi-monde of Toronto, but only noted the difficulty his friends had in finding scarlet women who were medically reliable. He also regaled his correspondent (James Coyne, who was later to be an august President of the Royal Society of Canada) with scabrous stories and verses from adventures around Toronto. One of these, since they are so rarely preserved across a century, might be kept. It was called "The maiden's prayer to the Virgin."

Mary Mother, we believe
That without sin you did conceive;
Teach we pray thee us, believing,
How to sin without conceiving.[6]

Hugh John did not agonize over his adventures much, unlike young Mackenzie King, twenty years or so later, who had similar Toronto adventures but whose Presbyterian conscience tortured him for it.

High life and low life often met at Ottawa in the sessions after Confederation. Cartier's stag parties were famous. Young Hugh John did not miss those. Madame Cauchon's musical evenings were ghastly, hot and dull, and Hugh John hated them. Adolphe Caron, a younger Conservative protégé of Cartier who came to Parliament in 1873, devised a drinking club, mainly Conservative in politics, but radical in everything else, that was based at Caron's Ottawa boarding-house. It was run by an old Communard, Bastien, who had had to leave France because he was implicated in the shooting of Archbishop Darboy in the Paris uprising of 1871. His wife was a superb cook whom the club boasted of. The club ran on food, wine, Caron's wit and good manners, and the sheer ridiculousness of the other members. The report about the club comes from the Liberal whip in the House of Commons, George Casey, who used to go there. Political lines often crossed when politicians observed, as they not infrequently did, parliamentary courtesies, or still more, when they were in search of a good time. John A. Macdonald helped to found the Rideau Club in 1865 with precisely that in mind. Even Alexander Mackenzie was not above having a champagne lunch at the Russell House with a Conservative friend.

That bill at the Russell House, for champagne lunch for two, would have been about three dollars. Most Canadian hotels sold wine, but it was sometimes expensive, sometimes poor, frequently both. Iced water was commonly served. Meals were generally *tout compris*, and tips not usually expected, except in the large cities. Canadian hotels were almost exclusively on the American plan, that is, with three, or more often four meals included in the price of the room. The Russell House charged from three to four dollars, American plan, depending on the room. Although the Russell House was the best hotel in Ottawa, it was not a first-class hotel by international standards. Its service was not always exemplary either, though in this respect most Canadian hotels were quite good. Ottawa did not get a really first-class hotel until the coming of the Chateau Laurier, built by the Grand Trunk Railway, in 1912. The fame of the Russell House was due to its traditions and associations with Parliament and parliamentarians. Hotels in the smaller centres of Canada could be terrible, and especially was this true, apparently, in Nova Scotia. However, the prices were also less, running to about $1.50 including meals.

The question of the relation of those prices with ours is difficult, but there is no point in burking it, since dollar values will appear again and again in this book.

The first working rule, and perhaps the only significant one, is to multiply all the dollar values by at least eight, in some cases ten, to get an approximate present-day equivalent. Then assume enormous individual variations. There were of course no payroll deductions from salaries. There was no income tax until 1917. There was no sales tax. If you earned $400 a year (about the salary of a lower-paid teacher in the Atlantic provinces), it came out as $33.33 a month, with a wonderful $33.34 coming every three months. That added up to exactly $400 per annum.

People lived altogether narrower, closer lives, and those on government salaries, even Supreme Court judges, or cabinet ministers, had a narrow enough time. Charles Hibbert Tupper said in 1884 that it was common knowledge in Ottawa that every judge of the Supreme Court of Canada except the Chief Justice had drawn his salary eight or nine months ahead of time by borrowing from the bank. Credit was common enough for merchants; those on salary, however, had to be more careful. Mainly the credit they acquired was in the form of long-term grocery bills (made up monthly, or even quarterly) or from money advanced on security of a mortgage or an expected salary.

Produce cost proportionately less than now. Thompson paid "only" eight cents a quart for strawberries in Ottawa in 1885; but there was nothing like our variety of fruits nor the extended season for them. Produce was seasonal. The whole object of the almost universal practice of home canning and

The Russell House, the leading hotel in Ottawa for half a century and a favourite rendezvous of politicians in Macdonald's day. Its glory did not fade until the Chateau Laurier was completed in 1912. It was burned in 1927 and the Government expropriated the site to make it part of Confederation Square.

jam making was to extend that range. You could store certain varieties of apples for two or three months in a reasonably cool cellar.

Anything manufactured cost much more proportionately than now, and not so much was manufactured. Sewing machines existed from about the 1860s but remained too expensive for extensive domestic use for at least another decade or two. The application of the working principle of the machine to leather was to bring down the prices of boots and shoes by the 1870s. Cheap, well-made manufactured goods were going to come by the 1880s, and with economies of scale produced by a national market.

How that national market was created, out of the conflicting tariff jurisdictions of five or more different colonies, each with their own traditions, postage stamps and sense of identity, is a story in itself. Macdonald's role in it was neither that of prophet nor popularizer. His task was not only to run up the blueprint of the new Confederation; he had also to supervise its building.

3
The Time of Unions 1864-1871

FOR MACDONALD, two new unions were celebrated in 1867. He returned to Canada from London in May 1867, bringing with him the British North America Act and Susan Agnes Bernard Macdonald, his second wife.

Susan Agnes Bernard came from a distinguished Jamaica family, and her father Thomas Bernard had been the Attorney-General of Jamaica. On his death in 1850 the family had left Jamaica; Susan Agnes' two elder brothers and the mother settled in Barrie, while she herself was still at school in England. Hewitt Bernard became a senior official in the Attorney-General's Department, a lieutenant-colonel in the militia, and Macdonald's private secretary from 1858 to 1866. He and Macdonald shared bachelor quarters after the Canadian government moved to Ottawa in the autumn of 1865. Macdonald had met Agnes casually in the 1860s. She was thirty when Macdonald met her again one day in December 1866 in Bond Street, London. He was now nearly fifty-two. They were married in St. George's, Hanover Square, one of the fashionable London churches, on February 16, 1867. Susan Agnes was handsome but not beautiful. The reader can look at the pictures and judge for himself. She was young, enthusiastic and capable. She loved managing her household, her dinners; and when she could she loved to manage Macdonald.

That was not so easy. Macdonald tended to follow Louis XIV's advice: don't let women manage your political affairs; follow your heart by all means, but keep control of your head. Macdonald tended to keep the control of matters political, and keep a good deal of his own counsel. There is a letter

The delegates to the Charlottetown Conference of 1864 gathered on the steps of Government House. Macdonald is in the middle, seated on the steps, with Cartier standing on his right. Although the discussions that led to Confederation began in Charlottetown, Prince Edward Island held aloof in 1867 and did not join until 1873.

Sir John and Lady Mac-
donald, photographed by
William Topley of Ottawa
in 1868. This is perhaps the
most attractive likeness of
Lady Macdonald that has
come down to us. The
expression is light-hearted,
in contrast to later pictures,
which reflect the tragedy
of her daughter Mary,
born in 1869, who was
never able to walk or look
after herself.

from Susan Agnes in the T. C. Patteson papers that illustrates
something of her relationship with Macdonald in these matters.
Patteson clearly wanted something and approached the matter
through Agnes. That route was not very hopeful, Agnes said.

My lord and master who in his private capacity simply lives to
please and gratify me to the utmost extent of his power, is
absolutely tyrannical in his public life so far as I am concerned —

If I interfere in any sort of way he will be annoyed, and
more, he will be "disinclined". I know him *so* well! . . .

Sir John knows my opinion and wishes on the subject
perfectly well — I expressed them at the time of the present
appointment and the other day when the continuance in another position became impossible, I expressed it again with
added decision — But Sir John, as is usual with him on these
domestic occasions, looked very benign [,] very gracious, very
pleasant — but — answered not one word! He never does!!

There is little doubt, however, that as time went on Agnes
developed her own little tyranny, especially as Macdonald
grew to lean on her more and more. In the later years of Mac-

donald's life Agnes' vigilance over his welfare never relaxed. No matter how late the sitting of the House, she would remain in the gallery and tried, and usually succeeded, in getting Macdonald away from his friends and home with her. One old Liberal M.P., John Charlton, who disapproved of many of Macdonald's habits, called her Macdonald's good angel. Like some good angels, however, she could be forceful and outspoken. She was not always calm and collected up there in the visitors' gallery, and her comments not infrequently drifted down to the floor of the House. When the 1878 session opened, for instance, Macdonald was in opposition, and led off the attack against the Mackenzie government before Black Rod had even summoned the members of the Commons to the bar of the Senate. Macdonald argued a contradiction dear to lawyers, but deliciously abstruse: that Timothy Anglin, who had been nominated Speaker by Mackenzie, could not, as a newly elected member, be made Speaker by Mackenzie because he had not been officially introduced, as a new member, to the Speaker! The Liberals quite properly won a division on that wildly improbable subject; and the whole affair was presided over by a somewhat uneasy Clerk of the House, who expressed some difficulty in so acting. Whereupon Lady Macdonald in the gallery stamped her foot angrily and exclaimed aloud, "Did ever any person see such tactics!" This story comes from Mackenzie.

Susan Agnes could be something of a tartar. Some who observed her were mean enough to suspect that Macdonald's home life was anything but a bed of roses, or that there were at least thorns to go along with the flowers. "His daily life at home," wrote John Thompson of Macdonald, "is of itself tormenting enough. . . ." This sentence raises more questions than it answers. And it is true that John Thompson, Macdonald's Minister of Justice, never seems to have been an enthusiast for Lady Macdonald. Making all allowances, it will not do to describe Macdonald's second marriage as "ideal." It may have been and it may not. The truth probably is that, as with most marriages, no one on the outside knows what the marriage was like on the inside. Besides, there is one view of this marriage we do not possess: Macdonald's. So far as this author knows, there is not a single letter from Macdonald to Susan Agnes in existence.

That Susan Agnes was sincerely devoted to him is undoubted. She was probably in love with him. She grieved for him long after he had gone. There is a rather touching letter written by her three years after Macdonald's death to his brother-in-law, Professor James Williamson, in Kingston:

Fresh, as the freshest flowers is the memory of my husband to me, is the sorrow and longing with which I hourly think on him — dearest, best, first of all! No change, nor time, nor absence has, or can, even for a moment weaken the tie that binds me to his precious memory and the recollection of that glorious life. How I miss his companionship and presence no words can tell. Nothing happens to me, even the most trifling event in my every day life occurs, but it brings a sickening longing to have him near to tell it to, as I used in the happy days gone by![1]

Susan Agnes could truly say, with some other widows, "think of the years I had of that splendid company!"

There are not many examples of Macdonald's conversations with Agnes, but Joseph Pope who became his private secretary in 1882 records some. In 1886, Lady Macdonald turned to her husband and asked a question about George Foster, at that time Macdonald's Minister of Finance, and a former classics professor from the University of New Brunswick. "Can you explain to me," asked Agnes, "how that timid, shy, retiring man is always so much at home before an audience, and not always a sympathetic audience at that?" Macdonald looked at her and said simply, "Consciousness of power, my dear." Macdonald was asked about a proposed punishment for a civil servant who had committed some misdemeanour. Sir John was disposed to be charitable. Agnes was not. "Sir John," she remarked, "don't you think Smith deserves it?" "My dear," said Macdonald, "if we all got what we deserved, some of us might be in a bad way."[2]

Macdonald had his failings, of course, and Agnes grieved over them. Not infrequently, in her own slightly starchy fashion, she tried to make them both better people. Agnes had her moments of joyful frivolity, but seriousness would come creeping in, as if Macdonald's twenty-years' difference in age made her feel conscious of time and mortality. After all, she reasoned, man's purpose on earth was surely not just the here and now; nevertheless, she was to watch the here and now come in on Macdonald's shoulders every evening with a certain sense of the pleasure of being in the middle of affairs.

Agnes had first watched these political processes on their return from a brief weekend wedding trip to Oxford in February 1867. They had heard out the debate on the British North America Bill in the Lords and, in the midst of great cabinet uncertainty about British electoral reform, had heard out the debate in the Commons. It had received its third reading there on March 8th and was signed into law on March 29th. It was to be effective when proclaimed, and by the time Agnes had got back to Canada with Macdonald, this date was set for July 1st.

The sheer audacity of Confederation is staggering. In a sense it could be said that the Americans had done it first. But they had done it in several stages over seventy years, beginning with the painful process of putting together the colonies along the Atlantic seaboard from New Hampshire to Georgia, and ending with the Mexican War of 1845-48 and the Oregon Boundary Treaty of 1846 that gave them the west coast. The British North Americans proposed and completed this process not in seventy years, but in seven, beginning in 1864 and ending with British Columbia's admission in 1871. Prince Edward Island annexed the rest of Canada in 1873. Newfoundland was courted assiduously, though intermittently, until 1895, and then largely ignored until the 1940s.

This tremendous movement has to be explained. It could not have been achieved in that short time if it had always had to wait for public opinion. There is no doubt that Confederation had strong popular support in Canada West, that is, Ontario, where it was regarded as a great measure of political reform and the means of acquiring the North-West. It had popular support in New Brunswick, enough to win a provincial election in 1866 after having lost one in 1865. It had some popular support everywhere. But in Canada East there was no election to test opinion, because Cartier knew that he could not count on winning such an election. In Nova Scotia, Confederation would have been defeated if there had been an election. Confederation was put through, quite constitutionally, because colonial parliamentary traditions, inherited from Great Britain,

The London Conference, at which the final terms of Confederation were hammered out and the British North America Act was drafted, met in this dignified old Conference Room in the Westminster Palace Hotel, across the street from Westminster Abbey. The building was demolished a few years ago, but the plaque placed in the room in 1911 to commemorate the Conference has been preserved.

allowed parliamentarians to assume initiatives like that, in the hope that in the long run the public would come around. And in the long run the public did. But in Nova Scotia it was to take a long time. As late as 1892 the Premier of Nova Scotia refused to go to a Dominion Day dinner when in London, England, because he feared that "the occasion will unavoidably elicit speeches from which I should have to dissent. . . ." Parliamentarians who took bold initiatives of the size and scale of Confederation had to have courage and conviction; perhaps even recklessness. Charles Tupper was one of these. George Cartier was probably another.

Macdonald's role is different again. Macdonald was no prophet or real reformer. Prophets and reformers have to fight long battles against things as they are, against the dead weight and inertia that institutions and human beings can summon up to resist change. Macdonald, it is fair to say, never really had persistence of that kind. He believed, sincerely, that new ways would not change things fundamentally. Laws should be improved, and changes made to correct palpable abuses; injustice ought not to be done. But so much that was trumpeted as being vitally necessary was largely unnecessary. Macdonald could never fight for something that looked visionary. His energies refused to be summoned for anything his mind told him was

ABOVE The two most famous historical paintings relating to Canada are undoubtedly West's portrayal of the death of Wolfe and Robert Harris's huge canvas depicting the Fathers of Confederation. Harris's original painting, completed in 1883, was destroyed when the centre block of the Parliament Buildings was burned in 1916, but fortunately his large preliminary black-and-white study and his oil sketch, here reproduced, have survived. There were many variations in detail between the studies and the painting, but in both Macdonald was shown, paper in hand, standing behind the table. The composition of the picture has been much criticized, but it must be remembered that Harris was handicapped by the necessity of providing 34 portraits in an arrangement that would give reasonably equal prominence to all. (Confederation Centre Art Gallery & Museum, Charlottetown)

BELOW The first page of Macdonald's handwritten draft of the British North America Act. The name to be given to the union was a matter that caused some difficulty. In a marginal note Macdonald jotted down six possibilities: Province, Dependency, Colony, Dominion, Vice Royalty and Kingdom. When he wrote this draft he evidently favoured Kingdom, but Dominion was the final choice.

CONFEDERATION DAY!

The Union of the Provinces of Canada, Nova Scotia and New Brunswick, under the new Constitution, takes effect to-day. We heartily congratulate our readers on the event, and fervently pray that all the blessings anticipated from the measure, by its promoters, may be fully realized.

So far as the people of Upper Canada are concerned, the inauguration of the new Constitution may well be heartily rejoiced over as the brightest day in their calendar. The Constitution of 1867 will be famous in the historical annals of Upper Canada, not only because it brought two flourishing Maritime States into alliance with the Canadas, and opened up new markets for our products, and a direct railway route to the Atlantic through British territory, but because it relieved the inhabitants of Western Canada from a system of injustice and demoralization under which they had suffered for a long series of years.

The unanimity and cordiality with which all sections of the people of Canada accept the new Constitution, gives the happiest omen of its successful operation. And, assuredly, if the people of the United Provinces are true to themselves and exercise a persistent and careful control over all public proceedings, there is not a shadow of doubt as to success. The only danger that threatens us is, lest the same men who have so long misgoverned us, should continue to misgovern us still, and the same reckless prodigality exhibited in past years should be continued in the future; but this we do not fear. We firmly believe, that from this day, Canada enters on a new and happier career, and that a time of great prosperity and advancement is before us.

Editorial column from the *Globe*, July 1, 1867.

ephemeral. He had seen the rise and fall of many movements, and in younger days had even been the *spiritus movens* of some of them. But years in office had strengthened his distrust for new and untried ideas.

There is a good deal of truth, therefore, in the argument that Macdonald took up new ideas when he was in opposition or when he was threatened with it. The British-American League he had espoused when in opposition, in July 1849. Confederation he had accepted as a loose and almost meaningless plank when he and Cartier had come back into power after the abortive Brown-Dorion government of July 1858. In June 1864 he decided to accept the nailing down of the plank only when defeated in the Assembly, and forced to join in a major reconstruction of the government. He took up the protective tariff in the mid-1870s, after almost two decades of quiescence, when he was in opposition and hoping to get into power.

So it should not be a matter of surprise that when Alexander Galt proposed Confederation resolutions to the Canadian Assembly in July 1858, they were ridiculed by Macdonald's government. Especially were they ridiculed by Cartier, and Macdonald had not a word to say. It is fair to add that the Assembly as a whole was not much interested in Confederation either. And to Macdonald, Assembly votes were always a present reality. The defeat of the Taché-Macdonald government on June 14, 1864 forced him to come to grips with Confederation, a subject he had largely ignored in 1858, had briefly sympathized with in April 1861, when the American Civil War and the exigencies of Canadian politics had compelled him to think about it. But he had opposed, in May 1864, the formation of a constitutional committee to enquire about federation, though he was made a member of the committee. When the committee reported on June 14, 1864, recommending constitutional changes and further discussion thereon, Macdonald refused to sign the report.

Yet, within two days, Macdonald had accepted Confederation, lock, stock and barrel. He came suddenly to the conclusion that unless some solution were found for the political grievances of Canada West (Ontario) no government could hold power for long. Any government that found a tangible, realistic proposal that would satisfy Canada West without alienating Canada East would obtain a satisfying and firm hold on power. Macdonald had the offer of an enormous block of political support to carry such a proposal. It came from George Brown and the Reform party behind George Brown. This offer, as Donald Creighton has put it, belonged "to the far different category of political realities. With its promise of an absolutely omnipotent majority in the legislature, it instantly removed the whole speculative business of British American union to the sphere of action. . . ."[3]

Terms were worked out; the great coalition of 1864 was launched. The clock was wound up. The power so established carried the Canadian government to Charlottetown in September 1864, carried the Charlottetown Conference, and the Quebec Conference that October and, though Brown resigned in November 1865, it was to carry the London Conference of December 1866. That Macdonald was made chairman of the London Conference was a recognition not only of the work he had already done in helping to shape the resolutions for Confederation but of his skill at their management in sometimes difficult circumstances. Drunk he was sometimes and at some inconvenient times; indeed, just before the Canadian cabinet went off to Charlottetown, a council meeting had been called for noon. Council waited. The Premier, Sir Etienne Taché, waited. Finally Macdonald was sent for, arrived shortly after three, half drunk, and was soon applying himself to the lunch on the side-table. Before business had been fairly started he was fully drunk, on ale. He then got into a quarrel with Brown over the new Parliament Buildings in Ottawa. Fortunately Galt succeeded in smoothing things over.

Macdonald was, however, an adroit and a responsible chairman. Sir Frederick Rogers, the Permanent Under-Secretary of the Colonial Office — our equivalent is a deputy-minister — watched Macdonald with admiration as he steered some of the delicate compromises through the London Conference, with Cartier and Hector Langevin very conscious of their own need for security on critical points, and the Nova Scotian and New Brunswick delegates sometimes jealous of Quebec. "He stated and argued the case with cool, ready fluency, while at the same time you saw that every word was measured, and that while he was making for a point ahead, he was never for a moment unconscious of the rocks among which he had to steer."[4]

George Brown, the leading Liberal of his day, who founded the Toronto *Globe* in 1844. It quickly became an influential journal that made him a power in politics, whether or not he had a seat in Parliament. He and Macdonald were long-term antagonists, but Brown joined with Macdonald in 1864 to form the coalition government that made Confederation possible.

Old Dufferin and Sappers Bridge by W. Chesterton, 1877.

The British North America Act spelled out the interrelations between the Dominion government and the provincial governments: it defined their respective powers; it set up governments for the new provinces of Ontario and Quebec; it determined the financial arrangements; it constituted the Senate and House of Commons at Ottawa. It did several other things, such as allowing room for Prince Edward Island, Newfoundland, Rupert's Land and British Columbia to come in. But there were some things it assumed. It assumed the continued existence of the same system of parliamentary cabinet government that all the colonial delegates had grown up with. It assumed, without saying so, party government. It assumed the conventions that had grown up around both cabinet and party.

It also assumed that the central Dominion government had in Section 91 all the power it needed to do what had to be done. The omission of any provision for the constitutional amendment for the Act as a whole was not an accident. The provinces were given powers to amend their own internal constitutional arrangements. The grant of power in Section 91 to the Dominion was sufficiently large and sweeping to give its government ample room for manoeuvre and there is good evidence that Macdonald was prepared to use it. Should any difficulty arise, however, that called for a change, a short act could be passed easily enough by the British Parliament. In Macdonald's lifetime this was done only three times, and on minor points.

On July 1, 1867, as part of the ceremonies of inauguration of the new Dominion, Lord Monck, the Governor-General, announced that Macdonald had been given a K.C.B., that he was now Sir John A. Macdonald. Macdonald himself had had nothing to do with that decision, and was soon regretting it. All the others who had been so important in helping to carry Confederation — Cartier, Galt, Tupper, Tilley and one or two others — were given only C.B.'s. The difference was, alas, all too obvious. Macdonald was the only one entitled to be addressed as "Sir." This was Lord Monck's mistake. And it did not pass lightly. Alexander Galt was so angry at not becoming "Sir Alexander Galt" that he refused to accept his C.B. By the late summer of 1867 there were already rumours that those who had not been knighted were forming a cabal against Macdonald. It never came to anything; but as soon as possible, in 1868, Cartier was given a baronetcy, a title superior to Macdonald's and hereditary in the male line. (Since Cartier had only two daughters and his wife was too old to have any more children, that part of it did not matter.) Galt got his knighthood, a K.C.M.G., in 1869. Tilley and Tupper waited until 1879 for theirs.

Knighthoods always were, and would continue to be, honours fraught with the greatest hazards. They were much coveted. Dr. James Grant, the official doctor to the governor-general ever since 1867, was dying for a knighthood. When the glorious news came to him at last, in 1887, he went straight home, bowed low to his wife, and said, "Lady Grant, you behold the happiest man in Canada." But for every knighthood given there were ten or more heartaches among those that did not get them. In matters of knighthoods the line from the Book of Proverbs was terribly true: "Hope deferred maketh the heart sick." Senator Miller of Nova Scotia expected his from about 1880 on, and when he died in 1912 he was still Senator Miller. How awful to have to live so long with hopes dashed regularly twice a year! The practice of giving titles to Canadians was to end in 1919, though briefly revived in 1934-35. It ended to the infinite regret of many Ottawa wives and not a few Ottawa husbands, but almost certainly to the everlasting gratitude of troubled Canadian prime ministers who had had to live so often, daily, in Ottawa, with the unhappy results of their recommendations.

Ottawa in 1867 was not of course the grandest of towns. Joseph Howe had ridiculed it and its turbid river, full of slabs and sawdust. Some liked it. Young Lord Rosebery described it in 1873 as a pleasant enough place, "with immense piles of clean looking and clean smelling lumber and wild woods reaching down into the town." Ottawa was a lumber town of 20,000 people or so, noisy, boisterous, clap-boarded, and snowy, muddy or dusty, according to the season. It was bitterly cold in winter, hot as Hades in summer. The summer was almost the worst. All who could leave Ottawa did. From the cool July breezes of Rivière du Loup where Macdonald usually went in the summers, he wrote cheerfully to John Thompson who was sweltering away at his Ottawa desk, "The weather is delightful here, and is all the more enjoyable when we know that there is only a sheet of brown paper between you Ottawaites and Hell. Yours always, JAMD." And almost invariably Ottawa was out of session in the summer, so besides being hot it was dull. Hugh

John Macdonald, with all the impatience of his twenty-one years, declared Ottawa out of session "almost like a City of the Dead."

Confederation Square did not exist. Instead, two bridges carried Rideau Street across the Rideau Canal. One was Sapper's Bridge that connected with Sparks Street and had been in existence almost from the beginning of Ottawa; the other was Dufferin Bridge, finished in 1872, that connected Rideau Street with Wellington Street. There is an agreeable old painting in the Public Archives, painted in the summer of 1877; a horse car is headed along Sapper's Bridge for Sparks Street; a small herd of four cattle is being driven east toward Rideau Street over the Dufferin Bridge, a stone's throw from where the Chateau Laurier now stands; smoke is coming up from a small steamer going through the locks in the canal below. Behind it all, rising like a fairy castle, are the Parliament Buildings. Photographs, less idyllic than paint, show both less and more: there is Ottawa, dusty in the summer sun; frame houses; high board fences unpainted and hot and splintery to the touch; innumerable back sheds, stables, barns, and beyond, on the hill, that sumptuous incongruity of stone with its wealth of pointed windows, perhaps defying this wooden town, or wooden country, to support it.

The handsome Gothic windows posed some inconveniences. Mackenzie once called the House of Commons a kind of cave, with windows that were illusions since they could not be opened. Some other architectural style would have given more light and better air. This was in fact a general complaint. Air for the House came not from the windows, but was pumped through underground ducts, over two hundred yards long. There was a strong suspicion that the ducts and the sewers had too much in common. Langevin had managed to improve matters by 1880, though complaints continued to recur.

These Parliament Buildings of the Dominion of Canada had never been intended as a home for a British North American Confederation. They had been conceived, planned and built for the Province of Canada. They were the result of a difficult decision, made late in 1857, to establish the hitherto peripatetic capital of the province at Ottawa. The main centre block and the Parliamentary Library were designed by Thomas Fuller in the neo-Gothic style. The first sod was turned on the Hill,

OPPOSITE LEFT Sir George Etienne Cartier, leader of the French-Canadian wing of the Liberal Conservative Party and Macdonald's closest political associate. They were first cabinet colleagues in 1855 and, with only one interruption of any length, served together in succeeding administrations until Cartier's death in 1873.

OPPOSITE RIGHT Joseph Howe, orator and journalist and Nova Scotia's most famous native son. He first rose to prominence in the struggle that in 1848 gave Nova Scotia the first responsible government in an overseas colony. Howe opposed Confederation, did his utmost to prevent Nova Scotia's joining the Dominion and tried to secure the repeal of the union after it had taken place. Having failed, he worked instead to secure better terms for the province, and early in 1869, as a reconciling gesture, he accepted a seat in Macdonald's cabinet.

D'Arcy McGee

Thomas D'Arcy McGee, whose assassination in April 1868 — one of the very few political murders that have occurred in Canada — shocked the country and was a personal sorrow to Macdonald. His funeral in Montreal, which he had represented in Parliament, was witnessed by huge crowds and it was estimated that 15,000 people walked in the procession. McGee's Irish wit and eloquence had made him an influential supporter of Confederation. He had denounced the Fenians, the Irish extremists who were threatening Canada, and his death was ascribed to them. RIGHT Columns from the *Globe*, April 8, 1868. OPPOSITE D'Arcy McGee's funeral.

The Globe.

TORONTO, WEDNESDAY, APRIL 8.

THOMAS D'ARCY M'GEE.

As was intimated in part of our last issue, the Hon. T. D. McGee was foully murdered at the door of his boarding-house when yesterday morning returning from the House of Parliament, where he had a short time before delivered a long and powerful address. The various particulars connected with this very shocking crime will be found elsewhere. The sad circumstances of Mr. McGee's death, as well as the position in Canadian politics which he occupied, the influence which he exerted, the prominence as a debater which he had secured in our Legislature, and his well known and generally recognized eminence as a lecturer on various literary subjects, require that we should, now that he has passed away in so sad and sudden a manner, give him more than a mere passing notice. We have frequently felt constrained to oppose him, and to say what might sound harsh and condemnatory in reference to his conduct as a public man, but we have not been backward to recognize his excellencies, and wherever we conscientiously could, to praise his zeal for the good of this the land of his adoption, however little we might often feel constrained to think that zeal was characterized by prudence, or those efforts distinguished for consistency, or likely to be followed by permanently beneficial results.

Mr. McGee's life has been a comparatively short one, but full of strange and stirring occurrences, and marked by more than the ordinary amount of change. In a few days he would have completed his 43rd year, having been born on the 13th of April, 1825, at Carlingford, in Ireland. After receiving his education at an academy in Wexford, he emigrated when only 17 to the United States, where he joined the newspaper press, began his career as a lecturer, and attracted considerable attention both as a public speaker and as a writer.

In 1845, an article on Irish matters drew the attention of Daniel O'Connell to him, and at his request Mr. McGee returned to Ireland and occupied a position on the editorial staff of the *Freeman's Journal*. The incidents connected with his public career in Ireland are tolerably well known, and are to be excused, if excused at all, on the plea that he was very young, very ardent, very impulsive, his experience of life very limited, his mental powers imperfectly developed, his imagination beyond his control, his anxiety to "make a bit" of history as well as to write it extreme, and his miscalculation of what was to be overturned and the means at his disposal for the accomplishment of that feat, simply what was to be expected from a young Irishman of 22, with the peculiarities of association and training through which Mr. McGee had passed. That the "Young Ireland" party showed

ASSASSINATION
OF
HON. T. D. McGEE.

We give below numerous despatches received yesterday, giving full details in regard to the sad tragedy which has taken place at Ottawa. The despatches are given in the order in which they were received :—

OTTAWA, Tuesday, 6 a. m.

The Hon. T. D. McGee was assassinated at half-past two this morning. He stayed in the House till 2 o'clock, made a long and eloquent speech in Dr. Parker's motion and when the house adjourned, walked home with Mr. MacFarlane, M.P., part of the way through the square in front of the Parliament buildings. He then went on a short distance to his boarding-house, Mrs. Trotter's, late of Toronto.

Arrived there, he put his hand to open the door with his latch-key, when some one behind him fired at him. The shot passed in through the back of his neck, and came out at his mouth. Mr. Trotter was up and Mr. Robitaille, M.P., had just before entered the house. Mrs. Trotter went to open the door, hearing McGee coming, and trying to get in. Just as she got to it, and was pulling it open, the flash of the pistol in her face horrified her and she shut it on him, seeing him crouch down, and not knowing who it was. The next who saw him was the son of Mr. Trotter, who, when at the corner of O'Connor St., saw a man fall over at the door, but saw no one fire the shot. He thought the lump looked like a Newfoundland dog, but gave the alarm.

After Mr. McGee left Mr. MacFarlane, the two last persons seen with him were the two Buckleys. Nothing more is known concerning him. He was dead when found.

All Ottawa is astir. Mr. McGee's body lies in the house, with his face all clotted with blood, so that you would scarcely recognize him.

There is no doubt here but that this is the result of the frequent threats of assassination made regarding Mr. McGee, in consequence of his exposure of Fenianism.

The tragedy has excited universal horror, and to-day the House will only meet and express its sorrow, and adjourn for the recess.

There are no traces of the assassin, and not the slightest clue can be had as to him.

The authorities have taken every means in their power, so far, to secure the murderer, but as yet nothing has transpired.

Mr. McGee would be 43 years old next Tuesday. His wife did not accompany him to the Capital; she remained in Montreal as also an only daughter 16 years old who is in one of the Montreal convents. Mr. McGee also leaves a brother with whom he lived in Montreal.

An inquest is to be held by Dr. Van Cortlandt at 10 o'clock this a. m. at Trotter's.

Hon. Mr. Holton, Police Magistrate, John Sandfield McDonald and others were speedily on the spot, at 7 o'clock.

It was clear moonlight, almost as light as day. Mr. McGee's lodgings were not more than 2 minutes' walk from Parliament Buildings.

When the shot was fired, all the other boarders rushed down, and Darcy McGee was

Samuel Leonard Tilley, the Saint John druggist who became the leading advocate of Confederation in New Brunswick. When the Confederates were defeated in an election in 1865, it seemed for a time that the cause had been lost, but Tilley fought back and won a decisive victory in a second election the following year.

Barrack Hill, in 1859. The design was spacious: two departmental blocks, east and west, were designed to complement the centre block. There were numerous objections to the costs; to Nova Scotians, the buildings were so big that Howe described their plaster as by the acre and the cornices by the mile; but the site was dramatic, and the buildings when completed were harmonious and satisfying. The departments of the government of the Province of Canada began to move into the buildings in the autumn of 1865.

The handsome, circular Parliamentary Library was finished in 1876. Alexander Mackenzie expanded the west block, put a clock on the centre block tower in 1878, and the whole complex then survived without much substantial change until the disastrous fire on February 3, 1916. This destroyed the whole centre block. The Parliamentary Library was saved, largely, it was said, by the efforts of Arthur Meighen. Between then and 1922 the centre block was rebuilt, virtually on the same plan as before but one storey higher, and a centre tower, strikingly different, was completed in 1927.

The old House of Commons, too, was different from what it is now. It was eighty-eight feet long and forty-seven feet wide, the same size as the old Senate. But unlike his counterpart in the Senate, the Speaker sat in the middle of the long eighty-eight-foot side, facing across the width of the House, with the seats seven rows deep to his right and his left. Thus government and opposition faced each other along the short axis of the House.*

The House in 1867 had 181 members; 82 for Ontario, 65 for Quebec, 15 for New Brunswick and 19 for Nova Scotia. In 1891 it had 215. Since the original House was intended for 130 members, seats were added early in 1867 to accommodate the 181, so the House often had a crowded look to it. It was here that the new Parliament of the Dominion of Canada opened on Wednesday, November 8, 1867.

Sir John Macdonald sat on the Speaker's right, of course, as the leader of the government. His seat was in the front row, third desk from the Speaker. His cabinet was disposed in the front seats on either side of him, and some behind him in the second row. When Chapleau came to Ottawa in 1882 he was eternally irked that he was in the second row, while Langevin was in the first!

Sir John's first cabinet was of thirteen members, of whom three were in the Senate. Some of his cabinet colleagues were to be around for a long time to come. Hector Langevin, who began in 1867 as Secretary of State, lived to pronounce Macdonald's eulogy from his place in the Commons. Leonard Tilley, the shrewd little druggist from Saint John was Minister of Finance, and retired to New Brunswick in 1885 as Lieutenant-Governor. Alexander Campbell, Macdonald's old law partner, was in the Senate and would have a variety of portfolios until 1887. George Etienne Cartier, Macdonald's old and trusted colleague from Province of Canada days, would

*The present house is 72' x 54', with the Speaker seated in the middle of the short side, and with the seats facing each other along the long axis of the House.

71

be the Minister of Militia and Defence until he died in May 1873. Senator Peter Mitchell was Macdonald's pugnacious and self-satisfied Minister of Marine and Fisheries. Alexander Galt, however, resigned as Minister of Finance in November 1867 and never entered a Canadian cabinet again. Missing from this group was, notably, Charles Tupper, who just could not be fitted into the cabinet at first but joined in 1870, and Thomas D'Arcy McGee, also one of the odd men out, who was shot in Sparks Street, April 1, 1868.

From the very first, the government and parliamentarians took up customs and conventions just where they had left off in the same building only the year before. The Dominion of Canada was just the old Province of Canada writ large. There had been 130 members in the old Assembly of the Province: there were now 147 from Quebec and Ontario in the Dominion of Canada. The 19 Nova Scotian members and the 15 from New Brunswick were new to Ottawa, to everything; many of the 147 members from Quebec and Ontario, while they may not have known Ottawa well, had known each other for years. So the habits of the old Canadian Assembly reasserted themselves effortlessly. On the very first day Parliament met, when Macdonald nominated James Cockburn, M.P. for Northumberland West, as Speaker, it was objected that Mr. Cockburn could not speak French. George Cartier replied that that was true, but Cockburn understood French; and in the old Province of Canada several Speakers had been in exactly the same position. That seemed to clinch the argument.

Even more significant, many of the old laws of the Province of Canada were simply resurrected and passed by the new Parliament to apply to all of the new Dominion. Tilley introduced a Customs bill on December 10, 1867, which was, he said, "in substance the Act which had been in force in the late Province of Canada." Two days later he was more specific. "The proposed changes in the tariff were very limited in number as far as [old] Canada was concerned, but very extensive as regarded Nova Scotia and New Brunswick." To take one example. Spirits entering Canada had to pay an increased duty. Ontario and Quebec men were used to drinking central Canadian rye; but Nova Scotians and New Brunswickers had tended to drink rum or brandy. They objected to the new tax. The new Finance Minister, John Rose, replying to this, cheerfully recommended the Maritimers to forget about imported rum or brandy and learn to drink Upper Canada rye. There were a number of other changes, some of them brought in after Maritime members had gone home for Christmas, 1867. Maritimers were furious. Even friends of the government were dismayed. Certainly, said Galt, "the policy of this Parliament should be to avoid every possible cause of irritation."

In other words, the protest movement in Nova Scotia, born of the way in which Nova Scotia had been brought into Confederation, was aggravated and extended by the legislation and the methods of the very first national parliament. Even New Brunswick supporters of Confederation became unhappy. And the unease in New Brunswick, and outright rebelliousness in Nova Scotia, spilled across into Prince Edward Island. It affected the Newfoundland provincial election of 1869, fought on the Confederation issue. Tilley had to ask Macdonald in May 1868 to strengthen his hands in New Brunswick; he had to warn Macdonald in July that the Nova Scotian situation could not be allowed to go on festering as it was. It matters not, Tilley said, *what* concessions are made so much as the fact that they are made.

Here, of course, we come up fairly against some weaknesses in Macdonald, and they have to be faced and understood if we are to appreciate him. First of all, there is little doubt that Macdonald thought of Confederation in a sense rather different from that a person in our time, looking backward, would expect him to. He perfectly understood Confederation under the British North America Act to be a new constitutional arrangement; but how much more than that is not clear. It is by no means certain that he thought of it as a new nationality. Constitutionally and legally it was, of course: but politically — that was another matter. As Macdonald himself put it in April 1868: "At the Union [of 1867], new elements were introduced, two large and important Provinces, having distinct governments and parliaments, were absorbed into the Union [of the Canadas]." Notice the "absorbed into." Notice the different usages of "union." This reflects Macdonald's perspectives, and his priorities. Those Parliament Buildings on the Hill were the visible symbol of Macdonald's political attitude to the new Maritime provinces. They were "absorbed into" Canada. Old Canada had just become new Canada, much bigger, much stronger. Macdonald now had solid majorities both in old Canada East (Quebec) and in old Canada West (Ontario). That meant far more to him than all the opposition in Nova Scotia and New Brunswick put together. After all, Ontario and Quebec commanded 147 seats; Nova Scotia and New Brunswick, 34.

Also he had never been to Halifax before his visit in September 1864 and he had not visited any other part of Nova Scotia, though he had been briefly in Saint John, Fredericton and Shediac in New Brunswick at that time. He did not know the Maritimes. He did not know many Maritimers. He was, moreover, not well served by Charles Tupper. Tupper had the courage of a lion and the constitution of an ox; excellent qualities, but they did not give Macdonald the sensitive antenna he needed in Nova Scotia. Tilley had to become that. Nova Scotia was, in short, terra incognita, and it is fair to say that if Macdonald was aware of his own ignorance, he did not fret too much about remedying it. He never seemed to develop a profound sense of feeling for a society different from his own. He tended to read people in his own generous, tolerant terms and if he couldn't then to generalize them into a special category. The French will always be French, he used to say to Lord Lorne. He might as well have said, the Nova Scotians will always be Nova Scotian, as if making them a generality, until he knew them better. He used to say of Thompson, whom he admired very much, that he was too much a Nova Scotian. What he invested that noun with is nearly impossible to say.

In the end he was forced to take Tilley's advice. He came to Halifax in late July 1868, stayed at the old Government House on Barrington Street, got hold of Howe after church, the first Sunday he could, and eventually succeeded in splitting the anti-Confederate movement. When in 1868 the British government refused to let Nova Scotia out of the British North America Act, the Nova Scotian anti-Confederates had nowhere to go. They had to accept the fait accompli, rebel, or take refuge in sullen resentment. With the Halifax Citadel full of British soldiers — they were to remain there until 1906 — revolt seemed fatuous, as revolt in Halifax often did. Some talked of annexation to the United States, which the American consul in Halifax happily reported home. Resentment was to last a good deal longer.

The Nova Scotian government, under the régime of Confederation, was undoubtedly hard up. Macdonald, for his part, was willing to make a few concessions. Howe, on his side, would have to become a member of the Canadian cabinet. Macdonald probably could not have carried concessions without that. But it was a bitter pill for Howe to swallow. He took it manfully, and he took the consequences: a hard, rancorous by-election in Hants County on April 24, 1869; moving to Ottawa; and, worst of all, the fact that whenever he was in Halifax old friends would sometimes cross the street to avoid meeting him. Let no one say that politics does not take courage. The split in the Nova Scotian anti-Confederates did not end the movement but it was weakened, and the prosperity of the next few years was a wonderful salve for political bruises.

That rule is a general one. Prosperity predisposes to the status quo; adversity urges change. The rule applied in Newfoundland. Adversity had urged change from 1860 on. It had shouted change. Newfoundland's population of 160,000 was divided into two, if not warring camps, at least jarring ones, Roman Catholic and Protestant, the latter being mainly Anglicans and Methodists. A bitterly fought election in 1861 had necessitated additional troops being brought in from Halifax. But what made Newfoundlanders desperate through most of the 1860s was a series of bad fishing years, especially the inshore fishing. With internecine warfare numbed by these disasters, Newfoundlanders started to look for a change. Confederation was offered in 1864. F. B. T. Carter, the Speaker of the House, and Ambrose Shea, the leader of the opposition, came to the Quebec Conference. They functioned virtually as delegates, and duly reported back to St. John's.

The Newfoundland Legislature hedged in 1865, again in 1866, and until 1869. It was all so new. Most Newfoundlanders lived far away from the Gulf of St. Lawrence. The gulf provided a common identity of problems for Gaspé, New Brunswick's north shore, Prince Edward Island, Cape Breton, and even perhaps the west coast of Newfoundland. Fishing firms in Gaspé established themselves in Cape Breton. But most Newfoundlanders lived with their backs to the gulf. As the old song put it:

Our face toward Britain, our back to the Gulf,
Come near at your peril, Canadian wolf!

On the Avalon Peninsula they faced eastward the 1,950 miles to Ireland or Cornwall.

Britain did all she could to push the Newfoundlanders into Confederation. Despatches were sent out. An able and energetic Governor, Anthony Musgrave, was sent out. Macdonald and the Canadian government were willing; Macdonald knew little of Newfoundland but he could read a map. He always used to say that Newfoundland held the key to our front door. It finally got to the point where the Newfoundlanders came to Ottawa to discuss terms in May 1869. These were at once put to the Canadian Parliament, approved, and the Newfoundland government took them to the people of Newfoundland in a general election in October 1869.

It didn't work. The year 1869 was the first thoroughly good fishing year Newfoundland had had in the whole decade. "A lighthouse on every headland!" was one appeal the hard-pressed Confederates used, but it was only too easy to arouse prejudice. It was easy to send out wild statements about Newfoundlanders making up the future Canadian navy, or worse, being drafted into a Canadian army to fight the Americans, leaving their bones (as one Newfoundlander put it with a superb sweep of exaggeration) "to bleach on the desert sands of Canada."

While Newfoundland was going through the turmoil of that election, an able, intensely vain, twenty-five-year-old Manitoban, Louis Riel, was leading his supporters to defend what he believed were the rights of his people. Indeed, on November 2nd, the very week when the Governor of Newfoundland was explaining to the Colonial Office what had happened in the election, Riel occupied the one strong point at Red River, the Hudson's Bay Company post of Fort Garry.

It was not as if the Canadian government had not been warned. That was the irony of it. The Hudson's Bay Company's governor, McTavish, allegedly warned them in June 1869*. Bishop Alexandre Taché, the Roman Catholic Bishop of

A sketch of the town of Winnipeg, published in the *Canadian Illustrated News* in December 1869, while Riel's provisional government was in control of Fort Garry. Most of the buildings were about half a mile from the Fort, clustered near what was to become the famous corner of Main Street and Portage Avenue (then known as Main Road and Portage Road).

---

*"Allegedly," because the evidence is conflicting. See L. H. Thomas, *The Struggle for Responsible Government in North West Territories* (Toronto: University of Toronto Press, 1956), 32n.

St. Boniface, came through Ottawa in July 1869 on his way to the Vatican Council in Rome. He talked to Cartier frankly about the problems in Red River. Cartier listened, not very politely; he was cocky, self-confident, his mind made up. Canadian rule would be welcomed, he was sure. Besides, he was currently having a war of his own with the Bishop of Montreal, Ignace Bourget. Cartier had, like Tupper, a marvellous faculty for ignoring what he did not want to hear. It was part of that mastiff quality in both men. But the Bishop of St. Boniface was offended, and apparently so reported to his coadjutor in St. Boniface. The Canadian government was really ignorant of the problems of the West and did not know it was. That was the worst of it.

It is easy to condemn the federal government for its blindness, and it has been freely condemned. But there is another perspective. The total population of the Red River area — French-speaking Métis, English-speaking people of mixed blood, whites — totalled 10,000 or so, a tenth of the population of Prince Edward Island. The North-West had no political power and considerable inconvenience. Macdonald would have been ready to leave the North-West quite alone, if only the Americans would do the same.

But it was quite clear the Americans would not. They had developed a fair skill at acquiring substantial chunks of North American real estate in the past hundred years. In 1869 most Americans were not ready to think that this time was past. Just two years before, Alaska had been bought from the Russians for $7.2 million; what might the Americans have been willing to pay for the title in fee simple of the Hudson's Bay Company territory, from the Great Lakes to the Rockies? A great deal more than Canada finally paid for it. Some figures ran to fifty times as much. The United States could not buy it, of course, because the British government would not have allowed the Hudson's Bay Company to sell it to them. But Americans would have loved to buy it. And if Canada did nothing, the Americans would squat the Hudson's Bay Company out, exactly as they had done in Oregon thirty years before. The Red River Valley would be the Williamette Valley all over again.

The pressures were very real. Minnesota had been made a state in 1858. In the United States census of 1860 its population was 172,000: in the census of 1870 it was 440,000. There were other pressures. The Union Pacific Railroad, with the Central Pacific, its western extension, completed the first transcontinental railway line in 1869, driving their last spike in Utah. The Northern Pacific Railroad, chartered in the United States Congress in 1864, was under construction. Running westward from Duluth at the western end of Lake Superior, they proposed to keep north as far as Georgetown on the Red River. They would run a spur northward to Pembina, and their westward route, beyond the Red River, would be turned northwestward, as close as thirty miles to the 49th parallel.* This came directly to Macdonald from Charles Brydges in Montreal, who had had a morning's conversation with the president of the Northern Pacific, Governor Smith of Vermont, on January 25,

*The Northern Pacific actually crossed the Red River at Moorhead, about 15 miles south of Georgetown, but from there it did not, finally, go northwest, but rather due west through Bismarck, North Dakota, some 150 miles south of the Canadian border.

1870. "I am quite satisfied from the way Smith talks to me," wrote Brydges, "that there is some political action at the bottom of this, and that the United States Government at Washington are anxious to take advantage of the organization of this Northern Pacific Railway to prevent your getting the control for Canada of the Hudson's Bay Territory. This is only a repetition of what I have already said to you; but it came to me so directly this morning, and from a channel that I am satisfied knows what he is talking about, that I think it only right to let you know...."

With that estimate Macdonald agreed. "It is quite evident to me," he wrote back, "not only from this conversation, but from advices from Washington, that the United States Government are resolved to do all they can, short of war, to get possession of the western territory, and we must take immediate and vigorous steps to counteract them." So the Red River question required solution, and immediately. The Canadian government had taken energetic steps, beginning in 1868, to acquire the territory. The Colonial Office had helped. Canada had decided to make an early beginning on the vitally important surveys in the summer of 1869, anticipating the transfer. That is where trouble started.

The surveys were admirable, technically. There have probably never been surveys quite like them, continually run,

Riel's tragically misguided action in permitting the execution of Thomas Scott was thus recorded in the diary of Alexander Begg, a Red River merchant, on March 4, 1870: "This morning the news spread that Thos. Scott ... was condemned to be shot today at twelve o'clock — this was not believed at first by anyone but some time after when it became known that the lumber and nails had been procured for his coffin people came to realize it.... A deep gloom has settled over the settlement on account of this deed." In Canada the execution was regarded as a murder and reaction was so violent that Riel was forced to flee to the United States. This engraving is from the *Canadian Illustrated News*.

over such a stretch of territory, as those Canadian surveys that began at the 49th parallel in the summer of 1869. But there is no doubt that the surveyors and their methods seriously alarmed the inhabitants of the Red River Valley. To the ordinary man there are few things more unsettling than surveyors. Surveyors do not tell people where they are going, what they are doing, or why they are doing it. They run their lines and their transits with a sublime disregard of everything but sun and earth. J. Stoughton Dennis, who was in charge of this survey, gave public assurances that local interests would be safeguarded, and also gave them to Riel personally. But to the Métis all Canadians were the same, and in the absence of *any* authoritative statement from *anybody* about what was happening or going to happen, the Métis, not unreasonably, believed the more extreme Canadian statements, those of the Red River Canadians.

The peoples of Indian and European descent in Red River, indeed Red River people generally, had no formal title to the land they lived on. There was lots of land; the great grasslands rolled westward as far as the eye could see. It was breathtaking, really; to some it was intensely moving. Charles Mair who went there as correspondent for the Montreal *Gazette* described it:

> Great prairies swept beyond our aching sight
> Into the measureless West; uncharted realms,
> Voiceless and calm, save when the tempestuous wind
> Rolled the rank herbage into billows cast,
> And rushing tides which never found a shore.
> And tender clouds, and veils of morning mist,
> Cast flying shadows, chased by flying light,
> Into interminable wildernesses. . . .

How much more was this so for the Métis who had lived their whole lives there, who had never known anything else. That was what the Métis lived for: the buffalo hunt, the horses, the open air, and the long, narrow, river-lot farms, tucked together in the French-Canadian style along the highway of the Red River. These farms were really squatters' farms. And the uncertainty of the Métis title to them was forcibly brought home by the coming of the Canadian surveyors.

The surveys were stopped, and by Métis action. When the new Canadian governor of the territory, William McDougall of Ontario, came up through the United States and arrived at

the border at Pembina at the end of October, he was stopped too. The leadership in Red River was assumed by a committee of people of mixed origin, both French- and English-speaking, with Riel as secretary. Fort Garry was taken over easily, peacefully, but by armed force. The Métis, like most people that live by hunting or herding, whether Arabs, Tartars or Plains Indians, had in the nature of their society ready to hand a semi-military organization. Their men could ride, hunt, shoot, and were used to the discipline of the hunt or the herd. The local Hudson's Bay Company governor was gravely ill and, still more, the moral presence of the company was dying on the eve of that sale of Rupert's Land to Canada.

The sale was stopped by Macdonald, at least temporarily. He was not willing to pay for a territory in insurrection. But the problem of settling the revolt was his rather than the company's. The transfer was finally made on July 15, 1870, and by that time the political arrangements for Red River had been substantially altered by the action of Riel and his colleagues.

What Macdonald had intended was clear enough in the North-West Territories Act of 1869, passed that spring anticipating the transfer in the fall. A governor and a small territorial council, both appointed by Ottawa, would make regulations

The Red River Expedition of 1870 under Sir Garnet Wolseley making a portage, probably at Kakabeka Falls, on the Kaministikwia River, about 18 miles west of Thunder Bay. The soldiers were following the old fur-trade canoe route from Lake Superior to the Lake of the Woods. They are shown bringing their boats ashore and laboriously hauling them over a corduroy portage path. The journey to Fort Garry took three months and demonstrated the need for a railway to provide ready communication with the West. The oil painting is by Frances Anne Hopkins, wife of a Hudson's Bay official. She and her husband travelled in the canoe shown in the middle foreground.

This photograph of Riel is believed to have been taken in 1873, after his election to Parliament in October. Though he looks much older, he was only 29. He was a fugitive at the time and unable to take his seat, though he came secretly to Ottawa, slipped into the Parliament Buildings one evening, and signed the Members' register.

subject to Ottawa approval. This was not unreasonable; a rudimentary organization for a large, virtually unoccupied territory. That Act still stood, notwithstanding Riel. What happened was that, as a result of the Red River uprising, a small, 11,000-square-mile piece of the North-West Territory was carved out and established as the Province of Manitoba. It was all of one hundred miles square, between the 49th parallel and Lake Winnipeg. It had every right and privilege of a province, except one: the Dominion government kept control of all the land, after having set aside land for Métis and Indian claims.

Thus did Manitoba come into existence on July 15, 1870. The new governor was not McDougall now, but a Nova Scotian, Adams Archibald, a big man with a plain, ploughed face, with no knowledge of the West whatever. But he had what Macdonald desperately needed there: tact, brains and a cool head. The Archbishop of Halifax once told Macdonald that Archibald was a Presbyterian, opposed to the Roman Catholic hierarchy on school matters, but "equal to any position in the Dominion," with "tact of a rare kind and ability of the first order." In Manitoba, Archibald was to be everything the Archbishop of Halifax said he was.

The aftermath of the Manitoba affair was complicated too. Riel had, unfortunately, shot a truculent, ne'er-do-well Irish Protestant, Thomas Scott, aged twenty-four, who had made trouble and who happened to come from Ontario. He was shot not in the heat of an argument, either, but formally, after court martial. In Red River the shooting tended to be regarded as an unfortunate incident in a difficult time. But in Ontario, where they knew almost nothing of Scott personally, it created terrible mischief not only for Macdonald and the Dominion government but for Riel too. Riel, who had really been the father of Manitoba, would never be able to take his place, perhaps his rightful place, in Parliament. He was elected three times, in a by-election in October 1873, in the general election of February 1874, and again in a by-election in September 1874, after being formally expelled from the House of Commons. But he never took his seat.*

The Manitoba Bill had been given assent on May 12, 1870. Macdonald was now out of action. He had had a trying year since the summer of 1869. His personal financial position was desperate. He was virtually in hock; he and his family lived in a plain rented house in the back streets of Sandy Hill behind Rideau Street, and there was a serious question of whether he would ever be able to provide adequately for his own family. Worst of all his troubles was Mary. She was born February 7, 1869. She had had a difficult birth and she was a difficult baby, but within a year it was obvious that there was something else. She did not seem to move, or to try to. At thirteen and a half months she lay in her carriage, smiling when she saw Macdonald or Agnes, cooing softly to herself; but physical abnormalities were already apparent: an enlarged head, getting more obvious all the time as the rest of her body failed to develop. Her re-

*He came close; in January 1874, with Dr. J.-B. Fiset he came quietly in a side door of the Parliament Buildings, signed the register and left.

sponses were strange and slow, as if her intelligence was only partly accessible to outside influences. The truth was — and the full truth Macdonald did not know yet — that she would never walk; she would never stand unsupported; she would never be able to take care of herself. Every man has his own private tragedies; but to live with Mary every day, to read to her, talk to her, bring her up, was terribly hard. For him, and for Agnes. Some of Mary's letters to her father are extant. In her own way, on her own terms, she seems to have adored him. "Dear father, when are you coming back?" she wrote* in 1877. "The house seems so dull and lonely without you and I miss my evening stories very much." And she was to live on and on. In 1902, at the age of thirty-three, in her basket chair she looked like a girl of twelve years of age. She finally died in Brighton, England, in 1933, a cripple to the last.

Macdonald was not borne under by these difficulties. Nor by drink, though he got very drunk for two or three days over the weekend of April 29, 1870, when the arduous discussions with the Manitoba delegates were concluded. It was the passage of a gallstone on May 6th, one of the most painful experiences, that almost carried Macdonald off. For a month he could not be moved from his office in the east block. Newspapers assumed he might not live. Finally in July he was got on board a steamer in the St. Lawrence and brought down to Charlottetown. There he laid himself up at a comfortable house on the outskirts, retired from the world for the summer, read, walked and gradually recovered. He did not leave Charlottetown until well into September 1870.

Macdonald's decision to take his convalescence in Charlottetown was probably not fortuitous. In August 1868, the Island had been visited by General Benjamin Butler, Representative for Massachusetts in the American House of Representatives. His professed intention was to persuade the still unconfederated Island to agree to a reciprocity-fishery treaty with the United States, something the Island was quite willing to do. But it was acutely embarrassing for the Canadian and the British governments. In the end nothing came of it, except Butler's re-election in November 1868 in the United States, and strong Colonial Office disapproval from London. But, clearly, the

*Mary eventually learned to write, but her early letters were dictated.

Island ought not to be allowed to drift. Two things had happened in 1869: one was an offer for better terms for the Island's entry into Confederation, an offer followed up by an August 1869 visit to the Island by the Governor-General and three of the cabinet, Kenny of Nova Scotia, Tilley of New Brunswick and Cartier of Quebec. Despite this, the Island rejected the terms early in 1870, a rejection confirmed in an election in July. But there was no doubt that Macdonald had an ample opportunity for getting the drift of Island sentiments and for talking with those politicians on the Island who were known to be favourable to Confederation.

The negotiations with the British Columbia delegates in June and July of 1870 thus fell upon Cartier, as Acting Prime Minister. The British Columbia delegates had come east via the Union Pacific and they were warmly received in Ottawa. The Canadian government was already convinced that a railway to Red River was essential for political reasons; the difficulties of Colonel Garnet Wolseley's expedition toiling a whole summer across the portages between Fort William and Fort Garry, in order to show the flag on the banks of the Red River, were becoming sufficiently persuasive. The British Columbia delegates for their part had had their own discussions in Victoria about this question of a railway. One of the most important of Vancouver Island politicians, J. S. Helmcken, had begun by thinking in terms of a wagon road westward from Winnipeg to Kamloops, and a railway from there to the coast. But J. W. Trutch, the British engineer who had built the Cariboo road, and was now the surveyor-general for the colony, put the question more graphically. He said to Helmcken that without a through line of railway from the east to the Pacific tidewater, Confederation would be nothing but a piece of paper. Without a railway no real union of any kind was possible. "Heavens, Trutch," said Helmcken, "how are they to build it?" Trutch believed he knew how they could, and although at first this proposal struck the British Columbia Executive Council like a bombshell, it was finally adopted, and taken east by the delegation. It was proposed to Cartier and the Canadian government. The Governor of British Columbia, Anthony Musgrave (he had been transferred from Newfoundland to see what he could do), did not believe the Canadians could possibly accept the

Joseph W. Trutch, leader of the three-man delegation that came to Ottawa in June 1870 and negotiated the terms of union under which British Columbia joined the Dominion in 1871. Macdonald appointed him the new province's first Lieutenant-Governor, and he inaugurated responsible government, which had not been granted in the colony before Confederation.

Pacific railway; to his utter astonishment, they did. "And the Railway, Credat Judaeus! is *guaranteed* . . . ! Sir George Cartier says they will do that or 'burst.' "[5] Construction of the railway was to start two years from the date of union. The union came into effect on July 20, 1871; therefore, construction was to start by July 20, 1873. Not only that. The railway was to be completed within ten years from the date of union, *that is*, by July 20, 1881. The little fifteen-member British Columbia special council unanimously adopted the terms early in 1870.

By now, in the East, the terms were news. The Liberal members of the House of Commons were surprised at them. Some were alarmed. So were some Conservatives, especially those from Ontario. The Conservative caucus insisted that some saving clause be put in the terms. Since British Columbia had already ratified the terms, Cartier got Joseph Trutch, one of the B.C. delegates, and the future Lieutenant-Governor, to promise the caucus that British Columbia would not insist on literal fulfilment of the ten-year time limit, if it proved beyond Canada's financial resources. And Trutch's assurance was repeated in the Commons. The party was tense and uneasy. Macdonald might have been still more careful than this, had he been in Ottawa. But Macdonald was now in Washington on the difficult negotiations connected with the Washington Treaty of 1871. So it was the old "lightning striker," Cartier, who reconciled the British Columbia delegates, the Conservative caucus and finally the House of Commons with appropriate glosses for those amazing railway terms. As Trutch wrote back to Victoria, "We must all remember in B.C. that to Sir George Cartier and his followers in Lower Canada we owe . . . the Canadian Pacific Railway."

British Columbia was a province of splendid possibilities, large size — right to the 60th parallel of latitude — and also of large pretensions. And with a meagre population. The population of British Columbia in 1871 was about 28,000 whites and 82,000 Indians.* To plan to complete a railway from Montreal to Pacific tidewater in ten years, across 3,000 miles of terrain, some of which was extremely rugged, none of which had ever been surveyed, was breathtaking: it was, probably, madness.

*The size of the Indian population of British Columbia was not really known in 1871, and the census of 1871 seriously underestimated their numbers. Joseph Trutch estimated them in 1872 at 40,000 to 50,000.

86

Some Canadian Painters

This group of paintings illustrates some of the moods and styles that were prevalent in the world of Canadian art in the course of Macdonald's political career.

Cornelius Krieghoff (see page 115) and Paul Kane were contemporaries (both the paintings reproduced were executed in 1871-72), and they died within a year of one another in 1871-72), but they had little else in common. Krieghoff was concerned almost exclusively with the folk life of French Canada, which he depicted in romantic style, with great spirit and verve. Kane was the first professional artist to travel from Central Canada overland to the Pacific Coast, and his paintings and sketches of Indians and Indian life are historical documents as well as works of art. Some of his pictures, including this view of Fort Garry and St. Boniface, have a romantic touch, but someone has aptly remarked that he saw most of his subjects with a reporter's eye.

The figures and animation in William Raphael's painting of immigrants at Montreal in 1866 reminds one of Krieghoff, but the treatment is much more realistic. Realism in full and highly effective flower is shown in Robert Harris's well known picture of a meeting of the trustees of a small rural school, in which the young school mistress is stating her needs to the four sceptical but not unsympathetic farmers composing her board. Harris painted the picture in 1886. Realism almost

as uncompromising characterized his famous painting of the Fathers of Confederation, commissioned in 1883.

The other two paintings, nearly contemporary with Harris's work, offer interesting contrasts to it and to one another. Homer Watson was born at Doon, in southern Ontario, and found most of his subjects in his native county. *The Stone Road*, painted in 1881, reminds one at once of Constable — an interesting point, as Watson was to insist later that he never saw a Constable painting until 1887.

Yet in 1882 Oscar Wilde visited him and immediately hailed him as the "Canadian Constable," with the unfortunate result that for a time Watson tended, both consciously and unconsciously, to imitate the English painter. Canadian-born Paul Peel, a highly sophisticated and technically skilled painter, spent much of his short working life in Paris. *Reading the Future*, also painted in 1881, introduces an entirely different social milieu — a world of fashion and leisure, in which frills and silks and satins were of the first importance.

Paul Peel, *Reading the Future*, 1881. (Vancouver Art Gallery)

Paul Kane, *Red River Settlement*, 1854. (Royal Ontario Museum, Toronto)

Homer Watson, *The Stone Road*, 1881. (The National Gallery of Canada, Ottawa)

William Raphael, *Behind Bonsecours Market, Montreal*, 1866. (The National Gallery of Canada, Ottawa)

Robert Harris, *A Meeting of the School Trustees*, 1886. (The National Gallery of Canada, Ottawa)

"ISN'T THAT A DAINTY DISH TO SET BEFORE A KING?"—Nursery Rhyme.

4
The Fall of Macdonald and After

It was a nasty, ungrateful business. "Never, in the whole course of my public life," wrote Macdonald from Washington, in April 1871, "have I been in so disagreeable a position, and had such an unpleasant duty to perform....[1]" Canada had always complained that she had been badly treated by British diplomacy. The popular view was, and still is, that Canada had been the sacrificial lamb for British efforts to contain the United States, to appease the United States, or to be friendly to the United States. Canadians suspected that Americans always knew the ground better; that they were shrewder and tougher players at diplomatic poker; that they had the effrontery to bluff when they held no cards; that, overall, the British Navy and British soldiers had won the wars, and the incompetent British diplomats had lost the peace treaties.

Like most stereotypes, this was all partly true. But also partly false. There is evidence that in the Oregon boundary settlement of 1846 the British knew the ground better than the Americans, and that British diplomacy, backed in this case by solid power in the British Navy, saved for Canada the southern end of Vancouver Island. Lord Elgin had proved an adroit and clear-headed negotiator at Washington in 1854, with some help from American internal quarrels, and had secured the Reciprocity Treaty of 1854-1866. Nevertheless, these accomplishments did not remove the Canadian prejudice against the settlement of 1783 after the American Revolutionary War, the settlement of 1814 after the War of 1812, or the Webster-Ashburton Treaty of 1842 that drew the Maine-Quebec boundary. *Grip* stated the prejudice very well:

OPPOSITE *Grip* comments on the Pacific Scandal: Blake (left) and Alexander Mackenzie present the pie, containing such birds as Macdonald, Allan and others, to Lord Dufferin, the Governor General.

91

LITTLE CANADA — I know my pa [John Bull] is very good natured and liberal, because he has given away almost everything I had. He often has settlements with my uncle JONATHAN. If he owes anything to my Uncle JONATHAN, he takes something of mine and pays him with it. . . . He paid him my big farm in Oregon, and my big farm in Maine, and as Uncle JONATHAN would like my fisheries, my pa says — What did you say, pa?

MR. BULL — Hi said hi shall hacquihesce hin hanythink to settle it. . . .

LITTLE CANADA — I do not like to make pa nor my uncle cross. . . . My pa is always forgiving. He has been for-giving my things away as long as I remember. I want to ask my pa if it would not be better to give me and all the farm to Uncle JONATHAN at once, so as to save trouble in future? Perhaps if my Uncle JONATHAN had me, he would not give my things away to any one who wanted them.

MR. JONATHAN — No! Omnipotent Snakes! I wouldn't. Say neow, J.B., couldn't yew let me have the little critter?

MR. BULL — No, no! Disintegrate my Hempire? Never. (Aside — But, say, hi couldn't let you 'ave him hopenly; happearances must be saved; but you are gittin' of 'im gradooal, you know.)[2]

The Americans thought of Canada as colonies to be negotiated for with Great Britain, or bullied into giving up territory whenever bullying would work. That Canada was a wholly owned dependency of Great Britain remained in the American popular mind for a long time to come. It was still a popular view in the 1930s. In 1870 it was a fixed idea in the administration of President Grant (1869-1877) that Britain really would be glad to get rid of her North American commitments. The American Secretary of State, Hamilton Fish, asked the British Minister in Washington whether the British government would have any objection if selected portions of Canada were acquired by the United States, on the free vote of the inhabitants. Fish was sure they would vote overwhelmingly.

Canadians all knew that if the Americans chose to follow up their ambitions with war it would be difficult, if not impossible, to prevent them from taking Canada. How far Great Britain could help was doubtful. There was a great deal of doubt whether Britain had the will or, by the 1870s, the power, to stop the Americans from doing it if they chose. Probably the Americans were not prepared to go to war over Canada.

Canada might have been desirable, but it was not *that* desirable. Wars were expensive. It was cheaper, better, cleaner, to do what had to be done diplomatically and politically.

By the autumn of 1870 Britain felt a powerful need for realigning her European arrangements. While Macdonald lay recovering amid the green farms and woods of Prince Edward Island, Germany won a decisive victory over France in the Franco-Prussian War of August and September, 1870. This destroyed many European diplomatic landmarks, and Britain moved to straighten out some of her overseas and especially her North American problems. As far as North America was concerned, this meant two things. It meant, first of all, the calling home of the British legions. The establishment of the British Army in North America had been reduced in 1855 at the time of the Crimean War, though it had been reinforced again at the time of the *Trent* crisis of 1861 with the United States. But a decade later the British Army left North America for good. No longer would British troops parade at Fredericton, Quebec, Ile aux Noix, Kingston or Toronto. Nor would British babies be born in the barracks there. Readers may remember in Dickens' *Bleak House* (1852) the happy family of ex-Sergeant Bagnet, whose two daughters were Quebec Bagnet and Malta Bagnet, named after the British army married quarters where they had been born.* The last of the British Army marched out of the Citadel of Quebec on November 11, 1871, the band playing "Auld Lang Syne," to go down to the waiting ships. There were two exceptions to this exodus: the bases at Halifax and Esquimalt still held British troops until 1906.

The second consequence wrought by the Franco-Prussian War was British desire to clear up outstanding issues with the United States, issues going back nearly a decade. Some of these involved Canada, notably the fisheries question; some of them did not, like the *Alabama*, a British-built Confederate States raider that wreaked havoc on Northern shipping in 1862 and 1863. Canada also had a long bill of expenses for the Fenians, for their raids on Canada in 1866, 1870 and 1871. Canada believed that the United States had not taken active enough steps

*The curious reader is here referred to Chapter XXVII, in the Oxford Illustrated Dickens at p. 383.

In 1871, in deference to Canada's interest in some of the matters to be discussed, Macdonald was one of the five British members appointed to a Joint Commission to settle outstanding differences between Great Britain and the United States. In this photograph of the British representatives and their secretary (standing at the left), the head of the delegation, Lord de Grey and Ripon, is seated in the centre. The proceedings were distressing to Macdonald, who saw Canadian interests, especially in the Atlantic fisheries, sacrificed in order to encourage agreement on other matters of more immediate concern to Great Britain.

to prevent the raids from occurring, and had not taken adequate steps to punish the offenders.

There was a slight precedent for the right given to Canada to approve any treaty. Newfoundland had been given that privilege at the time of the 1857 Anglo-French Convention, and had exercised it to the full by rejecting the convention completely. The whole convention thus fell to the ground. No doubt that event was in the mind of the British government; if Canada was given the right to ratify the new treaty, then some responsible Canadian was going to have to be on the delegation. But there was no precedent for the role of Macdonald and he was made a full member of the five-member British delegation. The Americans were puzzled by Canada's role, as well they might be. Were they dealing with Britain or Canada? It was not clear at all. Foreigners were frequently puzzled by the muddled nature of imperial authority.

Macdonald must himself have raised this question. He was in a difficult position. He had no real option but to accept the position on the British delegation, if Canada's interests were to be defended. But at the same time it was clear, all too painfully clear, that the British really wanted a treaty with the Americans. Macdonald had the very devil of a time trying to keep his fellow British Commissioners from giving Canada's cards away. He had to fight off not only the Americans but also the British.

"I stand alone," he wrote the Governor-General on April 7th, "the Americans are constantly depreciating the value of our property, and making absurdly low offers, which my [British] colleagues, in their anxiety for a settlement, are constantly pressing me to yield to." And as Prime Minister, he would have to take the result, whatever it was, to the Canadian Parliament and be responsible for it. The treaty was signed in Washington on May 6, 1871, ratified by Great Britain, the United States and by the Canadian Parliament by May 1872, and came into effect as of July 1, 1873.*

It is not easy now, a century later, to see around that immense arbitration of 1871-77. That is, perhaps, the measure of how big a watershed it was. Of course it is not true that Canadian-American relations since have been *couleur de rose*. No Canadian can forget the Alaskan Boundary arbitration of 1903. But it can be said that from about this time Canadian-

The rapid spread of settlement in the American West made it essential that the 49th parallel — the Canadian-American boundary between the Lake of the Woods and the Rocky Mountains — should be marked accurately as promptly as possible. An International Boundary Commission was appointed in 1872, surveys began in 1873 and the work was completed in only two seasons. In this supply train for the British survey party the first six wagons were drawn by horses but the eighteen others were hauled by oxen.

*The main provisions can be summarized. The San Juan Boundary question went to arbitration, that of the German Emperor. The *Alabama* claims went to arbitration, at Geneva. Canadians wanted a reciprocity treaty for the inshore fisheries, but got instead use of the American inshore fisheries (almost no value), free entrance of Canadian fish into the United States, and an arbitration over the difference in value between the Canadian fisheries and the American. That was held in Halifax in 1877. The fisheries clauses were to run for twelve years, that is, to July 1, 1885.

Portrait of Sir John A. Macdonald by Delos C. Bell, 1873. (Confederation Centre Art Gallery & Museum, Charlottetown)

American relations improved; not quickly, certainly not continually, but they did get better. Before 1871, Canadian memories of Americans had been of the War of 1812, the border raids of 1838, the Fenian raids, the sheer truculence of Washington in the later 1860s, the easy assumptions of poets and peasants, like Walt Whitman, that Canada was destined to be part of the great American polity. After 1871, these memories began to be memories rather than principles of action. But a note of caution is required. Thirty years or so in the life of a mature man is not that long; there were still a few Canadians around who had fought in the War of 1812, and many more, Macdonald among them, who actively recalled the border troubles of 1838. History tends to close in, unreasonably, one's sense of time, and here it is important to keep one's perspectives and to realize, with Macdonald, that in 1871 the Webster-Ashburton Treaty of 1842 was only thirty years old.

Macdonald always read American politics with a shrewd appreciation of American weaknesses. He would never regard the Americans as being potentially friendly to Canada. However friendly they seemed, they were always potentially dangerous. There was literally no other way Macdonald could see them; it was what he had grown up with.

The treaty passed in Canada, but with a great deal of noise and comment. The details were out almost at once, so the newspapers had nearly a year to talk about it before it came up before the Canadian Parliament in April 1872. Macdonald was in no hurry. And though it passed with a substantial majority of sixty-six, Macdonald and his party believed they paid a certain price at the polls in the election that followed late in the summer of 1872.

The general election of 1872 took place over most of August and into early September. It was the last Canadian general election held that way. (The next general election was held on one day — January 22, 1874 — in most constituencies.) Macdonald went to the election of 1872 confident of good support in all parts of Canada, including Nova Scotia, but not including Ontario. Everything the government had done seemed to threaten or to compromise the Conservative hold on Ontario, except possibly for the Trade Union Act of the 1872 session which had repealed the common law rules against restraint of trade as they applied to trade unions.

There would be also nine new members of the House of Commons as a result of the redistribution of seats after the 1871 census. That meant that including the Manitoba and British Columbia representatives, the new 1872 House of Commons would have 200 members. In Ontario there were now 88 seats at stake, 42 per cent of the House of Commons, and opposition more serious than even Macdonald expected developed there. He was forced to campaign as he had never done before, and most of it outside his own constituency, Kingston. He had, however, a good deal of money readily available and he was prepared to use it for fighting those Ontario battles. J. S. Mc-Cuaig at Picton was fighting to overturn Walter Ross, the Liberal member for Prince Edward County, and he was evidently having scruples about using money. Macdonald pushed aside McCuaig's tender conscience, not without a certain delicacy and sureness of touch:

...I quite appreciate your feelings about money matters. At the same time let me tell you that if Ross goes in with money he will stand a great chance of beating you. You must fight him with the same weapon. Our friends here have been liberal with contributions and I can send you $1,000 without inconvenience. You had better spend it between nomination [day] and polling [day].[3]

Whatever McCuaig did or did not spend, Ross was returned.

That voters were bribed into voting the right way was common knowledge. It is still common knowledge. That does not make it moral or legal, however. The question of the use of campaign funds is, even now, difficult. There are substantial and often legitimate expenses at election time. Printing, placards, meeting halls, assistants — not much of that is done with prayer. The candidate pays most of it. But he could, as Macdonald's letter to McCuaig shows, expect some outside assistance if he had a hard election or was trying to defeat the sitting member. The question could then slip over to treating the voters, from sandwiches and tea, to cakes and ale, to plenty of good booze and forget the food. From there it was a short step to the ubiquitous five-dollar bill.

Especially useful was the old "manly" practice of open voting, where you stood up and said to the world "I vote for James McCuaig (or Walter Ross)!" Then the candidate was sure that the voter who had been paid five dollars delivered the vote. When the ballot came in — it was introduced by Mackenzie in the 1874 session — no such control was possible. Indeed, the voters soon learned the trick of talking for one candidate and voting for another.

The Macdonald government was also fought by the Liberal organization that supported the Government of Ontario. An Ontario Liberal régime had come into power at the end of 1871. Edward Blake was then the Premier. Members of provincial legislatures were elected by precisely the same electorate that elected members to the House of Commons. And although Macdonald might protest that the course of provincial legislatures was their own affair, the essential oneness of the electorate was something that both parties were well aware of. None of them encouraged the separation of Dominion and provincial party support.

Some Ontario constituencies were hard fought. The new

riding of Toronto Centre was the scene of a difficult battle. As one Conservative described it, "The halt, the lame, the blind, and even the absent and the dead were brought out to vote and in many cases did vote,* and there can be no doubt a large sum of money was spent, and probably on both sides." Happily there was no violence in Toronto Centre and the whole election passed off good humouredly enough. But it did go Liberal, and for the Conservative workers this defeat was mortifying for, it was alleged, victory was almost in sight when the polls closed. In the old days of open voting, you knew how things were going as the day, or the two days, went along. At eleven o'clock in the morning of August 21st the Liberal candidate, Robert Wilkes, was 201 votes ahead. At noon he was 178 ahead, at 1:00 P.M. 157 ahead, and at 2:00 P.M. only 70 votes ahead! Wrote the Conservative organizer: "...we then began to

Fort Garry and the beginnings of Winnipeg about 1875, viewed at sunset from an Indian encampment on the east bank of the Red River. The steamer at the wharf is the *Dakota*. From the painting by Frank Lynn. (Winnipeg Art Gallery)

---

*So long as a man's name was on the voter's list, whether he was absent, dead, or *non compos mentis*, a vote was possible. Means of identification were meagre, so such a person could easily be impersonated.

Sir Hugh Allan, the bluff old shipowner and financier, probably the richest man in Canada, who tried to secure control of the Pacific Railway project by making lavish contributions to Conservative election campaign funds in 1872. Cartier, failing in health and in trouble in his Montreal constituency, was the party chief most involved; Macdonald had only a partial knowledge of what was going on. The Liberals got wind of the matter and precipitated the Pacific Scandal.

work and spend money but it was too late, we were beaten by 28. Half an hour more would have cleaned off the 28 and given us a good majority. I am dreadfully cut up [about it]."[4]

Altogether Macdonald lost ground in Ontario, taking only 40 of the 88 seats, and taking 38 of the 65 seats in Quebec. The party improved its position in Nova Scotia, where it broke even, as it did in New Brunswick; but it emerged with an overall majority of only 8 seats. It was eminently unsatisfactory for a man who had enjoyed a comfortable majority of 35 since Confederation. Macdonald always thoroughly appreciated being able to do what he liked with Parliament. That time was now coming to an end.

Cartier had had difficulties too. He had been defeated in Montreal East despite all his efforts. And although he was eventually given the nomination for Provencher in Manitoba, he never sat in the House of Commons again. He was seriously ill with Bright's disease, degeneration of the kidneys, and it was to kill him in May 1873, despite his continued accounts of improvement and all that the London doctors could do. And by that time Macdonald faced the Pacific Scandal.

To build that railway promised to British Columbia was going to take all the talent and capital available in Canada, and a good deal more from outside of Canada. "I don't know how many millions you have," said Walter Moberly to Macdonald in 1871, "but it is going to cost you money to get through those canyons." Money was the prime commodity. The Pacific Railway would not be built by the government, as the Intercolonial was currently being built. The government had had its fill of construction. The essential thing was to get private capital to undertake the railway. Macdonald tried to put Montreal and Toronto finance together. Montreal financier Sir Hugh Allan was greedy and selfish; Toronto financier David Macpherson was distrustful and suspicious of Montreal. But a vague and tentative agreement existed by August 1872, enough for Macdonald to feel that the main problem, Sir Hugh Allan's insistence on having the presidency of the new company which would be formed* to build the railway, could be resolved. On

*Both Allan and Macpherson were presidents of companies already, Allan's being the Canada Pacific Railway Company and Macpherson's the Interoceanic Railway Company.

Edward Blake, chief lieu-
tenant of Alexander Mac-
kenzie, the Liberal leader,
and Macdonald's most for-
midable opponent in the
struggle over the Pacific
Scandal. Blake's speeches
on what he deemed to be
important issues were in-
terminable (some lasted
five hours), but they could
be devastating. Undoubt-
edly he was the opposition
speaker that Macdonald
most feared.

that basis, the government could count on Sir Hugh Allan's
assistance with campaign expenses.

The Pacific Scandal was like a sharpened three-edged
bayonet. You could cut yourself on any one of the edges. Sir
Hugh Allan claimed to have ladled out $350,000 in campaign
funds to the Conservative party. That was one edge. The
second edge was that having dispensed the funds, Allan in due
course received the Pacific Railway charter from the government. Blake put it very simply in Parliament later: "... the
Government got the money and Sir Hugh Allan the Charter."
All of that was bad enough. But besides there was the third
edge. While most of the money that Sir Hugh Allan dispensed

was his, some was supplied by George McMullen and the Americans connected with the Northern Pacific Railway, who believed that they were going to be able to get control of the Pacific Railway in Canada. That was something that neither the Macdonald government nor the Canadian People had any intention of allowing. The trouble was, that edge was hidden from Macdonald's sight when he accepted the money in the first place. He found out about it soon enough after the elections were over. For the Americans kicked, and kicked hard, when they learned that they would be excluded from effective control of the Pacific Railway. They had not put up time and money for nothing. Then the Liberal Party heard about it, got hold of hard evidence, and stage by stage the whole affair grew rapidly worse.

Macdonald never at any time in the affair, not even on the night of November 3, 1873 when he gave his tremendous back-to-the-wall speech, really knew what the opposition had hold of. Beginning in April 1873, when L. S. Huntingdon rose in the House to make vague threats about a corrupt bargain at the time of the August 1872 election, Macdonald did not know how much the opposition knew. In April 1873 the best thing to do seemed to be to brave it out. But *he* knew, himself, how damaging some of that information could be. He had asked for and got $45,000 from Allan. His friends, as he had told James McCuaig, had indeed been liberal! Cartier had received $85,000 and Langevin $32,600. Altogether, Macdonald could count that $162,000 had been expended. That was the figure Blake was later to use. Allan claimed he had given out closer to $350,000.

There is a distinction between funds for party purposes and funds that go into one's own pocket. There was never any real accusation that Macdonald or Cartier or Langevin had used the money for themselves. Most politicians did not get rich fighting elections. They became poor. Cartier and Langevin needed the funds for the same reasons Macdonald needed them, though most of Cartier's money went to fight his own election in Montreal East.

Once the Pacific issue had been raised in Parliament, Macdonald's ingenuity went to work to devise roadblocks. They were not unsuccessful, for Macdonald always was a master of tactics. First there was the Oaths Bill, to allow a parliamentary investigating committee to take evidence on oath. Then the committee had to adjourn to allow Allan and Allan's solicitor, Abbott, to get back from England where they had been trying to float their Pacific Railway Company. By the time Allan and Abbott arrived, the Oaths Bill had been disallowed in London.

Even now, in the midst of these complications Macdonald kept his head. A good captain not only takes the reports of the watch but keeps his eye on the horizon. For example, the agreements with British Columbia required that the construction of the railway had to begin within two years of the date of union, that is, by July 20, 1873. Sandford Fleming had been appointed as engineer-in-chief of the Pacific Railway in April 1871 and had begun surveys that summer, which were now already ramified extensively. But Macdonald had not forgotten that construction *had to start officially* by July 20, 1873. There is a telegram to Langevin – Langevin was now Minister of Public Works – from Macdonald in Ottawa on July 13, 1873: "Instruct by telegraph Governor Trutch or Marcus Smith or some Dominion officer to begin Railway by survey planting stakes and otherwise before twentieth this is important." Five days later, on Friday, July 18th, this question was still being discussed by telegraph, Macdonald by this time being at Rivière du Loup. But on that day something else happened.

The opposition had grown increasingly angry over delays. Finally they bought, from Abbott's clerk, really damaging letters and telegrams stolen from Abbott's office. These were published in three opposition papers, on Friday, July 18, 1873: The Toronto *Globe*, the Montreal *Herald* and the Quebec *L'Evénement*. They were devastating:

> Macdonald to Abbott, St. Anne de Bellevue, from Toronto, August 26, 1872. Immediate. Private. I must have another ten thousand. Will be the last time of asking. Do not fail me. Answer today.

In the history of this country more damning documents had scarcely ever seen the light of day.

They shook Macdonald. They shook the cabinet. And the party. Macdonald came up to Quebec City and met with Langevin and Alexander Campbell. They attempted to devise some means of controlling, or of seeming to control, the course of affairs. For several days in early August Macdonald disappeared completely. Not even Agnes knew where he was. Affairs were almost, though not quite, out of his hands. Macdonald got a prorogation of Parliament on August 13th in the teeth of strong opposition resistance; he got a Royal Commission appointed to investigate the affair; and by the time Parliament opened again on October 23, 1873 , the government began to feel that they might weather it after all.

It was Prince Edward Island's first session as a province of the Dominion. She had come in on July 1st, after a long and rather sordid courtship in which the price of the lady's favour seemed continually to rise. Prince Edward Island's first experience of Parliament was not inappropriate:

| 3rd Wizard: (Toronto *Globe*) | Adjectives from Billingsgate, From my columns freely take, Add thereto McMullen's crams, Stolen letters, telegrams, All these matters mix & mangle, To form a great Pacific Scandal. |
| All: | Double, double cauldron bubble Bring the Premier lots of trouble.[5] |

OPPOSITE Many patriotic songs were composed in Canada in Macdonald's time, some of them in support of specific political parties and personalities. While he was out of office in the 1870s, this Loyal Opposition Galop was dedicated, as the legend on the cover states, to Macdonald "and the Liberal Conservatives of Canada." In 1874 Alexander Mackenzie had already been honoured by the publication of a New Premier Galop. (Oxford tells us that a galop is "a lively dance in 2/4 time.")

None of the Pacific Scandal money came east of the Quebec-New Brunswick border. Tupper of Nova Scotia defended the government, and did "lie like truth, and still most truly lie," in a way that left the impression that Sir John Macdonald was like a staunch old ship that had become barnacled and needed drydocking for a while. There was great tension in the corridors of Parliament and in the Ottawa streets. The Liberals smelt blood, and they put enormous pressure on Members of Parliament of all denominations to stand up for righteousness against iniquity. Within a few days of the opening of Parliament, the support for the government began to weaken. By Friday, October 31st, Langevin was already anticipating he would soon no longer be a minister.

Finally on Monday night, November 3rd, Macdonald made the speech of his life and, in a sense, for his life. Without a major defence he was finished as a public man. Most people believed he was probably finished anyway. He owed it to himself, to his party, to try. He rose to his feet shakily at 9:00 P.M. looking as if a breath would knock him over. Peter Mitchell,

LOYAL OPPOSITION GALOP.

OPPOSED AND RESPECTFULLY DEDICATED TO THE

AND THE LIBERAL CONSERVATIVES OF CANADA

FROM A PHOTO, BY W.J.TOPLEY.

RIGHT HON. SIR JOHN A. MACDONALD, K.C.B.

BY

G. L. ORME.

5

his Minister of Marine and Fisheries, kept him going on gin and water. The House was packed. The galleries were packed. Macdonald said plainly there had been no corrupt bargain. He denied that Sir Hugh Allan had ever been promised the charter in return for campaign funds. That was probably true. Macdonald said that the uses of campaign funds were well known to members on both sides of the House.

Macdonald's defence got better and stronger as he went along. Lady Dufferin was sitting in the gallery — Lord Dufferin could not, constitutionally, be there — listening spellbound to Macdonald. So was twenty-six-year-old Lord Rosebery. After five hours Macdonald concluded:

> I leave it [the decision] with this House with every confidence. I am equal to either fortune. I can see past the decision of this House either for or against me, but whether it be against me or for me, I know, and it is no vain boast to say so, for even my enemies will admit that I am no boaster, that there does not exist in Canada a man who has given more of his time, more of his heart, more of his wealth, or more of his intellect and power, such as it may be, for the good of this Dominion of Canada.

And that was true too. His followers cheered him to the rafters. But it has also to be said, as Blake did the next day, that no minister should stand in a position where his interest conflicted with his duty. Sir Hugh Allan was in a position, Blake averred, to say to the government at any time, "Either give me the contract or give me my money back."

Wednesday morning, November 5, 1873, a council was called for nine o'clock. There was no Sir John then, or at ten o'clock, and finally John Henry Pope, the Minister of Agriculture, was deputed to go and get him at Earnscliffe, the house that Macdonald had rented three years before. Pope found him in bed reading a novel. By the time Macdonald had arrived on the scene, about eleven-thirty, the members of the cabinet had virtually decided to throw in the sponge. According to Peter Mitchell, all that Macdonald said was, "I suppose I shall have to go to Rideau Hall and hand in your resignations." That was what Macdonald quietly announced to the House that afternoon when it met at three o'clock. The House was anything but quiet after that.

Only twice since 1867 has a government been defeated and the opposition installed without an election. It happened in June 1926, when the Meighen government replaced that of King. In November 1873, it was quite a scene. The Speaker left the Chair shortly after 3:30 P.M. and the House rose. The Conservatives literally moved out of their seats and crossed the floor. This happened just as the crowd was coming into the galleries. Most of them came down on the floor of the Commons, while the Conservative M.P.s pushed their way across with their books and stationery. More inexperienced ones had already headed for the bar. One erstwhile Conservative stayed right where he was. He was Amor de Cosmos, Member for Victoria, B.C. The Conservatives never forgave him.

It is altogether probable that the Macdonald government never expected to be in power again. That was the view of many of the party hangers-on too. They had been in Ottawa almost from the opening of Parliament. There had been a tremendous rush. The Russell House was bursting at the seams. The faithful, the deserving, the hungry and the unscrupulous, all wanted to get whatever it was they could get, before the Conservative ship broke up. And not only those from Ontario and Quebec; Nova Scotians and New Brunswickers were not behind in looking for judgeships, collectorships of customs, postmasterships, before the power to appoint was utterly gone. Leonard Tilley was appointed Lieutenant-Governor of New Brunswick on the very last day, November 5, 1873. That in itself suggested the government's own view that their future was hopeless.

Across the country the excitement was considerable. People were astonished that Macdonald resigned before the vote was taken in the House. In Ottawa the Orangemen, notwithstanding the defeat of the Conservatives, celebrated Guy Fawkes Day intemperately all night. In Quebec City the sole topic seemed to be the political situation. The Quebec *Morning Chronicle*'s description of the bars of Quebec that night could be generally applicable:

> . . . needless to say that the professional politician was equal to the occasion. He stood before the bar with his telegram in his hand, declaiming by the hour. As his eye grew fishier, his

Richard Cartwright, an unforgiving soul who never forgave Macdonald for not appointing him to the finance portfolio in 1870. He was still berating Macdonald 42 years later, when he published his *Reminiscences*. Cartwright joined the Liberals after the Pacific Scandal and was Minister of Finance in the Alexander Mackenzie ministry of 1873-78.

voice huskier and his perpendicularity uncertain, the loudness
of his remarks increased in proportion to their incoherency.
. . . The excitement spent itself as the night wore on. The professional politician went home in company with a shutter
when he failed in obtaining permission to take his natural rest
on the soft side of a plank. The enthusiast . . . called for his
"nightcap" and went home too. And sensible men, when tired
of the subject, did the same, and the world was at peace, re-
volving in its usual way as if nothing at all had happened.

The principals of the Pacific Scandal survived. It was the
railway that had to be begun again. Sir Hugh Allan's new railway company never got off the ground, and by the time the
government of Alexander Mackenzie picked up the pieces the
American depression of the autumn of 1873 was already beginning to make the financing of railways difficult. Canada was
still prosperous, but the bankruptcy of Jay Cooke's Philadelphia
banking firm and the stoppage of the Northern Pacific helped
to make doubtful all large railway schemes: Sir Hugh Allan
lived opulently enough for another ten years, with the Allan
steamship line and his other enterprises.

Macdonald believed his own political career pretty much
at an end. He was almost fifty-nine. The party needed a
younger leader. The party caucus he met on November 6, 1873,
unanimously declared their support for him, but he would not
commit himself. He might even have agreed with the *Globe* on
November 12th, that "his *role* as a Canadian politician is played
out." The *Globe* article that day, probably written by George
Brown, serves well enough to show Liberal reactions to Macdonald at the time, and through its very exaggerations points to
some of the warts and blemishes in Macdonald's portrait. That
he had great gifts of intellect and judgment the *Globe* conceded.

But these gifts have been poisoned by a cynical view of human
nature, which has led him to appeal to the least worthy side
of human character. His great facility in managing men applied only to a certain class of men, and broke down when
brought face to face with rectitude of character. . . . No one
could surpass him in power over men of the baser sort; his
adroitness captivated imaginations uninformed by high ideas
of conduct; while his resolve to approach every man through
his special foible or ambition placed the selfish and the vain

Alexander Mackenzie, the Scottish stonemason who became leader of the Liberal Party and who succeeded Macdonald as prime minister in 1873, when the Pacific Scandal forced him to resign. Though he won a resounding victory in the general election of 1874, Mackenzie was soon in difficulties. Canada suffered a depression, and overwork and worry took their toll of his health. He had been able to muster only a few able ministers, and Edward Blake, much the ablest of them, proved to be a difficult and erratic colleague in spite of his brilliance.

within his reach. . . . His policy has been first, steady resistance, and then, when resistance was no longer possible, to bow his head to the wave of public opinion which had been raised by more conscientious and far-seeing men.

And the *Globe* was not to let go of this theme for a long time. There were endless opportunities for gibes. Typically, seven months later, it remarked, "It cannot even be said,— 'All is lost save honour,' for alas! honour was the first to go." Liberals never forgot the Pacific Scandal. Why should they? The Conservative party remained for them a sink of iniquity. Sir Richard Cartwright published his reminiscences in 1912 still fulminating about the wickedness of Sir John Macdonald.

BLACKWASH AND WHITEWASH.

ILLUSTRATING THE RECENT GREAT OPPOSITION SPEECHES, AND THE DOINGS OF THE JOLLY ROYAL COMMISSION.

Bengough comments on the Royal Commission investigating the Pacific Scandal: Blake, Mackenzie and George Brown smear Macdonald with black political tar while the Royal Commissioners apply the whitewash.

The public condemnation in the press and Parliament had still to be reflected in seats in the House of Commons. That came with the January election of 1874. Mackenzie wanted a stronger majority and got an enormous one. The Conservatives were shattered. They were reduced to 67 in a 206-seat House. Macdonald narrowly escaped defeat in Kingston and soon had a petition out against him for corrupt practices. Was it not really time to quit? He walked down Sparks Street disconsolately one morning in February or March 1874 into the offices of the Ottawa *Citizen*. The *Citizen* was at that time run by the Holland brothers. They stopped work to talk to him. "Boys," said Macdonald, "I want you to publish an editorial paragraph in today's Citizen announcing my resignation of the leadership of the Conservative party." The party, Macdonald said, could never again come to power with him as leader. It would always be known, as long as he headed it, as the "Charter Seller's" party. The elder Holland threw down his pen. Such a resignation would be an admission that Sir John was guilty. "Sir John," he emphasized, "my pen will write no such announcement, nor will it be published in the Citizen."[6] Macdonald listened. He did not resign, not yet. A few weeks afterwards an uproarious banquet at the Russell House showed Macdonald how thoroughly he was still entrenched in the hearts and confidence of the party.

Macdonald continued to lead using a very light rein. He gave the Conservatives good advice. Don't badger the new government. Support good measures when there are good measures to support. Don't be captious. To the more captious of his supporters he suggested the motto of the party was, country first, party after. It was bread upon the waters. Even the *Globe* thought that Macdonald had been very cooperative in the 1874 session. And he was gradually drifting out of politics. He picked up again the threads of his law practice, and later in 1874 Macdonald, Patton, Fleming and Macdonald (the last being Hugh John) was established in Toronto.

He encouraged Hector Langevin to come out of retirement. Langevin had resigned his House of Commons seat in January 1874. "There was no one," Macdonald told Langevin over an evening dinner in Ottawa, April 14, 1874, "to take the direction of the French-Canadian wing of the party." There were certainly those who had ambitions to do so, he went on, but even they were beginning to realize that a French-Canadian leader was not made in a day. Langevin accepted this. "I told him I would take the first opportunity. . . . "

For his own part, Langevin seems to have believed that going out of office would do immense good for the party, and that a sojourn in opposition would be salutary. The Conservatives were in power in Quebec, and with that base they could regroup. They did, and in a way not unsatisfactory to Langevin. The Tanneries Scandal of July 1874 forced out of office some of the Conservatives and they were replaced with the purer, if more ultramontane, De Boucherville ministry. By the late autumn of 1875, Langevin had found a federal constituency, Charlevoix, and was elected there on January 22, 1876.

Cartier, three months before he died, had set forth for Langevin something of his own political ideology:

It was important not to forget that the union of races and religion in our province has been mainly the cause of the elevated, important and influential role that our province has played in public affairs both before and after Confederation. I have been able to see even from here [i.e., London] reading the speeches of the Grit chiefs of Ontario, that their politics always reduces itself to this,—"To rule Confederation by the

Grits and for the Grits"— the Quebec [Conservative] majority shipwrecked that policy within the Province of Canada
before Confederation when it had to struggle alone against
the Grits, and certainly it should now be easier to extinguish
Grit policy since the Quebec majority has for help in the
struggle the M.P.'s from Nova Scotia, New Brunswick,
Manitoba and British Columbia.[7]

Macdonald was as well aware of it as Cartier; French-Canadian
Conservatives were the strong core of Conservative defences.
The *Globe* was clearly not altogether wrong when it said that
Macdonald was kept in power not by his own strength but by
that of Sir George Cartier. Of the 67 Conservative M.P.s in
1874, 30 were from Quebec; of the 112 in 1872, some 38 had
been from Quebec. The Conservative and clerical *Nouveau
Monde* of Montreal put it in broader terms: Confederation
needs Quebec as a counterweight, and Quebec needs Confederation to guarantee its autonomy.

French-Canadian society had always retained this sense of
community, of belonging together. Quebec was a French island
in an English sea. It often had the insular sense of being be-
leaguered. But it had thrown up strong fortifications and the
church was one of the strongest. It was no small protection
against the English. It was also a guarantee of society's order,
its internal discipline. Even English Canadians would have
agreed that without religion society could not hang together.
Take away the priest, said *Le Nouveau Monde* in 1868, and you
will have to give the hangman a new role. You have to have one
or the other.

French-Canadian society was as rural as that of English
Canada. Seventy-seven per cent of Quebec's population was
classified rural in 1871. But it dropped below 70 per cent by
1891, and to 60 per cent by 1901. The transformation was
already under way in the 1870s. While Montreal had lost out
to New York in the contest for the Canadian and American
Midwest trade, it had now ambitions of transcontinental commercial hegemony. It began to develop industries in the 1850s,
and by the 1870s it was big enough to be hit hard by American
dumping of manufactured goods. At the same time, the expansion of agriculture in Ontario and, by the end of the 1870s, the

arrival of hard wheat from Manitoba, affected the traditional markets in Quebec for the produce of Quebec farms. Quebec farmers began to turn more to producing sugar beets for industry, to raising cattle for milk and butter and the export of beef to England. The surplus population from the large habitant families began to move outward. Some went to the Eastern Townships in the 1870s, some to the Saguenay and Lac St. Jean country. Some went to the towns or to Montreal or Quebec. Many left Quebec, for Ontario, Illinois, Minnesota and Manitoba. Many more headed for the nearby mill towns of New Hampshire and Massachusetts. At least in the nearby United States it was not that far to come home, as many did in the bad years in America from 1873 to 1878.

The English in the townships south and east of Montreal were gradually being displaced in the 1870s and 1880s. Sherbrooke in 1871 had already a slight Roman Catholic majority and in 1891 this became a French-speaking majority. The quiet French-Canadian occupation of land in the townships was a curious process, rather like the gathering of a hive of bees by the introduction of a queen. The symbol of French-Canadian expansion was the establishment of a parish church and a curé.

But basically the Quebec countryside changed only slowly. The habitant lived on about 125 acres, and in the area of the great Montreal plain or the Eastern Townships was apt to be more commercialized and prosperous than his counterpart in the counties down river from Quebec City, Bellechasse, Montmagny, L'Islet, Kamouraska. Broadly speaking, the habitant was content with life as he found it. He was largely untouched by cravings, now exemplified in Ontario, for things new and therefore better. In Ontario the farm parlours by the later 1870s and early 1880s were already acquiring a parlour organ, the horsehair sofa, lace curtains; in the barn would frequently be a light-running buggy of the newest design. Not so the habitant. His content came not from a philosophical desire to limit his desires to his means but because he did not know what to wish for. Newspapers, those rivers of restlessness and yearning, did not have large circulations in the Quebec countryside. By and large, habitants read very little. Books were regarded suspiciously, as sources of error and evil, veritable treasure troves of sin. Robert de Roquebrune recalled as late as the 1890s how l'Abbé Dorval, the local priest in L'Assomption (it is just northeast of Montreal), would say that the thirst for reading was simply an idle and dangerous form of curiosity, and a bad book was the doorway to Hell.

It was a typical English and Protestant assumption that all this meant the habitant was stupid and ignorant. This was nonsense, a question only of definition. The habitant lived much more in an oral world. The great channel of communication was outside the church door on Sunday after Mass. If men were wanted, if timber were needed, a call was made at the church door. In the countryside political speeches were nearly always made after Mass on Sunday — this to the scandal of Protestants in Ontario. But it was a civilized world. The priests and lawyers, even some farmers, had been educated at the French-Canadian classical colleges, an education built around Greek, Latin and philosophy, and the French classics. Lawyers and priests quoted Virgil and used quotations from Racine and Corneille in everyday speech. It was not unusual to hear farmers use them.

There was little real drunkenness in the Quebec countryside. That "abomination and curse of Ontario," the roadside tavern, "with its frowsy bar . . . its quota of sodden loafers waiting for a chance drink" was largely absent. The well-spoken, kind and hospitable people of the Quebec countryside, one Ontario correspondent remarked, were social results in which any society could take pride.[8]

However, the docility of the habitant was a popular English Protestant delusion. There was plenty of litigiousness in the Quebec countryside. The number of lawsuits taken out by the "docile" habitant, even against curés, was not inconsiderable, as a reading of the Quebec *Law Reports* will show. Chief Justice A. A. Dorion (he was appointed by Mackenzie in 1874) decided a number of celebrated cases of this kind in which, as one would suspect from his earlier years as editor of the Montreal *Le Pays*, he insisted that priests, like other citizens, were responsible to civil tribunals. That was not a position many bishops would then have accepted; but aside from that, the origins of such cases were civil suits of a great variety, suits about tithes, about pews, about all kinds of ecclesiastical matters. "La fabrique" meant the vestry-board that controlled and owned the local parish church and its property, and *fabrique* cases were an important part of most French-Canadian law practices. The "simple" habitant's acquaintance with the

technicalities of French-Canadian civil law was often quite phenomenal.

That was possible, of course, because French-Canadian law was not the mystery to French Canadians that English-Canadian law is to English Canadians. French-Canadian civil law was written down in the great *Code Civil* that Cartier brought in to the Legislature of the Province of Canada in 1865, the result of six years' work. It had been rendered essential by the abolition of seigneurial tenure in 1854 and 1855. French-Canadian civil law, because of the seigneurial system with which it was associated, the Roman law from which it was derived, was informed by a profound sense of the oneness of society, that interrelations between man and man are not so much between free individuals as between responsible ones. The French Canadian could rightly ask, who *is* free, anyway? Who *is* independent? Is anyone? In all society, primitive even more than civilized, all men are to a greater or less degree dependent on each other. This sense of interdependence, where each member of society has his role to play, was also fostered by the church. It could sometimes lead to a stultifying commit-

Cornelius Krieghoff, *The Habitant Farm*, 1854. (The National Gallery of Canada, Ottawa)

115

ment to things as they were.* But there was also a graciousness and peace in its quiet conservatism, and in its consciousness of mutuality. One of the legal obligations of children in the *Code Civil* was the support of parents when they had become too old to work, as it once had been the obligation of the parents to support the children. French-Canadian marriage law was more liberal in some respects than English law, at least before the Married Women's Property Act of 1882. But it *was* different. A man and woman who were to be married established, before a notary, a full list of what goods and property they were each bringing to the marriage, the totality of which was called *la communauté des biens.*

Logically, the *Code Civil* operated at the opposite pole from English common law. The Code stated a certain legal principle; its application to a particular case was deduced from the premises so stated. French-Canadian education generally, and legal education in particular, stressed deductive reasoning, and every French-Canadian graduate of the old classical college system was affected by it. English law worked the other way round. From individual legal decisions on all kinds of particular problems, one arrived inductively and empirically at a rough, working principle. That is the way the nature of our law of property, for example, can be discovered. It is no accident that the great English philosophers have been empiricists. It is, if you like, the English habit of mind, as it is the French habit to work the other way round.

It was part of young Wilfrid Laurier's genius that he knew and used both modes of thought, having been educated at Collège de l'Assomption — the same county as l'Abbé Dorval — and also at McGill University. He had first appeared in provincial politics in 1871 at the age of thirty, and he was elected M.P. for Drummond-Arthabaska in the 1874 election. In 1877 he was made Minister of Inland Revenue in the Mackenzie govern-

---

*The following is an example from a Roman Catholic paper in Halifax in 1874, but it is not unrepresentative of the church's position in the 1870s. "There must always be working men, men to work with their hands, to be poor, to be industrious, to be unfortunate, to suffer; it is the will of God and the destiny of the race. That will and that destiny are not to be counteracted by public meetings, by agitators . . . or other foolish means." *Halifax Evening Express*, February, 1874.

Wilfrid Laurier in 1874,
the year he was first elected
to the House of Commons.
He was then 33.

ment, and went back to his constituency for re-election. In that
by-election, October 27, 1877, he was defeated, to everyone's
surprise including his own. The Mackenzie government then
had no real option but to try Laurier elsewhere. Quebec East
was opened for him almost at once. Macdonald and Langevin
moved heaven and earth to defeat Laurier the second time.
Montreal friends were stirred up for funds. Macdonald offered
some diabolical advice. Spread the rumour, he told Langevin,
that Laurier and his friends have pots of money to spend. Push
up the expectations of the Liberal voters in Quebec East. Get
them to hold out until they are well paid. "I have known an

election lost," said Macdonald cheerfully, "by a candidate's friends holding back to get a share of what is going."

Charles Thibault, the great Conservative orator, was brought in. He had never been elected to anything, but he was a good stump speaker and, as Joseph Schull noted, "he had a portable grandmother who had been born within a mile of every stump he spoke from."[9] He had helped to defeat Laurier in Drummond-Arthabaska, and he would help again in Quebec East. Thomas Chapais, a nineteen-year-old law student, later to be editor of *Le Courrier du Canada*, was at one of Thibault's meetings on November 15, 1877, and described it to his sister Georgette. There are few better descriptions of Quebec political meetings:

> Well, at last I've heard Thibault, the famous Thibault, the distinguished Thibault. What a caricature! He's a good stump speaker, indeed, but he's vulgar, licentious, a braggart, a clown, he can earn any epithet. He certainly knows how to dominate a crowd and can get himself listened to, but he lies like a trooper.... But yesterday he couldn't speak at all, as you will see by the papers. For half an hour his voice was completely lost in the immense wave of noise from the crowd, who yelled at the top of their voice, stamping their feet in rhythm to
>
> > Pas d'Thibault!
> > Pas d'Thibault!
> > C'est Laurier
> > Qu'il nous faut!
>
> It was an indescribable scene, I'll never forget it. The smoke and haze you could cut with a knife. You could hardly see two feet. Darkness had come, a fine rain was falling, and the crowd (4,000 people) yelled, sang, stamped their feet, howled, miaowed, in a word gave the wildest and most bizarre concert you ever heard![10]

Laurier was elected this time, and to a seat he was to hold forty-two years until his death in 1919. He went to Ottawa to take up his duties, and was in his place when Parliament met for the raucous, lively and unpleasant session of 1878. The Conservatives were never so testy and bloody-minded as they were that session. Where was the defeated, demoralized, devastated party of four years before, the party "whose best and bravest had fallen ... whose bones lay on many a bleak hill-side and lonely valley, the prey of jackals...."[11] Where, indeed?

CANADIAN
Illustrated News

Vol. II No 5]   MONTREAL, SATURDAY, JULY 30, 1870.   SINGLE COPIES, TEN CENTS.
                                                                                        $4 PER YEAR IN ADVANCE.

EMIGRANTS ON THE FORECASTLE—From an original sketch.—SEE PAGE 67

5

The Rise of the Phoenix: Macdonald and the National Policy

WANTED---PROTECTION!!

THINGS HAD NOT GONE WELL with Alexander Mackenzie's government. A host of problems had descended. Ontario's unhappiness over the terms of union with British Columbia was the first. Fifty of Mackenzie's seats were from Ontario, and many Ontario M.Ps had opposed the terms of union right from the start. It was impossible for Mackenzie to do other than to try to wriggle out of them. It was a difficult and rancorous business. The British Columbians wanted the terms lived up to, whatever happened. The Governor-General, and even the Colonial Secretary in London, were soon hip deep in it.

Mackenzie's second problem was the depression. Government revenues fell. American-manufacturd goods, hit by the depression in the United States, found no difficulty in flooding into Canada over a low tariff barrier that amounted to 17½ per cent or less. Canadian manufacturers in Montreal and Toronto, Valleyfield and Brantford, and a dozen other places, were angry. Canadian workmen were thrown out of work when Canadian factories closed. The demand arose almost spontaneously for protection, that is a high tariff, of the order of from 25 per cent to 35 per cent. Protection sentiment had always been latent in Toronto and Montreal. By 1875 and 1876 the depression added tremendous new popular support. But the Liberal party had, at its highest level, convinced free-traders. Mackenzie; his Finance Minister, Richard Cartwright; an intellectual like David Mills: all believed that a high tariff was basically wicked. It was a tax on 95 per cent of Canadians for the benefit of 5 per cent. That was the Liberal doctrine. Tariffs were necessary only to provide revenue for the Dominion government. There was no income tax and thus no other real source. (In fact, the tariff provided some 75 per cent of all federal government revenue.) The Mackenzie government, supported by most Liberal newspapers, set its face sternly against protection. The depression, said Richard Cartwright, was just something that had to be lived through. No government could do anything about it. And to adopt protection would just make matters worse.

By 1876 the Conservative party and Macdonald had adopted protection as party policy. It was popularized in the summer of 1876 at Conservative country picnics across Ontario by a reinvigorated party. The revitalization of the party and of Macdonald is one of the most significant changes that had

OPPOSITE *Grip* supports tariff increases to protect and encourage Canadian industry — a cartoon by Bengough published in February 1876, in the depths of the depression. Uncle Sam is shown striking down Canadian industry with his protective tariff, while Alexander Mackenzie (the Government) stands idly by.

developed toward the end of 1875. It began with the winning of by-elections from the Liberals. A large number of them were held in 1875 and 1876 as a result of Mackenzie's election law of 1874; in February 1875 the Conservatives won Berthier, Deux-Montagnes in Quebec, and London in Ontario; in November 1875 they won Bellechasse in Quebec, Toronto West in Ontario and narrowly missed winning Montreal West. In January 1876 they won Chambly and Charlevoix in Quebec; in July 1876 they won both North and South Ridings in Ontario County. Altogether, the Conservatives had picked up a net gain of 14 seats by the end of 1876; they had reduced Mackenzie's thumping 1874 majority of 70 to 42.

The spirit of this change is reflected in *Grip*:

> In the land of the Kannay-Juns
> Frosty, freezy cold Kannay-Juns,
> Busy, steady, calm Kannay-Juns . . .
> In the great Depression Famine
> Starving were the poor Kannay-Juns
> Dying were the sad Kannay-Juns,
> Running off were the Kannay-Juns.
> Then the Medicine Man TUP-ER
> And the ancient war-chief JON-NAY
> Cried, "Be of good heart, Kannay-Juns
> We will bring the goose Protection,
> Bring the fairy goose Protection,
> Goose which is no sooner eaten
> Than again within the barnyard
> Instantly appears another,
> Fat as was its predecessor. . . ."

A scene near Ottawa:
MACKENZIE — Hoo dith it come.
    Ma braw majority slips fast awa' . . .
    Here comes SIR JONE,
    Full frae a hunner picnics.
SIR JOHN (jovially) — Teetotallers
    Can no reverses bear. My grieving Sir,
    See how I thrive. Despite your power and place,
    Your cringing placemen and bought newspapers,
    The country throngs my way. Alone I stand,
    Alone I do it; I. Where now your sheets
    That bragg'd my powers decayed? Where be they now?
    Where is the *Globe* — the *Advertiser* pack —
    That played-out did me call? If dead I be,
    How do I flourish thus?

MACKENZIE.— The deevil helps,
    Or ye were dune ere this. Why I hae got
    Ye're chiefest henchman noo; CAIRTWREET is mine,
    And diz adveeze in a'. . . .
SIR JOHN — Where e'er he goes
    Ill luck goes fast abreast. . . .

Cartwright did not seem to change. There is a cartoon of him in *Grip*, fourteen years later, in 1890, as a mounted knight, his shield bearing the legend, "Blue Ruin." Someone asked him, "But can't you let us see the other side of the shield, Sir Richard?" "It hasn't any other side!" the Blue Knight replied.[1] The Liberals were not a united party. Behind Mackenzie lay the power of Senator George Brown and the Toronto *Globe*. The *Globe* was regarded in some Liberal quarters, notably by Edward Blake, as being nothing less than a literary tyranny run by a man for whom bullying was second nature. Goldwin Smith, who had some Liberal leanings, ran afoul of Brown and never forgot or forgave. Three years after Brown's death he wrote a review of Alexander Mackenzie's book on Brown, and got his own back:

> Those who thwarted Mr. Brown's will or incurred his enmity were not merely assailed with . . . abuse . . . they were systematically hunted down. . . . there arose a literary despotism that struck without mercy, while a train of parasites seconded its blows, and its victims were utterly defenceless.[2]

Grip also shared Goldwin Smith's dislike of George Brown and the *Globe*, and more than once would show Brown at his worst, intimidating the younger intellectuals of the Liberal party. An example is Brown's interview with David Mills, Mackenzie's new Minister of the Interior, appointed in October 1876. Mills was a great free-trader, a former schoolteacher, and a man that Macdonald said had more disconnected information in his head than anyone else in Canada:

MR. BROWN — (alone) He's maybe no that bad, MACKEN-ZIE'S gane for him the noo. (Enter Mackenzie leading in Mills) A vara gude morning, gentlemen. I haena, as ye are dootless aware, Maister MILLS, lang expectkit ye're entrance tae *this* sphere, but ye will ken —
MR. MILLS — (takes up a position in centre, and pompously breaks in) No doubt, Sir, you did not expect. But the

Bengough by Bengough.

philosophic mind, Sir, expects all things in their due course. In logical sequence, Sir, I take a leading position here, as necessarily, as logically, as I ruled the London Board of Trade. Your power, Sir, is of the press; mine is logic alone. "Magna est Logicus, et prevalebit." Quint. [ilian].

MR. BROWN — (rather staggered by the quotation) Maister MILLS, I doot ye hairdly recognize the presence wherein ye noo stand. But I mak allooance for the effeck o' sudden elevation —

MR. MILLS — (striking a Demosthenic attitude with startling rapidity) — Sir! Elevation! What elevation rivals the vast height from which the PHILOSOPHER surveys cringing Politicians, crawling Cabinets, writhing Grit editors and hissing Protectionists? Logic, Sir —

MR. BROWN — (screechingly sharp) Maister MACKENZIE, gin Maister MILLS suld be sae eccentric as tae intraduce logic intae a Cawbinet whaur nae sic nonsense is sufferit, I tak it for granted ye will correck sic conduck in a severely practical manner.

MR. MACKENZIE — (aside) For Heeven's sake, no a word! He's a' I could get. Sax others refusit, and declarit we could no survive a session, and it wad be madness tae join. I ken he's pairtially crackit, but it's joost MILLS or naething.[3]

Grip was a power in its own right. A satirical weekly, it was run with tremendous verve by J. W. Bengough in Toronto. It appeared for the first time in May 1873. Every Saturday for nearly twenty years *Grip* was published and enjoyed on all sides of English-speaking society. It was Ontario-centred, inevitably, but was read nationally. It had made its reputation (and its fortune) out of the Pacific Scandal, and its devastating cartoons had done not a little to help bring down the Macdonald government. The one of August 16, 1873, just after the prorogation, for example: Macdonald has his foot on a recumbent and weeping Miss Canada, a bottle of "Taktix" sticking out of his coat pocket, looking up heavenward and saying: "These hands are clean!," while on one of the hands is written, "Send me another $10,000!" Probably in his heart of hearts J. W. Bengough was a Liberal in sympathy but, if so, he was a satirist first and foremost who, like *Punch*, made everything, but especially governments in power, the butt of his humour. Political leaders read it from cover to cover. Bengough was famous enough to have had interviews with most of the leading politicians, and he would go to Ottawa every once in a while

Vol. XXX.   TORONTO, MARCH 17th, 1888.   No. 771.

GRIP

THE TIDE HAS EBBED, THAT'S ALL!

" BEFORE LONG THE GREAT CURLING WAVE OF PUBLIC OPINION WILL
SWEEP ALONG THAT SHORE AND SUBMERGE POOR RUMMY AND HIS BAR-
REL BEYOND ALL HOPE. LET HIM LAUGH WHILE HE CAN !"

PRICE 5 CENTS PER COPY, $2 PER YEAR.

PUBLISHED EVERY SATURDAY,
By the GRIP PRINTING AND PUBLISHING CO., 26 and 28 Front St. West, Toronto.

A few weeks after Huntington asked the questions in Parliament that were to touch off the Pacific Scandal, John Wilson Bengough, a young Liberal writer with a ready wit and remarkable gifts as a cartoonist, founded *Grip*, a weekly journal of comment and humour. It has been said truly that he was responsible for the rise of the cartoon as an editorial force in Canada. Bengough seized upon the Pacific Scandal and ever after, in hundreds of cartoons, pursued Macdonald relentlessly but without malice. One suspects that they developed a grudging admiration for one another. *Grip* did not long outlive Macdonald; it ceased publication in 1894. Bengough was a man of strong opinions; the cover of this 1888 issue of *Grip* was part of his running fight against the liquor traffic. His *Caricature History of Canadian Politics*, published in 1886, is a classic of its kind and a brilliant commentary on Canadian affairs.

just to study a man's figure or his expressions, since photographs did such a poor job of both. He had one interview with Sir John Macdonald about 1886 and received a great compliment. "*Grip*," said Macdonald, "has been conducted most fairly and impartially so far; I hope you will never let it get into the control of either party."[4]

Grip tended to dissolve governments, not make them. Satire and irony are always most effective against power. *Grip* helped to bring down Macdonald in 1873 and it helped to bring down Mackenzie in 1878. That it did not defeat Macdonald in the years from 1878 to 1891 is a compliment to Macdonald, not a derogation of *Grip*. It was not from want of trying. Macdonald's tribute of 1886 is, therefore, all the more telling. *Grip* was *for* the protective tariff when it was the policy of the Conservative opposition: it was *against* the protective tariff when it was the policy of the Conservative government. That is a form of consistency.

Grip was also a Canadian nationalist. Bengough was born and brought up in Whitby, east of Toronto, and got his early experience on the Toronto *Globe*, and had no great sympathies for Great Britain. He would make tremendous sport of the peculiarities of Englishmen.* He would have entirely sympathized with Macdonald's prejudice against "an overwashed Englishman, utterly ignorant of the country and full of crotchets, as all Englishmen are. . . ."

One other consistent theme *Grip* had. It hated liquor, it hated saloons, it hated the results of both, the poverty and crime that they allegedly engendered. That they did indeed cause povery and crime *Grip* never doubted. Temperance would therefore improve society. Here one gets close to Bengough's liberalism; he believed that society could be made better and, if it could be, it should be. It was the task of political life to undertake this reform.

"Temperance" meant different things, of course. Even applied to movements for ending the liquor traffic it differed. In the early years, the 1850s and 1860s, temperance meant prohibition of distilled liquors, whisky, rum, gin, and so on. Natural fermentations, like blueberry wine, apple cider, peach wine and beer, were all right in moderation. If a man said he did not drink in these years it usually meant he did not drink whisky or rum. Alexander Mackenzie was called a "teetotaller" but he drank wine. It was only later, in the 1880s perhaps, that temperance acquired its prohibitionist tinge, that is, the abolition of all drinks that had any alcohol in them. The difference is merely one of degree. Whisky has about 50 per cent alcohol; wine has about 11 per cent.

New Brunswick had adopted temperance legislation in 1852, effective January 1, 1853, and then promptly had to re-

*See, for example the account of John Bull, at beginning of Chapter 4.

Toronto in 1873, as seen from the top of the Northern Railway grain elevator. The population was then about 85,000.

peal it in 1854, as it was utterly unworkable. Another version was brought in in 1855, effective January 1, 1856. It brought down the government and it was repealed too. After that New Brunswick governments left the whole question severely alone, as well they might. No other colony made such an attempt; it ran counter to too many strong feelings and well-established institutions and customs. And, it is fair to add, the machinery for enforcement was still too primitive.

Support for temperance did exist in certain counties in Nova Scotia, New Brunswick, Ontario and even Quebec, those counties where Methodists and Baptists tended to predominate. The Presbyterians were split, and the Anglicans were too, the low-church Anglicans being more apt to be on the side of temperance than the high-church. The Roman Catholics did not care much about the movement believing, one suspects, that if God had not meant wine for man, he would not have invented it. Notwithstanding that argument, the House of Commons had a select committee in 1874 that urged temperance legislation. The heartland of Mackenzie Liberalism, southwest Ontario, was strongly prohibitionist. From there in fact had emanated some of the earliest blue laws at the county council level, in 1859.* Temperance advocates formed a powerful lobby — they

*Perth County Council adopted on December 23, 1859, a number of blue laws, restricting Sunday work, prohibiting hunting, dancing, the playing of "profane music," playing of ball games or any noisy game on Sundays. It also prohibited, on all days, indecent exposure, the keeping of bawdy houses, the "covering of mares" by any stud horse in an exposed place.

127

These two houses are typical of the stone castles that the wealthy built for themselves in the 1880s. Above is the Montreal residence of Senator George Drummond, whose many business interests included the Canada Sugar Refining Company and the Bank of Montreal, of which he was vice-president when this house was built. Below is Craigdarroch Castle, the imposing residence built in Victoria by the Hon. Robert Dunsmuir, owner of coal mines and builder of the Esquimalt & Nanaimo Railway. The house was not quite ready for occupancy at the time of his death.

always would — but they sounded more powerful than they really were.

The Canada Temperance Act of 1878 was the result. It was temperance by local option. Each parliamentary constituency was a local option unit, and could have a temperance referendum when one-quarter of the voters petitioned for it. Temperance went into effect when a simple majority was secured. It could also go out of effect in the same way. For a time it gathered support. The high point was 1886 when 62 out of Canada's 215 constituencies had gone dry. Its constitutionality had by that time been tested in the Supreme Court of Canada and in the Privy Council in London. A bootlegger in Fredericton had fought the Act on that ground, giving to Canada its first great constitutional case *Russell vs. The Queen* (1882). There was also to be *Hodge vs. The Queen* (1883), and some others. (Our early constitutional annals are replete with liquor cases.) After 1886 a retreat began. By the time of Macdonald's death there were only 30 dry constituencies left, none of them in Ontario.*

The problem was enforcement. One of the original supporters of the Act, Dr. Darley Bergin, M.P. Cornwall and Stormont, said in 1887, "We never knew what drunkenness was until the enactment of the Canada Temperance Act." If the demand was there, soon enough there would be illegal means to satisfy it. Licensed tavern keepers had some responsibilities in order to justify their licences; bootleggers had no responsibilities at all. It was just as bad elsewhere. Keeping Charlottetown dry was uphill work. There the Canada Temperance Act was adopted in 1879 and Charlottetown duly became dry. The issue was revoted on in 1884 and 1887 and the drys won. In 1891, however, Charlottetown went wet. In 1894 it voted dry, and in 1897 it went wet again. In other words, Charlottetown was dry from 1879 to 1891, and from 1894 to 1897. When it was dry there were allegedly 146 places where you could get a drink, night or day, seven days a week.[5]

That there were real social evils in taverns few doubted. In the 1870s there were probably more places to buy liquor in Toronto than to buy groceries; there was one tavern for every

*Nova Scotia, 12; New Brunswick, 9; P.E.I., 4; Quebec, 3; Ontario, 0; Manitoba, 2; British Columbia, 0.

120 men, women and children in the city. Drinking was alleged to be the main cause of poverty and the main source of crime. Powerful movements for reform centred on these points. Perhaps the greatest temperance song ever written, "Father, dear Father" focused on poverty and the disruption of family life. It was written by H. C. Work, the author of "Marching through Georgia," and it marched triumphantly northward from the United States. It is about a child sick at home, while the father drinks away the family money in the tavern:

> Father, dear father, come home with me now!
>   The clock in the steeple strikes two;
> The night has grown colder, and Benny is worse,
>   But he has been calling for you.
> Indeed he is worse — Ma says he will die,
>   Perhaps before morning shall dawn;
> And this is the message she sent me to bring —
> "Come quickly or he will be gone."
>
> Father, dear father, come home with me now!
>   The clock in the steeple strikes three;
> The house is so lonely — the hours are so long
>   For poor weeping mother and me.
> Yes, we are alone — poor Benny is dead
>   And gone with the angels of light;
> And these were the very last words that he said
> "I want to kiss papa goodnight."

By the time a temperance meeting got through with that song, there was hardly a dry eye in the house.[6]

It is no good making fun of temperance. The people that fought for it were in deadly earnest, hot with the emotion engendered by a song like that, or experiences in life that were almost as bad or worse. There was something infinitely sad about a temperance meeting, attended mainly by anxious mothers or wives, their minds filled with the danger to their man who had wandered from the straight and narrow, almost as if he could be reformed by act of Parliament. The real temperance people, and those who made the cause so dubious, were the grim-visaged prohibitionists and their wives. Goldwin Smith poked fun at them in *The Week*. "For a lifetime they have been attacking the digestive apparatus of those about them with puddings, pies and bread as hard as their own features. The victims of their bad cookery suffer from chronic dyspepsia; and in a perpetual state of thirst they are warned off the only article of drink that might do them good . . . Instead they were soaked with leather-producing tea or coffee that tasted like brick-dust." But mere politicians might well quail before the power of such an issue. And it was not to be settled for another fifty years.

Macdonald was probably opposed to temperance legislation on principle, but his reaction was, typically, entirely political. As early as August 1877, he was writing Tupper, "Now we won't lose a single Conservative teetotaller at next election, while the Grits have alienated every Grit Brewer Distiller & Licensed Victualler in Ontario — " Nevertheless, the Canada Temperance Act went through Parliament without a division. What Macdonald's personal feelings about it were is not clear. He did send a note to Langevin, May 2, 1878: "I am so unwell that I shall go to bed. If the Teetotal bill comes up send a cab for me." Parliament may have passed the bill in a mood of repentance for the almighty drunk it had got into just three weeks before. But whatever the reason, it was to prove unfortunate for Mackenzie when Canada went to the polls on Tuesday, September 17, 1878. Every tavern in Canada on that Tuesday, said Cartwright, became a committee room for the Conservative party.

Macdonald swept into power with an eighty-seat majority. The extent of the victory surprised everyone. *Grip* was caught out famously, predicting that Miss Canada would renew Mr. Mackenzie's lease, and being forced to eat humble pie the following week, with Mackenzie's bust knocked to the ground and Macdonald suggesting that the September 14th cartoon needed a little "readjusting." Joseph Pope, who was to become Macdonald's private secretary in 1882, was in Halifax in 1878, working for the Bank of Nova Scotia; he described how not only the victory, but the extent of it, was totally unexpected. The celebration at the old Temperance Hall in Halifax went on intemperately until daylight on Wednesday. Pope didn't recover his voice until Saturday.

There were many explanations for this triumph. Depressions tend to destroy governments in power. (Mackenzie King was to win an even bigger majority in the election of October 1935.) It was the first time the secret ballot had been used in a general election. The voters could now avoid comments of

THE GREAT POLITICAL CONJURER.

"ALL SORTS OF WINE POURED OUT OF ONE AND THE SAME BOTTLE."

RIDING INTO POWER.

friends and neighbours; they could forget about voting for the "party of purity" and vote for anyone that appealed to them. There were also intimations that the party of purity had been too pure. English Canadians said that Mackenzie could never wink hard enough. French Canadians put it more delicately. One French-Canadian Senator remarked that Mackenzie had never learnt tolerance for the foibles (and needs) of devoted friends. Some Liberals, indeed, saw Macdonald's victory as a reflection of the inherent wickedness of the electorate, that the Canadian people had thrown out an honest man who had conducted the business of the country as honestly as he could. Mackenzie himself certainly thought that, and he was understandably bitter. Few men had given so much of their time, energy and health to the service of the people of Canada. Mackenzie worked like a horse. He had been rewarded with a defeat more crushing than that which the Pacific Scandal had dealt Macdonald. The election of 1878, said Cartwright, was nothing less than a declaration by the Canadian people that they did not want their politicians honest or truthful, and they have certainly had their reward.

LEFT Although Bengough favoured protective tariffs, he nevertheless continued to be suspicious of Macdonald and to lampoon his National Policy. This cartoon appeared in *Grip* in August 1878, a few days before Mackenzie called a general election.

RIGHT A *Grip* comment on the success of the National Policy, published in September 1878, just after Macdonald had won his resounding victory at the polls. Mackenzie, Cartwright and George Brown are being trampled underfoot.

The Macdonald government was sworn into office on October 17, 1878. John Ross Robertson's new Toronto *Telegram* thought he was going to be in for a long time. "The indications are, indeed, that Sir John has a long lease of power, and that unless he does some mad thing, he will be in office until the close of his career." He was almost sixty-four, his magnetic victory had pulled the party behind him as never before; he was now in command and proposed to stay there. The talk of retiring from politics receded and was only heard infrequently; even in the very last months before June 1891, he could not be persuaded to give up.

His parliamentary technique was by now fairly polished and subtle. He did get into a blaze of temper now and then — as at prorogation in May 1878, when he and Tupper vented their hatred up on Donald Smith. *Grip* then had a cartoon showing the two of them sounding off with that language in a barroom, and the bartender saying: "Hold up, Gents! This isn't the House of Commons; it's a decent groggery — None of your 'parliamentary language' here!" But gradually these exhibitions became less and less, and in later years Macdonald rarely lost his temper. He would look instead for holes in his opponents' armour. He hardly ever met argument with argument. He rarely attempted to cover the ground of Liberal attacks. He would parry them with some wry caricature of what his opponent had meant, some happy and improbable exaggeration of their position. Sir Richard Cartwright landed one day upon an awful admission in the Mounted Police estimates from the officer at Fort McLeod, about the disappearance of 2,000 bushels of oats and 10 kegs of nails, which had been "eaten by rats." How could the government explain *that* scandal? Macdonald rose with a smile. "The explanation which I had to offer my honourable friend, for what he considers an extraordinary circumstance, is a very simple and reasonable one. The rats, having gorged themselves upon 2,000 bushels of oats, evidently felt they were in need of a tonic." Macdonald would on these occasions even turn his back to the Speaker, and talk half to his own followers, as if more intent upon convincing them, and rousing their loyalty and laughter, than the hopeless task of converting the opposition. So he would spin his stories with a deft touch, a marvellous sense of timing, tickle his followers and exasperate his opponents.

132

He would support his own followers, even if their speeches were bad. In April 1879, Arthur McQuade, M.P. South Victoria, was on the floor late at night, discussing some exhausted, threadbare aspect of the National Policy tariff. McQuade was a terrible speaker, and an infrequent one; but after his speech, when the House adjourned, McQuade happened to go out just in front of Macdonald. Macdonald put his arm around McQuade's shoulders and said, not too quietly, "McQuade, you spoke like an angel. I am proud of you."

He was friendly with opponents. G. W. Ross, Liberal from West Middlesex, tells how in March 1833 he got into a hot argument with D. B. Woodworth, Conservative, from Kings, Nova Scotia, during estimates. About midnight Ross went down to the restaurant for tea (he was a prohibitionist), when Sir John came in, sat down with Ross and ordered whisky and sherry. After a pleasant talk, Macdonald got up and said to some Conservatives nearby, "Come, boys, hurry up. Doug Woodworth and Ross have been into a devil of a row for the last hour, and I am going to take a hand in the sport." Ross went up to the House himself, and a few minutes later was listening while Macdonald sternly castigated him for his remarks against Woodworth, not an hour before.

Macdonald still retained his marvellous memory for names and faces. He would tour some constituency — more often in Ontario than elsewhere — and meet some party worker he had seen only briefly two or three years ago and say, "How are you, McClintock, old man? And how are your wife and your two pretty daughters?" It is not as easy as it seems. Hiram Blanchard in Nova Scotia tried this technique, went up to a constituent he had not seen for a couple of years and said, "And how is your father now, Mr. Winter?" "He's still dead," was the outraged answer. Macdonald was, in short, just about indispensable. "If anything were to happen to him," said a visitor looking at Macdonald from the Parliament gallery one day, "the Conservative party would not hold together for ten days." An old Conservative friend looked too and said, "Not for ten minutes." Macdonald had always had great ability to draw recruits from the enemy side, to repair the waste inevitable in the frictions of party life and the natural decay that is incident to all governments. There had been few occasions when he could not get the right man at the right time.

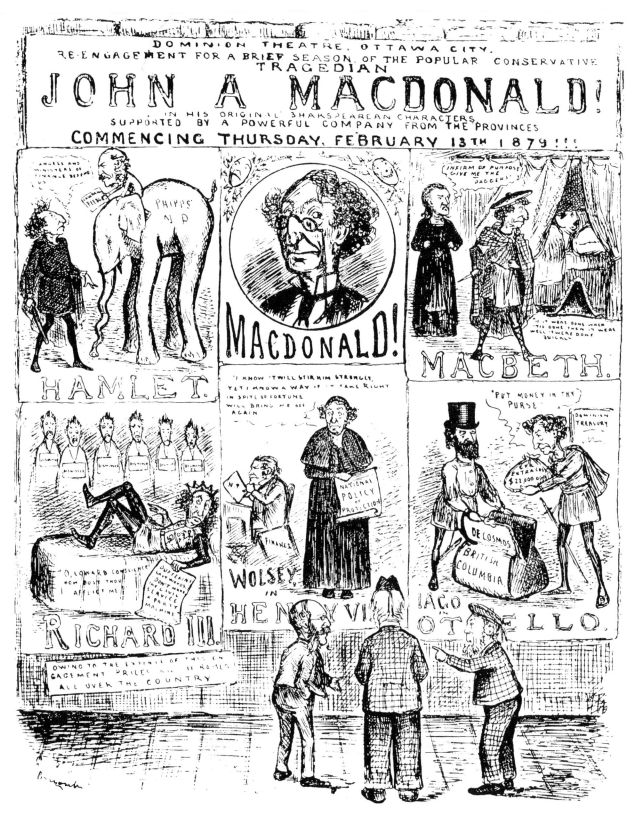

THE COMING ATTRACTION!

But he was now becoming more and more closed in, natural enough at his age, but nevertheless effectively imprisoned, in a sense, by his old circle of friends and associates. In his new 1878 cabinet there was little that was new. There were half a dozen new men, but none lasted long, and none was of any importance save possibly L. F. R. Masson who stayed into 1884. Some of these weaknesses were not yet apparent but they soon were going to be. Macdonald held the portfolio of Minister of Interior for five solid years; he gave it up in 1883 to, of all people, Senator David MacPherson.

Nor had he ever pioneered the advocacy of great questions. That was the defect of other, greater virtues. He hated precipitateness; he had an abiding faith in the healing virtues of procrastination. But he generally knew when the time to change had come. When the balance of opinion had shifted, his own position was usually adjusted to square with it. He never believed in finality in anything.

He had picked up the National Policy in precisely this way. The name had been developed probably by the Toronto *Mail*, encouraged in Montreal and popularized by *Grip*. But he never intended it for one class in society. Protective duties would be made to help everyone, farmers (who can be as protectionist as anyone when it's in their interest), workers and manufacturers. Macdonald had adopted it in 1876 to apply to all three. The tariff was to be "adjusted" rather than raised. Macdonald kept the name, "National Policy" — that was a stroke of genius by someone — and added in 1878 the battle cry "Canada for the Canadians."

The problem was real enough. The United States had established its high tariff in 1863, and it applied to British North America after the Reciprocity Treaty ended in March 1866. The American gates opened outward readily enough; American manufacturers had no difficulty in exporting to Canada manufactured goods at slashed prices, just to get rid of inventory, in the 1870s. Like all good valves, the American one closed quickly enough when there was pressure from the outside in. Canadian exports to the United States had a completely different fate from American exports to Canada. Free trade was fine to talk about, but was it not in these circumstances an illusion? *Grip* had expressed the popular view very well in May 1877:

OPPOSITE *Grip* looks forward to the session of Parliament that was to open on February 13, 1879 — the first since Macdonald had been returned to power in the general election of 1878. Cartwright, Brown and Mackenzie are discussing the billboard.

... You this great truth should know,
Countries alone by manufactures grow.
What would you gain — what would it profit you
If wheat today through all your borders grew,
While all you sell it for must go, next day,
British or Yankee dry-good bills to pay? ...
Know you this fact Canadians — When you see
One country manufacturing to be,
Another agricultural — the first
Grows richer, but the other still is cursed
With poverty, for all that it can grow
Much as the life-blood to the other flow ...
The profit goes to him, who fat and fair
In other and more cunning regions dwells,
And manufactures, and complacent sells
The fruits of twenty minutes work to you
For that which took you two full days to do ...
Your tools, your arms, your raiment, make hard by.
Your farmers will your workmen all supply
With food, your workmen them with all they need,
Each helping each, and profits shall succeed ...
Strength shall arise, and Canada be known
Not as a petty colony alone. ...
The present's here; the lazy past is done,
We'll have a country, or we will have none.

There the whole argument for the National Policy is summed up.

The new tariff was brought in on March 14, 1879, rates to be effective the next day. A great deal of work had gone into it, and not a little hard bargaining, with expertise imported from as far afield as Halifax and Washington. The sugar tariff, for example, was designed to strike a balance, a rather delicate one, between Canadian sugar manufacturers, who wanted their imported raw sugar as cheap as possible, and sugar importers who wanted their imported refined sugar as cheap as possible. The basic aim of the tariff was to strengthen Canadian manufacturing by admitting raw materials at very low duties and manufactured materials at high duties. The schedules were quite complex, using both specific and *ad valorem* principles, but the purpose is clear enough.

Confederation had given Canadian manufacturing its first national market and its real start. Ontario manufacturers of scythes, forks and other agricultural equipment and tools, Montreal manufacturers of boots and shoes and clothing, went to New Brunswick and Nova Scotia, and in six or seven years had succeeded in driving most of the Americans out — even before the Intercolonial Railway was completed. Using the Gulf of St. Lawrence steamers they could usually offer many manufactures as good, and cheaper, than the Americans could. By the end of the 1870s this trade was already beginning to affect Maritime industry. One Liberal M.P. from Charlotte County, New Brunswick, complained about it:

> The manufacturers of the Lower Provinces have been going down since Confederation. Instead of having our commercial agents up here in the west, looking out a market for our agricultural implements, we find quite the opposite. We find our Lower Provinces traversed by commercial agents from Montreal; every hole and corner of the Lower Provinces is flooded with them.[7]

The National Policy tariff thus solidified and confirmed a strong trend that was already a decade old. The tariff had never been politically neutral even when it was low; it was now in politics with a vengeance. Tilley, Macdonald's Minister of Finance, had delegations innumerable; the corridors leading to his office were choked with them for over two months. Manufacturers, as they never had had before, now did have a vital interest in what was happening at Ottawa.

In order for the National Policy tariff to be successful, it had to promise something like permanency. No one could be expected to invest in, say, a cotton manufacturing plant, without some reasonable expectation that the tariff on cotton clothing (30 per cent) was going to stay for a while. Perhaps twenty-five years was close enough to permanency. The trouble for the Liberals was that many of the senior men in their party — Mackenzie, Cartwright, Mills — believed the new tariff was incurably wicked, confiscatory in purpose, class legislation of the worst kind, benefiting only, as Cartwright was wont to say, those poor, needy manufacturers whose hovels were to be observed in Westmount, Oakville and other miserable suburbs. The Liberals fought the National Policy tariff through three more general elections, 1882, 1887 and 1891, with only superficial results. This naturally put the manufacturers more and more on the side of the Conservative party. Edward Blake, the new Liberal leader who replaced the ailing and unyielding

Supporters of the demand for a nine-hour working day parading in Hamilton in 1872. In the early 1870s Toronto, Ottawa and Hamilton became the first Canadian cities in which individual trade unions came together to form local councils or assemblies to give organized labour a basis for common action.

Mackenzie in 1880, fought hard to keep the Liberal party more broadminded and abreast of the times by attempting to keep open lines of communication with Liberal-minded manufacturers in Ontario. But the party defeated him time and again.

No one can pretend the result of Canada's industrial revolution was altogether pretty. Factories rarely are. They had been in existence for some years, of course, but it was with the National Policy that they became an important feature of Canadian life. The Canadian industrial plant appeared to contemporaries to come almost at one bound, in the expansive years of the 1880s. There was tremendous contrast just between 1878 and 1884. In Ontario and Quebec particularly, the number of labourers employed had doubled, as had total value of wages. Whole sets of new industries had appeared — cutlery, clocks, felts, tableware, lines of woollen goods. The first piece of printed cotton in Canada was turned out in July 1884 from a factory with a total capacity of 30,000 yards a day. This vast productivity had promoted the physical prosperity and well-being of the country. But there were concomitant evils as well, and by the mid-1880s these were severe enough to persuade the Macdonald government to create the Armstrong Royal Commission on the relations of capital and labour.

A factory and its machinery is a considerable investment of capital. The cotton machines mentioned above were brought in and installed directly from Manchester, England. Machines are untiring; they work best at long stretches of time, and in order to repay the investment in them it was highly desirable that they should. Thus factories of necessity imposed a discipline on the personal life and habits of workers. This discipline was often unpleasant and unyielding, and behind it lay a general philosophy of making money by keeping wages as low as possible and hours as long as possible. Probably the conduct of the majority of factory owners was not unreasonable, or so at least *The Week* believed in 1886; but the increasing necessity of regulations was already apparent.

There were marked differences between provinces. The nature of the legislation was not always a good clue to conditions, for much depended upon enforcement of the regulations a province chose to lay down. Quebec factory regulations were much the same as Ontario's, but were not well enforced. The Armstrong Commission believed they were not enforced at all. Those concerning child labour are one example. The chairman of the commission asked W. R. Webster, a cigar manufacturer in Sherbrooke, if he knew that there was a law fixing the age of children and the hours of work in factories. Mr. Webster replied, "I believe there is a law but I have never looked it up."[18] Labour of boys under twelve and girls under fourteen was prohibited in both provinces, but there was plenty of evidence that in Quebec numerous exceptions to these rules existed. In Nova Scotia it was worse. There the only restrictions were that boys had to be ten years of age (and how was that to be proved?). Until they were twelve years old they could not be employed for more than sixty hours a week! They were used especially for opening and closing doors in coal mines. The brutal truth was that the cheapest labour available was that of women and children. Factory jobs required some training or craft but this could be learned, and in some types of factories labour of women and children made up half the work force or more. Child labour was a conspiracy of parents and employers. The parents needed the money and the employers the labour.

Take the case of Théophile Charron, journeyman cigarmaker, age fourteen. He was apprenticed at eleven years of age,

Alexander Graham Bell, inventor of the telephone. This photograph was taken in 1876, the year the first telephone message was transmitted over eight miles of wire between Paris, Ontario, and Bell's home in Brantford.

almost certainly by his father or mother, under a duly notarized indenture. He would earn $1.00 a week in his first year, $1.50 in his second and so on. After three years he became a journeyman. Such young fellows were a little difficult to control and they were usually fined as punishment. The commonest sin was talking too much. For mistakes in cutting the leaf they would be rapped across the knuckles by the foreman.

The employers were not necessarily wicked. Some of them were, no doubt, like some of the employees. W. R. Webster of Sherbrooke said, and it has a ring of authenticity:

> . . . it is not an easy thing to run a factory where the employees are largely composed of young people, and you must have some system. Now, the moment your back is turned, it may be, three or four of the hands will jump up and commence to knock each other down, and have, what they consider, a good time. If this kind of thing is allowed the material [tobacco leaves] is wasted, and the machinery or plant may be broken.

What was the answer? The answer was not easy because this was the system, the way things were done, and its continuation meant something to everyone. Probably one had to begin, as provincial legislatures did, with some kind of controls over ages of children and perhaps more enforceable hours of work.

In the cotton factories of Montreal and Valleyfield, work started at 6:30 A.M. and stopped at 6:15 P.M., with three-quarters of an hour off for lunch, and a half-day on Saturday. An eleven-hour day was not uncommon in Quebec. In New Brunswick and Nova Scotia a ten-hour day was common; in Ontario it could be shorter than that. It varied enormously. In nearly all the cities in Canada streetcar drivers and conductors were especially victimized by long hours.

One great complaint that the Royal Commission presented to Parliament was the relative absence of any sense of obligation between the factory owner and his workers. "To obtain a very large percentage of work with the smallest outlay of wages appears to be the one fixed and dominant idea." Inevitably this meant bad working conditions, the absence of any comforts or conveniences, and in most instances imposition of a rough-and-ready discipline by the employer. The cigar manufacturers were, apparently, the worst of these. Young apprentices who

DOMINION DAY.

SOMETHING FOR THE FATHER OF CONFEDERATION TO THINK OVER.

SIR JOHN.—"MY DEARS, I CONGRATULATE YOU ON THE TWELFTH ANNIVERSARY OF YOUR GLORIOUS VICTORY. WHAT CAN I DO TO ADD TO YOUR HAPPINESS?"
MADEMOISELLE QUEBEC (VIGOROUSLY).—"MIND YOUR OWN FEDERAL BUSINESS, AND PERMIT US TO MANAGE OUR LOCAL AFFAIRS TO SUIT OURSELVES, ACCORDING
TO THE TERMS OF UNION,—*THAT'S* WHAT YOU CAN DO, SIR!"

Provincial rights were already a lively issue in 1879. In this *Grip* cartoon Bengough made Mademoiselle Quebec the spokesman for the Provinces, and her comment might have been made today: "Mind your own federal business, and permit us to manage our local affairs to suit ourselves."

showed the least breach of discipline could be incarcerated in the factory's own, home-made prison. If the term extended after working hours, a special constable came to release them or to carry out the punishment awarded by proprietor or foreman. The commissioners were indignant:

> ... Occasionally this Oriental despot would himself be the executioner of his own decrees, and did, upon an occasion, personally chastise, in a flagrantly indecent manner a girl eighteen years of age. And for all this the law provides no remedy — nay, incredible as it may appear, law, in the person of the Recorder of Montreal, expressly authorized the punishment inflicted. This gentleman, on being examined, stated that he had authorized employers to chastise their operatives at their discretion, so long as no permanent injury was inflicted; and this evidence was given in the Year of Our Lord One Thousand Eight Hundred and Eighty-eight ...

It can be argued that if labourers did not want to submit to such conditions they did not have to. They had always the option of getting out if they did not like the pay or working conditions. But it was early recognized by the commission that the exchange of labour for wages was not a simple exchange of one commodity for another.

Some businessmen seemed to think otherwise. William C. Macdonald, the founding father of the great old tobacco firm of Montreal, had some great old ideas. His firm employed about eleven hundred workers, half of whom were women or girls. For thirty years, from about 1857, when the firm was founded, he had reduced wages 25 per cent or more in the fall when labour was plentiful, and raised wages again in the spring when labour was short. Samuel Heakes, a carpenter on the commission, asked him if the cost of living did not increase substantially during the winter months?

"Oh, yes," Mr. Macdonald replied.

"Is it not a hardship to them," Mr. Heakes asked, "to have their wages reduced at the time they need it more than in summer?"

"That will depend upon how they provide for rainy days," was Mr. Macdonald's comforting reply.* "When they have good wages they should save for the short period."

That was easier to say than to do. The blunt truth was that the labourer had to sell his labour or starve. Money can be stored. A labourer cannot store labour, or hunger. He had few options, and some protection for him was necessary.

The evolution of labour unions helped to protect the workman from the fierce pressure to lower wages and lengthen hours. If he were making six or eight dollars a week, not uncommon for a fifty-five- or sixty-hour week, the reduction of an hour's labour a day, or the increase in pay of even twenty-five cents a day, made a substantial difference. One great change between the 1870s and 1880s was the much wider acceptance of unions and union principles. Despite Macdonald's legislation of 1872, workingmen in 1875 or 1876 would still go to a union meeting along the shadows of walls so they would not be seen by employers. Broadly speaking this was much eased by 1885, although it is right to say it varied enormously from employer to employer. Some employers, like banks, retained strong prejudices against any union membership by employees up to and after the 1930s.

*It would be a little unfair to leave Sir William Christopher Macdonald (1831-1917) thus. A Prince Edward Islander, he came to Montreal when he was 23 and worked his way into a very large fortune. In 1897 he owned 150,000 shares of the Merchants' Bank, and was perhaps the largest single shareholder of Bank of Montreal shares, 410,000. At par these bank shares alone were worth $5,600,000. But he was a generous benefactor to McGill University, and to the Ontario Agricultural College at Guelph, and he endowed the Macdonald Agricultural College at Ste Anne de Bellevue. He was Chancellor of McGill for many years.

A tailoring workshop, photographed about 1890. This illustrates the crowded working conditions but long hours, poor ventilation and inadequate lighting have to be left to the imagination.

The most significant labour organization of the 1880s was "The Noble and Holy Order of the Knights of Labour of North America," a secret society that received guarded support from the church in Quebec and much open support in Ontario, and which started in Canada in 1881. It was the dominant force in Canadian labour until the 1890s, when it lost ground to more trade-oriented unions. For the Knights of Labour was inclusive, not exclusive. They included all labouring men in their ranks, however labour was defined. Even small businessmen joined the union. They excluded only bankers and lawyers, people whom the Knights regarded as non-producing classes of society. The Knights greatly helped to bring labour questions into the natural forums of public discussion.

A good example of the difference between the 1870s and the 1880's was the public reaction to the Grand Trunk strike of December 1876, and to the Toronto streetcar strike of March 1886. The drivers and firemen on the Grand Trunk received notice just before Christmas 1876 that falling revenues and traffic on the railway would compel a 20 per cent reduction in the work force. There was also to be a cut in wages. The drivers and firemen struck as of 9:00 P.M., Friday, December 29, 1876, leaving one train stranded halfway between Toronto and Weston, with 120 members of the local Orange Lodge on Board plus their ladies, who were on their way to a dance at Weston. It was in the middle of a heavy snowstorm. There were also a number of well-publicized incidents at Belleville. This strike weakened the position of the union and alienated a substantial section of public opinion. In 1886, however, much more sympathy was expressed. The union, the Knights of Labour, handled the strike with rather more tact, and the president of the Toronto Street-Railway Company, Senator Frank

Smith, had categorically prohibited his men from joining the union, a position that seemed unreasonable to many. The men won. The strike lasted long enough to impress Torontonians with the indispensability of streetcars, and Senator Frank Smith* with the necessity of backing down from an untenable position.

As to the broader issues, however, implied in labour's use of the strike, it has to be said that Canadian labour was on the whole indifferent. The socialist idea touched them only marginally. The labour papers complained bitterly of the *petit-bourgeois* character of their labour constituency. It was nearly impossible to persuade labourers that the remedy for their problems lay in the broader and nobler spheres of political action. The Toronto *Labor Advocate*, a paper which lasted from December 1890 to October 1891, said in its last issue that workers were still, unhappily, clinging to their

> old worn out and discredited trade union policy of strikes and petty restrictions . . . Stupid, prejudiced and selfish, they cling to their fetiches of partyism, sectarianism and loyalty, and resent any attempt to present broader views. They can see no further than their noses, and their ideas of labor reforms are limited to some petty advance in pay in their particular trade. They do not know, and do not wish to know, anything of the underlying causes that depress labor.

At the same time, however, even the Toronto *Globe* conceded that a social order that produced senseless luxury for millions on the one hand, while on the other willing labourers could not find work to keep starvation from wives and children, would have to be changed.

The fact probably was, however, that over the fifteen years from 1876 to 1891 wages improved steadily. Moreover, a dollar bought more as time went on. There was a slight but continual deflation from 1870 to 1900. A dollar in 1900 bought more flour, meat, sugar and tea than it had in 1870. Savings deposits in Canadian banks increased 2.5 times in the same period as did the Gross National Product. Canada's physical

---

*Frank Smith was appointed to the Senate by Macdonald in 1871, and was Minister without Portfolio from 1882 to 1896. He was knighted in 1894. He was not poor. His holdings of bank stock alone, as of December 31, 1896, amounted to $1,717,000 in the Dominion Bank, and $866,700 in the Imperial Bank (Canada, Sessional Papers, 1897, No. 3).

growth was substantial. It is true that this development took place unevenly; that Canada, like the United States, suffered cyclical depressions in 1874-79, 1884-87 and 1893-95. But the incidence of such depressions fell unevenly too, some businesses flourished, others did not. *Grip* boasted in 1877 that it had never been healthier. Massey, Harris, Frost and other implement manufacturers seem to have grown steadily. The predecessors of the Steel Company seem never to have looked back in the period from 1873 to 1893.

As labour had combined, so had the manufacturers. Combines to keep up prices and mitigate competition were alleged with increasing frequency in the later 1880s. As early as 1881 a Conservative M.P. said that a "coal-oil ring" existed, keeping up the price of coal oil at thirty-five cents a gallon, when it ought to have been only eighteen cents. The Macdonald government appointed a select committee in 1888 to report. The main abuses the committee uncovered were on the distributing side of business, in groceries, fire insurance and other enterprises. One particularly effective and pernicious example was the Coal Association of Toronto, which controlled the price and distribution of coal in the city.* Gooderham and

*Mainly American coal. Nova Scotia coal was not sold at retail much west of Montreal.

The Canada Southern Railway at Niagara by Robert Whale, probably painted about the time the Canada Southern line was completed in 1873. The picture proved so popular that the artist and his sons produced many near duplicates, in some of which a Michigan Central train was substituted for that of the Canada Southern. (The National Gallery of Canada, Ottawa)

Worts, the well-known distillery in Toronto, tried to break this control by ordering a schooner-load of anthracite (250 tons) from a coal company in Buffalo, New York, at a price that undercut the established Toronto one. The Coal Association made stern representations to the Buffalo colliery. Buffalo did not want to lose the really big Toronto business; it promised to be good in future, and was let off with a thousand-dollar fine. The Coal Association was powerful; private detectives kept track of dealers and where they got their coal. Similar though apparently less effective organizations existed in London, Ottawa and Montreal. An anti-combines act passed parliament in 1889, mainly a restatement of old common law rules against conspiracies in restraint of trade, from which Macdonald had exempted the Toronto printers and other labour unions in 1872. There were also allegations of the unscrupulous use of freight rates, rebates from published rates being given to preferred customers of the Grand Trunk, for example. Other complaints centred around lower rates at competitive rather than at non-competitive points.

Most railways were monopolies by their nature and possessed power to make or break shippers and villages. The very existence of questions of this kind shows what a distance Canada had come in the thirty years since the Grand Trunk was first built in the 1850s. And railways had changed Canadian society irremediably. They extended the metropolitan influences of cities and their institutions. They covered distances at a speed no horse, or two horses, could match, and did so, night and day, 365 days a year. Railway stations became the highly visible centres of a whole new age of transportation. *The Week*, just before Christmas 1887, published Lampman's impression of them and what they meant to him:

> The darkness brings no quiet here, the light
> No waking; ever on my blinded brain
> The flare of lights, the rush, and cry, and strain,
> The engine's scream, the hiss and thunder smith:
> I see the hurrying crowds, the clasp, the flight,
> Faces that touch, eyes that are dim with pain;
> I see the hoarse wheels turn, and the great train
> Move labouring out onto the bourneless night.

Great trains moving through the night had a magic quite their

ANOTHER MILE-STONE PASSED; OR, FATHER TIME AS SPRY AS EVER.

Grip greets Sir John on his 67th birthday, in January 1882. Political rivals in the background wonder, "When is he going to stop?"

ABOVE RIGHT *The Old Guard*, a Topley montage of the dinner at which leading Conservatives assembled to honour Macdonald after the election victory of 1882. Macdonald stands in the centre; the portrait of Queen Victoria, directly above him, is flanked by those of the Governor General, the Marquis of Lorne, and his wife Princess Louise, the Queen's daughter. W. J. Topley was for many years the leading photographer in Ottawa.

RIGHT Lady Macdonald in 1882. This is the photograph that Topley included in his montage of the "Old Guard" dinner, where she is shown in the small balcony above the portrait of the Queen.

own. The Grand Trunk engines must have had whistles built by Thor himself, for they seemed to some observers wonderfully suited to the northern climate and splintery air of a winter's night. One old railroader remembered the great Grand Trunk engines going by his home in Vermont just fifteen or twenty miles south of the Canadian border, on the way from Portland to Montreal.

> It was the echo of a mogul whistle in these same old [Nul] Hegan woods that made me a railroad man for life. . . . The Grand Trunk engines possessed whistles built by a master. . . . The steam shot quickly up from the big round dome on the mogul's heaving back, then a blast of mighty noise shattered the woods and the night. . . . It was a blast to roll on and on. . . . before the echo had worn itself out . . . the Grand Trunk engine was making the [Nul] Hegan Woods with a full head of steam and would soon be over the hump, to drift easily downgrade along St. Lawrence waters. . . .

That whistle near Island Pond, Vermont, was the symbol of Montreal's triumph in 1856 over the frozen St. Lawrence. The city had broken out to the sea at Portland. The Intercolonial of 1876 was its second reach eastward, to Halifax. Now, in 1886, came the greatest triumph of all: the whistle of a transcontinental train out of Montreal in the Rockies, 2,000 miles to the west; the reaffirmation of the great hegemony of the North West Company one hundred years before.

6
Tracks West, Seas East

The Rogers Pass by John Fraser. (The National Gallery of Canada, Ottawa)

THE FIRST CANADIAN transcontinental train pulled out of Montreal at 8:00 P.M., Monday evening, June 28, 1886. Five and a half days later it reached Port Moody on Burrard Inlet at noon on Sunday, July 4, 1886. Macdonald himself left Ottawa on July 10th in a special car, the *Jamaica*, with a party of seven. The CPR could do things handsomely when it chose. The *Jamaica* was upholstered in grey-green velvet. The sides of the seats and the berths were of carved cherrywood inlaid with brass. Two lounges took up the centre of the car. The washrooms were furnished with dark marble washbasins and even a small three-foot bath which, on most trains, received some patronage.

Macdonald had never been further west than the Bruce Peninsula in Ontario, where he had been nearly shipwrecked in 1859. Few ministers of his government had been west. Tupper had been briefly in Red River in 1869, and had been as far west as Moose Jaw in 1882. Alexander Campbell had been in Victoria in 1883, going west via the Union Pacific. Hector Langevin had visited British Columbia in 1871. But that was about all. There was no western minister in the cabinet. Macdonald held the portfolio of Minister of the Interior until October 1883, and that of Superintendent-General of Indian Affairs until October 1887. No one in the cabinet knew the West, and it is probably fair to say they were not expected to. The government here relied on its civil service. The West possessed little political power. British Columbia returned six MP's, Manitoba five, and the North-West Territories were wholly unrepresented in Parliament. Its population would have entitled it to four MP's, which it was to get in 1887. The whole West, from the Ontario-Manitoba border (one could even say from Fort William, Ontario) westward to the Pacific Ocean counted for less, politically speaking, than New Brunswick. Its total population in the 1881 census was 270,000, *including* about 100,000 Indians.

All of this has to be considered in assessing eastern reactions to western problems. The East believed the West was already getting a disproportionate share of money and attention. It was true that the Pacific Railway was now, after 1880, being built by a private company, but it was being mightily subsidized with 25,000,000 acres of western land and $25,000,000 of Canadian money, plus another $32,000,000 worth of railways built or to

OPPOSITE Tariff changes made by Macdonald in accordance with the National Policy gave Canadian manufacturers increased protection and many of them flourished and expanded their factories. One such was the Massey Manufacturing Company (later Massey Harris and now Massey-Ferguson), makers of "harvesting machinery," which greatly enlarged its works in 1883.

be built at the expense of the Canadian taxpayer. There was a big CPR government loan in 1884; there was another in 1885. How much was the mainly eastern taxpayer to bear? Canada's total population in 1881 was 4.3 million. It was easy for westerners to compare life above the 49th parallel with life below it, and assume that the amenities ought to be roughly the same. In many respects they were. The surprising thing really was not how little had been done for the West but how much, and in the face of what odds!

On the other hand, easterners looked at the West, inevitably, from viewpoints east. Macdonald tended too often to regard complaints from the West as complaints from mere speculators who were not making their fast bucks fast enough. "I wish you could be induced to come and see this country for yourself," wrote an old associate, C. J. Brydges, in 1883, "and that you would get out of your heads in Ottawa that this part of the world is solely filled by speculators." It was often regarded as a source of jobs for political friends. The Department of Interior had jobs in western land offices; Indian Affairs offered positions as Indian Agents; any Dominion government post in the new western provinces of Manitoba and British Columbia, and all the government posts in the North-West Territories, were Dominion government patronage appointments. Many of those appointed were easterners. Some were good and some were not. Westerners not unnaturally resented seeing the jobs going to many easterners who were certainly inexperienced and not infrequently incompetent. Goldwin Smith went westward in the summer of 1884 and reported in *The Week*:

> Nobody doubts that the intentions of the Ottawa Government towards the people of the North-West are good. But it is a distant Government; its all-powerful chief has never himself been in the North-West; and references or appeals to it are tedious and precarious. It is a party government, and it cannot resist the importunities of hungry partisans who mark the new and defenceless territory as their perquisite. . . .

The West and its ways had to be learned. Western life put a premium on certain capacities and virtues, and it demoralized some others. It put a premium on resilience, toughness, resourcefulness; it depreciated learning, elegance, sophistication,

MASSEY'S ILLUSTRATED

A·JOURNAL·OF·HARVESTING·MACHINERY

Sept. **FALL FAIR EDITION.** 1883.

THE MASSEY MANUFACTURING COMPANY

Build double the number of Reapers, Mowers, Binders and Horse Rakes of any manufacturers in Canada.

10,300 MADE FOR 1883! - - - 11,500 to be Made for 1884!!

The greatest number of Machines ever built by any one concern in the Dominion.

We employ a Staff of over 400 men. We pay for wages about $18,000 per month.

The Largest Factory and Best Equipped in the Dominion of Canada.

THE WORKS OF THE MASSEY MANUFACTURING COMPANY FOR 1883.

Now being greatly enlarged, 400 feet, 4 stories high, 50 feet wide, being added to meet the demand of our celebrated machines the coming season.

☞ Read description of our Factories on Page 4, and visit them before leaving the City.

especially when unaccompanied by any of the necessary western virtues. The frontier had its own strengths; but there was also a cultural Gresham's law: lower tastes tended to drive out higher ones.*

Farming itself was always something of a grumble and a gamble, even in the East; but there, with a variety of crops, and usually over thirty inches of rain, something was bound to grow. Farmers were constitutional grumblers, anyway; if the potatoes were looking good, then the fall wheat was not; or if the cattle were fat on good pasture, then it was too wet for haying. But the West was all rather more vulnerable. A lot was staked on a good hand of cards. You grew as much as you could of what you were going to eat; but you had to count on selling that grain. It was not easy living on one hundred and sixty acres of prairie. Begin with the questions of fuel and water. And markets meant the necessity of railways and branch lines. A horse and wagon could only take wheat so far. A sign on a deserted cabin in the Dakotas suggests the problem:

> Four miles from a nayber
> Sixty miles from a post ofis
> Twenty miles from a ralerode
> A hundred and atey from timber
> 250 feet from water. God bless our Home.[1]

The first immigrants began to come into Manitoba in 1875, and the years of the early 1880s were phenomenal. In 1883 134,000 immigrants came to Canada, the biggest year in Canada's history until 1903, when 139,000 came. And while not all went west, many did. There were success stories, too. One Scotsman, John Fraser, wrote back home to Edinburgh from Brandon, in September 1884. He had come to the North-West in 1882 with $2,000 and bought half a section of black-loam land from the CPR. The farm was, in September 1884, worth $4,500; Fraser had 40 acres in wheat, giving 20 to 30 bushels to the acre; 20 acres in oats and 20 in barley. His cattle survived the winters on nothing but prairie hay. All the vegetables were flourishing. Nicholas Davin, editor of the Regina

*See the splendid book about the West, Wallace Stegner's *Wolf Willow* (New York: Viking Press, 1955), especially the last chapter. This particular reference is to p. 298.

Leader, described a farm in Riding Mountain country, seventy miles north of Brandon in 1888. Sixty-five acres were under crop. Cattle, pigs, hens produced the butter, eggs, bacon and pork that the good Beacon Hill farm lavished on its guests. It was after a rain, in an early June evening, the calves like deer lying on the grass, the wheat already looking good,

> the grasses and flowers sending up their odours to a blue sky flecked with clouds of grey and shining fleece, not a house nearer than four miles in this beautiful, fruitful land . . . a vigorous pioneer couple near, and the little fairhaired girl of a year and a half that toddles down towards the stables, and looks back and smiles, conscious she is going on to forbidden ground. Even the attentions of a stray mosquito could not mar the sense of peace. . . .

There were not only immigrants, but easterners of all kinds, from all provinces. C. B. Sissons remarked that when he was teaching school near Barrie in the 1890s, the farmlands of Simcoe County were systematically drained of young people whose parents had gone west for the past two decades. "The poor little girls of Ontar-ay-o" was a song that called after the young men who had gone west:

> I'll sing you a song of a plaguey pest
> It goes by the name of the Great North-West
> I cannot have a beau at all
> They all skip out there in the fall.
>
> One by one they all clear out
> Thinking to better themselves no doubt
> Caring little how far they go
> From the poor little girls of Ontar-ay-o.

The West was not, however, going to make many people's fortunes overnight. George Grant, the principal of Queen's who came from Pictou and Halifax in Nova Scotia, had some salutary reflections. He knew the West better than most people; he had crossed the continent with Sandford Fleming in 1872. Then, he said, he could get few people to believe there was anything good in the West. Ten years later he could hardly persuade people there was anything bad. "Bye-and-bye," he remarked with his usual good sense, "we shall understand that like every other country it is a mixture of good and bad." Canada

TOP Big Bear's Camp, Maple Creek, Saskatchewan, 1883.

ABOVE LEFT Wekemouskunk, a Saulteux Chief, with his son and canoe, Lake St. Martin, Manitoba, 1888.

ABOVE RIGHT Métis, Maple Creek, Saskatchewan, 1884.

ought not to be in a hurry. The settlement of the North-West not only *will* take time but it *should* take time. No one ought to come West hoping to make a fast buck. In Grant's view, there was no way to make an honest living in the West except to get it out of the ground.[2]

Nevertheless, lots of people came west with the aim of getting rich faster than that. Some of them succeeded. Hugh John Macdonald moved to Winnipeg in 1882; Tupper's two sons ended in the West; also Elliott Galt, A. T. Galt's son, and numerous others. Some went into farming; some others into law or business; others went into ranching. The great early ranchers in Alberta Territory came from the East; A. E. Cross from Montreal; Dan Riley from Prince Edward Island; M. H. Coch-

A police force "in and for the North-West Territories" was officially constituted by an Order-in-Council approved by Lord Dufferin, the Governor General, on August 30, 1873. The first commissioned officers of the North-West Mounted Police were appointed the following month. Officers and constables of the North-West Mounted Police are here shown wearing the first official uniforms. Jackets were scarlet from the beginning. Sub-Inspector Francis J. Dickens, son of the novelist, is standing second from the right.

rane from Compton, in the eastern townships; Fred Stimson from Montreal; Pat Burns from Oshawa. There was also a sprinkling of others from England, and a good deal of imported capital both from the East and from England.

Ranching had started after the arrival of the Mounted Police in southern Alberta and when the buffalo were nearly gone. In the fall of 1881, 6,800 head of cattle and 300 horses arrived from Montana for the Cochrane Ranch. The Americans taught the Canadians the business of ranching; the saddles, horses, techniques: all came from below the border. The gun law did not. Ranching required capital and experience, but the former was just as essential as the latter. The system of closed, long-term leases put the Canadian ranching system along a different path from that of the United States. For the first fifteen years — until Laurier came to power — the Canadian ranchers had things pretty much their own way. As early as the summer of 1884, in an area fifty miles east of the Rockies and from the 49th parallel northward to the CPR main line, were some 60,000 head of cattle. The grazing-lease principle adopted by the Dominion government for southern Alberta was sensible; but as settlement developed, it would provoke conflict with farmers, especially over fencing and water rights. The ranches had their difficulties; they too had to learn the ways of the West, and bad winter storms were to prove terribly destructive. In the January blizzard of 1887 some ranches reported losses of up to 75 per cent. Even the trains had a hard time. Edgar Dewdney, Indian Commissioner in the North-West Territories since 1879 and, from 1881 also the Lieutenant

Indian land titles in the West were the subject of seven treaties concluded between 1871 and 1877. The first two covered the new and then very small province of Manitoba and larger areas west and north of it. This sketch of the conference with the Indian chiefs appeared in the *Canadian Illustrated News* on September 9, 1871.

Governor, took a week to come from Calgary to Regina by train. The blizzard blew four days and four nights, and it took eight engines to free the train. By 1888 most ranches had devised some system of protection for cattle and some reserve winter feed. The warm chinook winds could not always be counted on. But profit there was. And with the developing cattle trade to England, by the later eighties the western ranches made money.

It was country spectacularly beautiful, that range country, in full sight of the Rockies fifty miles distant, glowing with wind and sun; the great swales of grassland were wide and deep enough to roll half a world in. No one who had ever ridden it could forget it; it haunted the memory, it exalted the heart, and it made a man humble before the majesty of a splendid world. In those days of the open range the great round-up came in May, lasting over a month; a camp with sixty men and three hundred horses, for the branding of the new calves. They were remarkable animals, those western horses. They were small, twelve to thirteen hands high.* They travelled in the peculiar gait of range ponies, a slow canter, and were guided by pressure

*A hand is four inches. Most eastern and English horses were bigger, fourteen hands or above.

of reins on the side of the neck rather than by the bit and, unlike eastern horses, could travel day after day feeding only on native bunch grass and never tasting corn or oats.

Many of these open-range ranches were directly on old buffalo territory, from which the buffalo had gone within the past decade. The Prairie Indians, the Cree, Assiniboine, the Blackfeet Confederacy (Blood, Piegan, Sarcee and Blackfeet), had lived by the buffalo and for the buffalo. Long before the horse had come northward from Mexico in the late eighteenth century, Plains Indians lived by the buffalo hunt. Head-Smashed-In Buffalo Jump, twelve miles west of Fort Macleod, had a history of use going back to 3000 B.C. (The buffalo were stampeded over a cliff or cut-bank.) The arrival of the gun from the East did not spell the end of the buffalo; it was the Winchester repeater of the 1870s that did that. By 1876, Crowfoot, the Blackfoot chief, had already discerned in the distance the end of the old Indian way of life: " . . . the day is coming when the buffalo will all be killed, and we shall have nothing more to live on . . . then you will come into our camp and see the poor Blackfoot starving."[3] At the time of the signing of the Blackfoot Treaty in 1877, few Indians believed that the buffalo would ever go; nevertheless, the treaty included a provision

The North-West Council in session at Regina in 1884. Tradition insists that the table shown was used at the Quebec Confederation Conference in 1864. Later it migrated with the government to Ottawa, where it was used for some years at cabinet meetings in the Privy Council Chamber. It was then sent to Battleford to serve the North-West Council, and was taken to Regina when the capital of the Territories was established there in 1883. It is now in the Legislative Buildings in Regina.

for assisting the Indian to become a farmer or a small herder.

That the Indian understood what was meant by giving up his hunting lands to the newcomers is very doubtful. The Blackfeet hardly knew what a farm was. Most of them had never seen one. The only white authority they had ever known was the Hudson's Bay Company or, more recently, the Mounted Police. Both established posts, not farms. So the issue never came to their intelligence as giving the white man a deed to fence up and farm all the lands in the West. Even a chief of Crowfoot's intelligence saw the treaty more as an act of faith between the Indian and the white man. No interpreter alive could explain to a nomadic Indian exactly what a reserve meant.

By the spring of 1879 Blackfeet were already starving, and Edgar Dewdney provided flour, tea and beef for the camps at Blackfoot Crossing.

> ...I found about 1,300 Indians in a very destitute condition, and many on the verge of starvation. Young fellows who were known to be stout and hearty fellows some six months ago were quite emaciated and so weak they could hardly work; the old people and widows, who, with their children, live on the charity of the younger and more prosperous, had nothing....

American hide hunters set fires south of the border in September 1879 to prevent the buffalo herds moving north, and so the Blackfeet moved south in Montana after the buffalo. By the time they returned to Canada two years later their numbers were virtually cut in half by whisky, starvation and disease. Nothing was the same any more. "The formerly neat lodges of the Blackfeet were ragged and torn, the once-gallant warriors were subdued, and even the children had lost the spark of life. The buffalo were gone, the old life was gone.... Warriors who had defeated every enemy in battle were reduced to bony derelicts...."[4]

The Blackfoot problem extended also to Crees and Assiniboines. Most Indians believed that white men, though powerful, were few, and could easily be wiped out by Indian warriors. Edgar Dewdney, as Lieutenant-Governor of the North-West Territories based at Regina, arranged to have three of the Blackfoot chiefs go to Winnipeg at the government's expense in the summer of 1884. Winnipeg was now a booming city of

REGINA, WEST N.W.T.

Regina in 1884. The city was named when the first train arrived on August 23, 1882. Four months later it became the headquarters of the North-West Mounted Police and in 1883 replaced Battleford as capital of the North-West Territories.

15,000; it was abundantly clear to the Blackfoot chiefs that white supremacy was inescapable.

In 1883 federal government Indian officials started to tamper with the western Indian rations, to cut down on expense; in particular to substitute bacon for beef, the former being cheaper. The Indians hated bacon. Then came the winter of 1884-85. The rebellion broke out in March and April 1885, not in the Blackfoot country but in the Cree country to the north and east, in the valleys of the North and the South Saskatchewan, near where they meet not far from Prince Albert.

The Saskatchewan rebellion was put down by a fledgling Canadian militia army in April and May 1885. But it cost the government five million dollars to do it, and settlers in the Saskatchewan and Battle River valleys lost heavily. Louis Riel, who had come to the Saskatchewan Valley at the behest both of old Métis friends and the whites of Prince Albert, had led the rebellion. He was now imprisoned and tried. The dreamy, clever, rather handsome youth, half-mad with ambition even in 1870, was now a man of forty-one, still as ambitious and probably more insane. But he remained an attractive figure even to the eastern doctors who came to examine him for insanity. A western jury was compelled to find him guilty but recommended mercy. It was one of the few recommendations of that kind that Macdonald ever ignored. Sir David Macpherson, the Minister of the Interior, who resigned on August 4, 1885, asked

Macdonald the next day: "I shall be curious to know whether you consider the testimony of his insanity too strong to allow him to be hanged. If he is not hanged — unless the evidence of insanity be clear — Ontario will be furious and if his sentence be commuted to imprisonment in a lunatic asylum, Quebec will be unceasingly clamouring for his discharge." Riel believed that "politics will save me," but it was perhaps politics that killed him, at Regina in November 1885.

The government itself had not been well served, and the Department of the Interior was not well run. Good local officials there were, but too many of them in the Indian Branch were expected to teach the Indians habits of hard work from the cocoon of their own laziness. The department was especially weak at the top. A. M. Burgess, the Deputy Minister of the

An artist's conception of the Battle of Batoche, May 12, 1885, the last major engagement in the North-West Rebellion. Riel's forces were beaten decisively and he himself surrendered three days later.

Riel a prisoner. The day after he surrendered Riel was allowed to walk about briefly. This picture was taken by Captain James Peters, of A Battery, an enthusiastic amateur photographer.

Interior, was an example of promotion to the level of incompetence. The Minister of the Interior was Sir David Macpherson, an old friend of Macdonald, aged sixty-six in 1884 and in the Senate, whose appointment in October 1883, considering the importance Macdonald attached to that department, was a little curious. Tupper, in London, was delighted to hear Macdonald was at last relieved of the Interior portfolio; he thought Macpherson would be useful, provided he could be made to realize that the North West was rather different from Macpherson's comfortable estate, Chestnut Park, in Toronto. The appointment is best explained by the developing pattern of Macdonald's later cabinet appointments. He liked to surround himself with old friends and old loyalties, people upon whom he could rely. Macpherson was able but he was not robust, though he lived on until 1896; he spent much of the summer and early autumn of 1884 in London on business and in St. Moritz on health. Macpherson was aware of his difficulty and he warned Macdonald that "the Minister of the Interior should always be at his post or at least within hail." The job was big enough for an active man. But no change was made until after the rebellion, in August 1885.

In Indian Affairs, it was a little worse. The senior civil servant was called the Deputy Superintendent General, and was Lawrence Vankoughnet. He was the son of an old political friend, P. M. Vankoughnet. Hugh John Macdonald had married Gertrude Vankoughnet, a niece, in 1883. Macdonald himself was the minister, but he left administration heavily in the hands of his deputy, who was narrow-minded, and who based a whole set of departmental decisions on one brief trip westward at harvest time in 1883. Martin Griffin, editor of the Toronto *Mail*, wrote to Tupper in July 1884 that North-West affairs looked very doubtful. Lawrence Vankoughnet was "simply an imbecile" and everything depended upon the harvest of 1884. If that turned out to be very good all would be well. The harvest of 1884 was late and wet, and in the Prince Albert area crops were a total failure.

The irony is that Macdonald had information from other sources available all the time, telling him what the problems were. Edgar Dewdney may have made a lot of enemies in the West in the course of his progress upward in the world, but he knew the Indians and was apparently respected by them. Macdonald had plenty of warnings had he chosen to act upon them. In particular, a private letter from Dewdney of August 1884, enclosing one from J. M. Rae from the Indian Office at Battleford, detailed the current problems of the Indians with great clarity. The saddest part of all is the endorsement on the back of each in Macdonald's hand: "Discuss situation with Vt [Vankoughnet] after session, 30 June, 1885."

Yet there were excuses for Macdonald. The very month of 1884 that Dewdney was writing the warning letter from Regina, Macdonald was writing to Tupper from Rivière du Loup. Nothing was going right, he told Tupper. Every by-election, Dominion or provincial, the Conservatives were fought with the full strength of the Liberals. "My colleagues with exception Pope, Langevin and Caron are not worth a cent in counteracting this tremendous effort and with my failing strength and advancing years I cannot do everything. Next month I shall have a clear understanding with my colleagues, & they must work or others will." Here Macdonald is thinking, characteristically, of the mending of electoral fences. But *mutatis mutandis* for cabinet vitality and initiative. A letter six months later to Tupper indicated nothing better. If anything, the ministry was worse, now broken down in health. Pope and Tilley were virtually out of action. The rest were of little help in the House. Chapleau was coming along but needed maturing. "I find, however, that I cannot be absent for an hour without some blunder taking place. We want new blood badly." That was in February, just four weeks before Duck Lake, March 26, 1885.

The events of March to May 1885 solved the CPR's problems and in a sense solved the western ones too. Métis grievances were to some extent met; Indian grievances did not end, but they were more carefully considered and unenlightened departmental penny-pinchings stopped; the North-West Territories were given representation in Parliament; and there was a drastic shake-up in the cabinet. Tilley, broken down in health, gave up after seven solid years the Finance portfolio, and went to New Brunswick again as Lieutenant-Governor. There was a new Minister of the Interior, Thomas White, who was soon to win golden opinions; the Minister of Justice, Senator Campbell, was retired back into the Post Office Department, and an able forty-one-year-old Nova Scotian, John Thompson, was brought in. Marine and Fisheries was taken over by an austere and capable former classics professor, George Foster, from New Brunswick. New blood the ministry indeed got: it should have had it two years before.

So Macdonald travelled westward in July 1886, over the tracks that had taken Canadian troops to the Saskatchewan in April 1885, just fifteen months before. That was past now, and Winnipeg turned out to greet Macdonald at the train with the same enthusiasm that had been manifested for the first transcontinental train two weeks earlier. A vast crowd came to the station, and when the cheering died a little a young Tory near the train, who had been cheering lustily but who had never laid eyes on Macdonald before, turned to a friend beside him, and remarked, "Seedy-looking old beggar, isn't he?"

Brandon, 125 miles to the west, was already a town; Fred White, of the North-West Mounted Police, had camped there on virgin prairie just five years before. Eight miles west of Brandon, the CPR crossed into the jurisdiction of the North-West Territories. It had its own laws, under Ottawa's supervision. One of them was prohibition. Westward to the British Columbia border, all alcohol was prohibited but beer. One could only bring in whisky under special permits issued by the territorial government at Regina. Bars there were, at Regina, Moose Jaw and Calgary, but they all dispensed beer, and the

The Great Railway

The first railway locomotive in Western Canada arriving at St. Boniface on October 9, 1877. With six flat cars and a caboose the engine, soon to be named *Countess of Dufferin*, was brought down the Red River on a barge pushed by the steamer *Selkirk*. Although engine and cars belonged to Joseph Whitehead, the contractor who was building the line south from St. Boniface to the American border, and no C.P.R. Company was yet in existence, it will be seen that all were lettered with the name Canadian Pacific.

To speed construction of the Canadian Pacific hundreds of rivers and ravines were spanned by temporary timber trestles, all of which were replaced later by embankments or steel bridges. Mountain Creek Bridge, on the eastern slopes of the Selkirk Mountains, was one of the finest structures of the kind. It was over a thousand feet long and contained over two million board feet of timber.

Driving the last spike in the transcontinental line of the Canadian Pacific at Craigellachie, in Eagle Pass, British Columbia, on November 7, 1885. This is probably the best known of all historical photographs relating to Canada. Lord Strathcona is driving the spike. Behind him stand Sir Sandford Fleming (in the stovepipe hat), who had been engineer in charge of the early railway surveys, and W. C. Van Horne, then vice-president of the Canadian Pacific, who had superintended the building of the line.

The arrival of the first transcontinental train at Vancouver on May 23, 1887. The next day was Queen Victoria's birthday in her Golden Jubilee year, and the locomotive carried her portrait on the headlight. Three weeks later the first trans-Pacific passenger liner to connect with the railway tied up at the wharf to the left of the picture.

In July 1886 Sir John and Lady Macdonald travelled to Vancouver over the railway he had been instrumental in creating. They were photographed at Fort William on the platform of the Canadian Pacific's official car *Jamaica*. This was Macdonald's only visit to Western Canada.

usual collection of loungers contented themselves with beer, cigar smoke and talk. And the use of spittoons. The CPR was practically built with chewing tobacco.

Most people were prepared to admit, at least in 1884, that prohibition in the North-West had been a blessing. CPR contractors, Indian agents and settlers, according to G. M. Grant (no teetotaller himself) agreed with that verdict. Many of the railway labourers had come from the States; "many of them lawless and spendthrifts by nature and habits, accustomed to the free use of the revolver and the bowie knife, have lived quiet, sober, industrious, cleanly lives, because whiskey . . . had been kept out of the country." Grant must surely have been exaggerating a little! But he was right in saying that all the elements of pandemonium along the CPR line were present — except the one vital ingredient, whisky. It was perhaps proof of this that the only place along the CPR where anything resembling a serious riot occurred was at Beavermouth in British Columbia, where whisky was legal and available.

The North-West Mounted Police watched the trains carefully for smuggling. Grant described how at Maple Creek Station (near the border of Alberta Territory) a clerical-looking gentleman had been noticed getting off the train with a large and apparently heavy suitcase. The man was stopped and the bag opened.* Underneath the spotless shirts and improving sermons were bottles of brandy. And it would not be the watery stuff presently masquerading under that name but real

*The Mounted Police had power to search for liquor and to seize and destroy any they found. Certain Mounted Police Officers were given judicial powers as well.

firewater that ran up to 65 per cent alcohol, that is, about 30 per cent overproof, and burned with a pale blue flame. The bottles were opened and spilled on the spot. Some nearby Crees hanging about Maple Creek Station could only kneel down and smell it. The man himself could not pay the hundred-dollar fine and went by the next train to Regina jail. But he would have his revenge; he would probably write anonymous letters to the Winnipeg papers denouncing the wicked tyranny of the Mounted Police. And ordinary people who read the papers would believe there was something in the story.

But increasingly, as time went on, enforcing prohibition in the North-West Territories became more difficult. It became especially so after the CPR was completed. No duty was more discouraging or more distasteful to the Mounted Police than this constant effort to catch the uncatchable. Smuggling was widespread by 1887 and 1888. A favourite method was to bring it into Alberta Territory from British Columbia. One harassed NWMP constable at Banff reported that the smuggler would actually fill his berth on the CPR with kegs of whisky. When the train got near Calgary the liquor would be thrown off to waiting accomplices just before the train pulled into the station. An even more ingenious method was the use of rubber mattresses and pillows which, instead of being filled with air, would be filled with whisky. Liquor was in fact brought into the Territories by every conceivable means: inside tins specially prepared in the shape of a book, and labelled "Bibles"; as canned fruit, a single peach perhaps floating in pure alcohol worth about five dollars. It was even brought in inside of eggs.

Finally the North-West had had enough. The North-West Assembly appealed to the Dominion government to give it power to legislate on the question, and Ottawa did, in September 1891. In January 1892, the North-West Assembly adopted a licensing system for bars, and the history, and perhaps it can even be said honourable history, of prohibition in the Territories was for the time being over. And it was soon quite clear that the change was not an improvement.[5]

By that time other changes had taken place in the West. Macdonald was sufficiently impressed with Banff — as indeed were others — that Mary, his crippled daughter, was sent there the very next summer, in 1887. Banff National Park had been established already, in November, 1885; the CPR had a hotel up and town leases were going rapidly.

Lake Louise had been discovered by Tom Wilson just five years before. Tom Wilson was an Ontario farmboy who joined the North-West Mounted Police at Fort Walsh and was eventually hired by CPR survey crews. He was packing supplies from Padmore to the Kicking Horse Pass in the summer of 1882 when, near the summit, he heard distant avalanches. The Stony Indians knew what it was — a mountain of snow above the "lake of the little fishes." Wilson got himself guided into the lake. The two men, Indian and white, rode out of the evergreen forest suddenly, and there before them was the emerald-blue lake, the great glacier behind it. "As God is my judge, I never in all my explorations saw such a matchless scene." It is still matchless.

Agnes Macdonald rode through the Kicking Horse Pass not on horseback but on the buffer bar-platform above the cowcatcher on the very front of a CPR engine. She was like most people who go through for the first time, or the tenth; she could not take her eyes off the scenery. Agnes stuck to her platform the whole six hundred miles to Port Moody, with the men of the party, Macdonald included, taking turns to stay with her.

Macdonald's train arrived at Port Moody, B.C., at 1:00 P.M. Saturday, July 24th. There was Pacific tidewater; there were the steep forested hillsides coming down to Burrard Inlet. Macdonald, with Pope standing beside him watching him, talked to the crowd around the train at the Port Moody Station, his grey hair blowing across his forehead from a fresh Pacific breeze. What a triumphal moment it must have been for him, Pope thought! The whole party settled down for three weeks at the Driad House at Victoria, a splendid old place three blocks from the harbour. It was a place local people knew and loved. It was mentioned by a CPR engineer in the 1870s as one of the best hotels on the continent. The food, at least, was sublime:

> fresh salmon, small coppery oysters . . . a few hours out of the sea, English pheasant, beautifully cooked splendid crabs, every known vegetable, a real master piece of a sweet . . . all washed down by the finest vintages that ever came "round the Horn", and then such cigars and such coffee![6]

168

Vancouver in 1886. This photograph was taken only a month after the city had been virtually swept out of existence by fire on June 13, and shows the remarkable speed with which it was rebuilt.

Victoria had also a good deal of leisurely and somnolent charm. Macdonald described it in a phrase, "the day was always in the afternoon."

There was more bustle than that in Vancouver. It was chartered as a city in April 1886, and promptly had a fire that wiped it out in June, the month before Macdonald arrived. The CPR wanted to transfer its Pacific terminus to Vancouver, and transfer it it did, almost over the dead bodies of the anguished Port Moody-ites. The city of Vancouver was re-built with great speed and determination, and on May 23, 1887 it took its permanent place as the Pacific terminal of the CPR. Three weeks after that the first of the Canadian Pacific trans-Pacific Steamers arrived in Vancouver, thirteen and one-half days out of Yokohama, with tea, silk and a cargo of tremendous potentiality for the future. That link was to make money for the CPR. Prior to this time it was bringing East some thirty-eight empty freight cars a day; and since it cost little more to haul them full instead of empty, the CPR made substantial cuts in freight rates from Vancouver, not only to Montreal to get through business, but to American points, like Omaha, Nebraska, via Winnipeg and St. Paul. And it was doing a sub-

stantial business that seriously alarmed the pool that controlled the rates of American transcontinental lines. Nor was this temporary. "The jealousy of the United States' Railways," wrote Macdonald to Lord Lansdowne in 1889, "... amounts to panic – They are seriously trying to prevent our railway from carrying U.S. traffic across the continent and would succeed were it not that Chicago and the New England States like the competition."[7]

Vancouver soon presented odd contrasts. Real estate was the name of the business. In 1889 it seemed to be the pre-occupation of barbers, sailors, tailors, tinkers and druggists. And the contrasts of Vancouver that one Australian correspondent noted in 1895 were just as striking fifty years later:

> one lot would have a grand grey granite building ... costing One Hundred Thousand Dollars; and the next a wretched little wooden shanty, or a bit of the original bush, with tall mountain ferns and mountain ash and dogwoods. ...

Vancouver citizens were as enthusiastic about their city then as later. They saw Vancouver "in their mind's eye as the future third City of the Dominion. ..." A remarkably prescient note from 1889 by T. M. Martin in *The Week*. He also insisted that the CPR had now the effect of welding Canada together. "The people of Ontario are no longer styled Canadians in distinction from British Columbians or Manitobans. ..." Even Edward Blake, that determined Ontarian, came around eventually. From the Aurora speech of 1874, through the long CPR debates of the early 1880s, Blake had been unhappy with British Columbia and the costs of her acquisition. But the CPR was now a fact, and Blake (actually on CPR business) went West. In Victoria, in May 1891, he made generous amends for the nasty things he had said in the past. How could he possibly have imagined that British Columbia was a difficult country for railway construction? There was the "quiet ... undisturbed Kicking Horse ... the calm Columbia, [we] were gently driven down the dead waters of the Beaver, meandered past the placid Illecillewaet, then over the vast prairie levels [to where] ... the Fraser slowly, quietly, serenely winds its sluggish way ... and I come here a convert (Laughter and applause)."

By this time British Columbia interior development was well under way. The Kootenays got their start with silver, lead and copper discoveries in the 1880s; Nelson, in east Kootenay, was founded on the Silver King Mine where the ore assayed 465 ounces of silver to the ton. It was not placer mining or pick-and-shovel mining; it demanded equipment, capital and skill, much of which in these early years came from contiguous areas of Montana, Idaho and Washington. Rossland got a big silver-lead strike in 1890. But there was more than mines. By 1891 the Okanagan Valley was already developed. Lord Aberdeen acquired a property there before even becoming Governor-General in 1893, and he was to spend much time there, an enthusiastic advocate of the beauties and versatility of the Okanagan. Charles Mair, the much travelled poet, moved there in 1892 and was ecstatic:

> . . . the lake beside me rivals Loch Lomond, only that it is 75 miles long; there is a climate which might fetch the angels down . . . every kind of fruit matures here . . . what with fruit, fine vegetables, tomatoes, hops, vines and wine-growing this region will be an exceedingly rich one.

Mair was a bit sceptical that the region was being Canadianized fast enough, but even this impression had worn off in a few months. In May 1891, almost the last letter that William van Horne wrote to Macdonald dealt with the prospects and politics of a railway through the Crowsnest Pass.

By 1889 the CPR was complete from end to end, from Pacific to Atlantic. The "short line," five hundred miles from Montreal through Maine to Saint John, was the price exacted by the Conservative Maritime M.P.s for supporting the CPR 1885 loan. Not only did they insist on the CPR building it, they continued to insist on the CPR running it. The first train out of Montreal arrived in Saint John, on June 3, 1889. Now, at last, Saint John would get off the siding she had been on ever since the Intercolonial Railway had been completed into Halifax in 1876. And the "great ships of gray Saint John" — Bliss Carman's phrase — would now get their winter cargoes from Montreal in half the time.

> Gently now this gentlest country
> The old habitude takes on,
> But my wintry heart is outbound
> With the great ships of Saint John.

ABOVE For half a century, in the days of wooden ships, shipbuilding and shipowning were major activities in Canada, especially in the Maritimes. Ships were built in scores of coves by the sea where a stand of timber was conveniently close by. This scene at Dorchester, New Brunswick, shows logs in the millpond, the sawmill that cut them into timber and planks, and a ship under construction on the slipway nearby.

RIGHT The *William D. Lawrence*, 2458 tons, launched in 1874, the largest of the many hundreds of square-riggers that came from Maritime shipyards. With a favourable wind she could make 15 knots. In 1878 Canada had the fourth largest merchant fleet in the world, a position she soon lost, thanks to the advent of iron and steel ships.

Past the light house, past the nun buoy,
Past the crimson rising sun
There are dreams go down the harbour
With the tall ships of Saint John.

But I sight a vaster sea-line
Wider lee-way, longer run
Whose discoverers return not
With the ships of gray Saint John.

The great old ships were not memories yet, but that was coming. These years of the later 1880s were in some ways the most remarkable for Maritime shipping. As in many great efforts for supremacy, the best of the great square-riggers were being built when the end was in sight. New Brunswick shipowners were already beginning to give up, though in 1884 Stewart & Ritchie in Saint John built the *Canara*, 1,545 tons, so well made that she was classed by Lloyd's for fourteen years and was still afloat in 1916. Bigger ships were built in Nova Scotia:

They built 'em in Annapolis, Windsor, River John,
Jest as able packets as you ever shipped upon,
Yarmouth ships, Maitland ships, hookers from Maccan,
The kind o' craft that took the eye of any sailorman.

In July 1891, C. R. Burgess launched at Kingsport, not far from Lunenburg, the *Canada*, 2,030 tons, 257 feet long. She could carry 3,600 tons of cargo and still make good passages. The *William D. Lawrence* built twenty years before at Maitland, at the mouth of the Shubenacadie River, was even bigger. She was at the time of launching the largest wooden sailing ship in the world, made chiefly of Nova Scotian spruce, a great ark of a vessel built to carry a big cargo, and fast. On her second voyage, carrying guano from Peru to Europe, running eastward in the South Atlantic with a heavy breeze astern, she was logging fifteen knots. The captain, W. D. Ellis, the son-in-law of the owner, W. D. Lawrence, wanted to reduce sail, but Lawrence said, "Hang on a bit until the log reads sixteen knots. She'll make it." A few minutes after that she dived into a big sea — and how big they are in the Southern Ocean! — at fifteen knots, and in fetching up all her upper spars went over the side — a beautiful mess. She spent most of the seventies and early eighties in the eastern trade, between England and India. She cost her owner $108,000; she made him $141,000 clear profit over *eight* years; and in 1883 she was sold to the Norwegians for $86,000.

Her career is in some ways typical. Canadian square-riggers rarely saw home port. They were scattered all over the globe and came home only every so often. They were found in Rio, Capetown, Bombay, Manila, Canton, San Francisco. They were usually owned in shares, the captain often having a percentage himself. Where she went and the cargo she carried was the responsibility of the owner, the ship's agents and the captain though, as cable communication improved, the owners back home could play a more significant role. But Bluenose ships were to be found wherever in the world there was money to be made in ship cargoes.

The name "Bluenose" was usually applied by the Nova Scotians to themselves and to Nova Scotian ships, but the name was applied by others to all British North American ships.

Timber Raft on the St. Lawrence by Frances Anne Hopkins. As the painting shows, some of the rafts were very large and the crews manning them lived on board, complete with tents and campfires. For many years they were the chief means of moving timber from the lakes to the markets in Montreal and Quebec. (Royal Ontario Museum)

Sailors talked of "bucko Bluenose mates," or "hard-case Nova Scotia packets," when they might be speaking neither of Nova Scotian mates nor Nova Scotian ships. New Brunswickers and Quebeckers built, owned and operated a considerable tonnage of Canadian ships. In the early 1880s Saint John was rated the fourth largest wooden-ship-owning port anywhere.

These Canadian square-rigged ships earned their reputation. They were run with a firm hand. They flew the Red Ensign, like all British ships, but sailors recognized them as Canadian almost as soon as they saw them, from the rig, the style, the up-to-date gear they preferred to use and their spotless appearance. The Canadian captain was a stickler for discipline and cleanliness. One Englishman who had sailed as a foremast hand in those ships across the Atlantic remarked:

> The captain, mate and second-mate were as hard drivers as their countrymen always are. . . . No one was struck by an officer the whole passage — no one ever gave occasion, that

is the secret. As is often the case in some of the hardest-worked British North American ships, to give the devil his due, the food was of the best quality and the quantity un-limited. By the time we reached New York, a general good feeling existed fore and aft, a healthy pride in smartness and respect for skill in our officers, who took more than their share of our risk.

They were young, those officers. Second-mates at sixteen years of age were not uncommon. Mates were often twenty or twenty-one years of age, and there were numerous masters not much older. Such captains often had their wives and children with them on board. The officers had very little polish; they did not affect uniforms or brass buttons; they had a great deal of capacity. Most of them had gone to sea at thirteen or four-teen, and learned their trade from the fo'c's'le up. The second mate would go aloft with the men if either of his superiors were on deck, and in all-hands work, when both port and starboard watches were turned out to stow or reef a big sail in heavy weather,* the mate himself would be up on the yard. The crews respected two things, seamanship and physical and moral courage. They were tough crews, and they could not be handled by a beardless second mate of seventeen or eighteen

*A properly made mainsail in a ship like the *W. D. Lawrence* weighed something around a ton, and a lot more than that when wet.

A sailing ship loading in the timber coves above Quebec about 1880. The huge squared timbers are being hauled through two special ports in her bow.

years of age if he did not have capacity. Sailors can be rough customers, drunk or sober, but especially drunk. Not that the life of the crew was easy. The first thing a young apprentice had to do, going on board the *Moshulu* in Belfast for the first time, was to obey the orders of the mate and climb to the top of the mainmast, two hundred feet up (the same as the *William D. Lawrence*) from keel to truck, to touch the little hardwood cap at the top mast.

It was in the mid-1880s that iron hulls began to make their appearance. Many of them were built on the Clyde and they had, unhappily, several advantages. Larger ships could be built, with bigger cargo capacity, because of lighter framing; Lloyd's gave them a much higher classification for marine insurance; their repair bills were lower; and they would outlast a wooden ship at least twice as long. Fifteen years was good for a soft-wood ship. The Clyde-built iron sailing ships could last fifty. Moreover, they didn't leak, they did not spoil cargoes, as did occasionally even the best softwood ships after half a dozen years at sea. It was not the tramp steamer that killed the great Canadian square-riggers; it was the iron-hulled sailing ship, like the *Moshulu*. The tramp steamer did not put in an appearance until about 1910. By 1924 the big old softwood ships were mostly memories:

> I can't help feelin' lonesome for the old ships that have gone,
> For the sight o' tropic sunsets and the hour before the dawn,
> And the white sails pullin' stoutly to a warm and steady draft,
> And the smell o' roastin' coffee, and the watches must'rin' aft.
>
> I'd like to ship off-shore again upon some Bluenose barque,
> And shout a sailor chantey in the windy, starry dark,
> Or fist a clewed-up tops'l in a black south-easter's roar,
> But it ain't no use a-wishin', for them days will come no more.

But the schooners were left; they would continue to exist well into the 1920s and 1930s in all parts of the Atlantic provinces, but especially in Nova Scotia and the still uncon-federated colony of Newfoundland.

> Lively on the' chorus thar'
>   Ez hearty ez ye can
> For we're outward bound this mornin'
>   On a Novy Scotia-man!

So, a Nova Scotian schooner with her Newfoundland crew. Heights of canvas loomed aloft, tight with the wind; one was caught by the sense of quiet, only the cheeping of mast hoops or the clink of sheet block fetching up against a shackle when the vessel bowed to a surge or where, below the black bowsprit, the forefoot ripped steadily into the sea. She was heading for the Banks.

The Newfoundland fishermen followed the age-old practice of turning their fish over to the merchant, sometimes called in Newfoundland, "the planter." To take an example. A fisherman has 70 quintals (allow 50 fish to the 112 pound quintal), which he turns over to the planter at $3.00 per quintal. He has $210 coming to him. But last year was a bad season; he owes the planter $150 from last year, and now has but $60 to his credit. But he has to spend; "ye'll have your new shawl, Mother; an' Katie yonder'll have her calico, and I'll borrow a bit against the sealing time." And the fisherman would hug himself with the thought that next year his good time would come. Fishing encouraged the gambling instinct, already lively enough in that gloriously unstrung nationality, the Irish, who made up half the population of Newfoundland.

Newfoundland toyed with Confederation in 1885-87, and in 1894-95 went after it more seriously. The projected Trans-Newfoundland Railway contributed a good deal to both ventures. But Newfoundland's main business was still at sea, and the lines of communication from St. John's lay outward, as much to Lisbon, Malaga and Barcelona, as to Barbados, Boston and Halifax. The interior of Newfoundland until the 548-mile railway was finished in 1898 was still in the 1880s a haunting wilderness; much of it, like the interior of Nova Scotia and New Brunswick, still is. Newfoundland's west coast was still in a state of uncertainty between the claims of the French to the littoral, through the French Shore, and Newfoundland's own desire to possess what was, but for those privileges, hers.

Few came to Newfoundland without being impressed with that splendid and brooding coast. At St. John's, cliffs were three hundred feet or more up from the sea, and dropping nearly straight into thirty or forty fathoms of water. One could lay a ship right up against some of them. In the summertime the green heaths on the top were a carpet: in June full of purple wild rhododendron, in August blueberries sweet and hot in the sun, and in September would come the bake-apples, and in November the cranberries. Lying on top of those cliffs one watched the sea the whole 1,900 miles to Ireland or the 1,250 miles to the Azores. One visitor who came from Montreal in the summer of 1886 stayed three months at Tilt Cove, a mining area up on Notre Dame Bay on the northeast coast, and described her Newfoundland summer as having left her "fresher and rosier than I ever looked before in my life, with more exuberance of good health and spirits than I knew what to do with."

Summers gone and recalled: one thinks of Charles G. D. Roberts' evocation of the fishing nets in "Tantramar Revisited" in 1886:

> . . . the net-reels
> Wound with the beaded nets, dripping and dark from the sea!
> Now at this season the nets are unwound; they hang from the
>   rafters
> Over the fresh-stowed hay in upland barns, and the wind
> Blows all day through the chinks, with the streaks of sunlight,
>   and sweeps them
> Softly at will; or they lie heaped in the gloom of a loft.

It is the verisimilitude of this that strikes the reader; one has stepped inside the door of the barn, and is listening to the sibilant hush of it. "You see it is like this," said Bliss Carman, Roberts' cousin, "old Nature lies out there in the sun, all so beautiful and fair; and poetry is what she would say if she could speak. . . . It is not their own word, [that is, the poets'] not their private grief or sorrow or joy, but the echoed joy of the whole earth. . . ."[8] But Roberts' great poem of 1886 has more to it even than that. He had lived near those marshlands until he was fourteen, and he came back to them at twenty-six after being editor of *The Week*, homesick for the sea.

> Summers and summers have come, and gone with the flight of
>   the swallow . . .
> Even the bosom of Earth is strewn with heavier shadows,—
> Only in these green hills, aslant to the sea, no change!

There were changes, of course. One wonders if the charming inn by the harbour at Sydney was still there from thirty years before, its pretty maid announcing tea with a bell, and with a look that was its own bell. The Maritimes seem to produce their own brand of nostalgia, on natives and visitors alike.

> It is just a year since I was seated in the cosy inn-parlor at Sydney, and how strangely it all comes back again; the little window overlooking the harbor, the lights on the twinkling waters; the old-fashioned house-clock in the corner of the room; the bright brass andirons . . . the old sofa; the cheerful lamp, and the well-polished table.

Soon enough would the Dominion Steel and Coal Company, formed in 1899, make an end to all of that if, in fact, an end had not been made already.

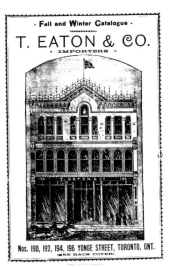

Cover of the first catalogue of T. Eaton & Company, issued in 1884. Although the foreword refers to the "Mail Order Department," for many years it was railway express services that made it possible to send small shipments to customers over a large part of Canada. Country-wide parcel post service was not available until 1914.

Nova Scotia had taken in and enjoyed some of the benefits of the National Policy. Or, to put it more accurately, parts of Nova Scotia had done so. The coal was mined in roughly equal proportions in three counties, Cumberland, in the Isthmus of Chignecto, Pictou, facing Northumberland Strait, and Cape Breton, at the southeast end, literally, of Cape Breton Island. Nova Scotia coal production grew steadily without any major downturns, from 800,000 tons in 1876 to 2,500,000 tons in 1896. Mining coal was not easy; it was dangerous and hard. Especially was this so in Cape Breton, where the most extensive seams ran under the sea, and for every ton of coal that was taken out another three tons of water had to be pumped out. In case of accidents, at least at most mines, there was no compensation or reward from the mine company. The men themselves made up a fund at the Londonderry Mines in Cumberland County, into which they each paid ten cents a month. The national market for Nova Scotia coal was extensive and important. Nova Scotia only absorbed 35 per cent of her own coal production. Quebec took 40 per cent, and the remaining 25 per cent was divided between the other Atlantic provinces. The American market was at this time insignificant. When Premier W. S. Fielding called a provincial election in June 1886, on the issue of repeal of Confederation, Pictou and Cape Breton Counties voted for Confederation.

The Nova Scotia government had been kept rather hard up by the Confederation settlement. All Atlantic colonial governments had been traditionally weak in municipal institutions. Partly it was owing to the lack of imperative needs for roads; the sea would do, if nothing else. That was not true in Upper Canada. Partly also, there was a chronic shortage of ready cash, especially in Newfoundland which operated so much on the truck system that made collection of local taxes difficult, even if the municipal institutions had existed to levy them. There was a long tradition of dislike of local taxation, associated with the sturdy independence of fishermen and sea captains. On his own vessel, however small it might be, a man was his own master. In Nova Scotia every government that developed or extended municipal institutions suffered at the polls for it. There are few better examples of the wilful wrong-headedness of the public than the bitter opposition to Tupper's compulsory assessment for education in 1864 and after, which set up the Nova Scotian system of public education; or the equally wrongheaded opposition to Thompson's legislation establishing county municipal institutions in Nova Scotia in 1879. Both governments were duly punished at the polls; the legislation itself stayed.

Upon the governments at Halifax, Fredericton, Charlottetown and St. John's, therefore, fell much of the responsibility, the patronage and the costs of maintaining local roads and bridges that in Ontario and Quebec would be handled at the municipal level. When these governments, Nova Scotia especially, complained to Ottawa that the Confederation financial settlement left them chronically hard up, Ottawa, not unreasonably, replied, "Divest yourself of the costs of maintaining roads and bridges by setting up proper municipal governments, and you'll have lots of money!" The Nova Scotia government replied, "We can't do that, our people wouldn't stand for it," manifesting a natural desire to stay in office. So the Ottawa government was quite cool and distant when the Fielding Liberal government protested in 1884, and when it threatened repeal in 1885. For despite Thompson's municipal legislation the depression of 1884-87 had made Nova Scotia's financial position bad; and she had invested heavily in railway enterprises.

The Liberal government, in power since 1882, had not had a robust record, and a vital new issue was needed. Repeal of Confederation was almost certainly dead in practical terms, but not emotionally. Nothing had been said about repeal in the 1886 Speech from the Throne at Halifax, and nothing was said officially until two days before the end of the session. Fielding then proposed, and carried, a resolution for a union of the Maritime provinces outside of Confederation, failing which Nova Scotia would go it alone and ask to become a colony of Great Britain again. This resolution carried fifteen to seven, though in a House where sixteen other members either did not vote or stayed away. The House was then dissolved.

Fielding had his election on June 15, 1886. The anti-Confederate sentiment in Nova Scotia voted Liberal with enthusiasm, and those opposed to repeal thought Fielding was being so ridiculous they made insufficient effort to counteract it. The result was that everyone was surprised. Conservatives were pained. Fielding was pleased, perhaps even astonished. He wanted a good working majority; he got an overwhelming one, twenty-eight Liberals in a House of thirty-eight. It was all a little embarrassing. He had called the genie out of the bottle. "And now what, master?" the genie said eagerly. "Uh — er — let's think about it," was the gist of Fielding's reply.

The Dominion cabinet ministers who had gone down to Nova Scotia to help the local Conservatives fight Fielding returned to Ottawa a little chop-fallen. "Never was there such a rout," Macdonald wrote Tupper, "McLelan has come back from his inglorious campaign & gives no intelligent acct. of the disaster. Thompson is to be here on Wednesday [June 23rd] and we shall know more about it. . . . We are not in a flourishing state in the present state of public opinion. . . . We have rocks ahead and great skill must be exercised in steering the ship — "[9] But he said little about it in cabinet. Thompson came and offered to resign if Macdonald wanted to bring Tupper back from London. Macdonald put his arm on Thompson's shoulder and said, "It's no go. You've got to stay here and work as long as I am here." But serious though Macdonald was, his sense of humour always rose to the occasion. A. W. McLelan, Minister of Finance, came in to cabinet newly barbered and trim, with his hair wetted down. Macdonald looked up, and said, "Why McLelan, you look as if you've just had a good *licking!*"[10] He did not intend to have any more of those if he could help it. When he returned to Ottawa from the West, at the end of August 1886, he was to set about preparations for the next Dominion election, the necessity for which was now clearly visible on a stormy horizon.

7

The Last Years, 1886-1891

"SIR JOHN has got his war paint on and wants us all to take the field in Ontario," Thompson wrote to his wife in Halifax two weeks after Macdonald's return from the West. A September 1886 by-election in Haldimand, a constituency in Ontario that had been Liberal since long before Confederation, had been held by the Liberals, notwithstanding great Conservative efforts to take it. It was the time to strengthen the government with Ontario voters. In any Dominion election, ground would probably be lost in Quebec. On October 30th, the cabinet decided to have the elections before another session of Parliament was called, and expected to go to the polls in January and probably secure an overall majority of about twenty-five. By November 1886, Ontario announced a provincial election and the Conservative campaign went vigorously forward into Ontario.

Macdonald and three or four cabinet ministers spent almost two solid weeks campaigning in the last half of November. The pace was ferocious. Macdonald was astonishing. He went through meeting after meeting with ease. "Sir John surprises me," Thompson wrote to his wife, "he goes through all these hardships quite gaily..." The Dominion ministers, Macdonald, Thomas White* and Thompson, together with W. H. Meredith, the leader of the Conservative opposition in Ontario, installed themselves in a special Grand Trunk car, lived there and slept there, like gypsies. Thursday, November 18, 1886, they travelled from Palmerston to Goderich in a

OPPOSITE Sir John Macdonald about 1886, the year he paid his only visit to Western Canada. Over a hundred photographs have survived; this is one of the best of them.

*Thomas White (1830-1888) was a newspaperman, who founded two papers, the *Peterborough Review* and the Hamilton *Spectator*. In 1870 he assumed control of the Montreal *Gazette*. He became Minister of the Interior in August 1885.

perfect blizzard all day. At every station there was a crowd, sometimes with a brass band, who always cried out for "John A." Thompson would watch Macdonald go out, "shake hands everywhere with everyone, and kiss all the girls and . . . come back to the car covered with snow." When they arrived at Goderich at 10:30 P.M. there was a torchlight procession which the Dominion ministers were too exhausted to attend, so they gave Meredith to the natives as a peace offering.

The next day the blizzard subsided into wind; they drove twelve miles in open carriages northeast to Dungannon, arrived perished from cold, to have the crowd there take out the horses and themselves haul the carriages through the crowded streets of the village. Then back to Goderich for another five-hour meeting until 1:00 A.M. On Saturday they were in Hamilton, to the biggest meeting so far, a very rough crowd. Thomas White could not manage them at all. They stamped their feet until they got Macdonald but even he had a difficult time. "You have to say very wicked things," said Thompson frankly. "You cannot hold such crowds as we have had unless you give them your best and your worst." They often felt like travelling minstrels, from railway car to meetings and back again, often in dirty clothes; and in spite of their own exhaustion, both of mind and body, were "supposed to be quite up to the boiling point of excitement which prevails among the audiences." At Stratford the press was so thick that Thompson's guide was stopped dead, and when he was on the point of being suffocated by the pressure, by shouting and cursing he got himself lifted up bodily by the crowd, was hoisted over their heads and handed forward to the platform amid deafening cheers and laughter.[1]

When the general election of February 22, 1887 was over Macdonald was still firmly in the saddle. Quebec's 65 seats broke even, 33 Conservatives, a retreat from the 51 of 1882. But Nova Scotia returned to the fold — rather dishing the repeal movement — and Ontario held firm; altogether Macdonald could look forward to a comfortable 35-seat majority.* By now Macdonald was really more necessary to the party than ever — that was Thompson's shrewd estimate. Thompson had not been uncritical of Macdonald. He had come late to Ottawa when

*In the Ontario provincial election, however, Mowat increased his majority.

184

Macdonald was already showing some of the failings of age, and had never really walked in the old man's shadow. Putting off, Macdonald's most ancient sin, had grown upon him in recent years, though he had been rapped over the knuckles for it in 1885. But it irritated colleagues who had been asked by cabinet to prepare a paper on a subject — as Campbell had been in 1884 on the Ontario boundary question — only to have Macdonald postpone consideration of it for reasons that seemed quite inexplicable.[2] Macdonald could get annoyed and could get away with bullying in cabinet. Macdonald was annoyed with Thompson for something, in January 1887. Thompson, instead of submitting, showed fight. He ignored Macdonald's opinion on a legal point, talked to Macdonald's colleagues in cabinet over his head, and generally showed he could be annoyed too. He told his shocked colleagues privately that Macdonald could go to hell and get over his nastiness there. They both got over it. And Thompson had to admit that Macdonald was indispensable. Voting for Macdonald, Thompson reflected, "is one of those things in which the people are right without knowing why."

Edward Blake, the leader of the Liberals since 1880, was crushed after the 1887 elections. The Conservative party had

"The Doctor Arrives." Whenever Macdonald was in serious political trouble he sent a cry for help to Sir Charles Tupper, a pugnacious and effective campaigner. Even after Tupper became High Commissioner in London, Macdonald summoned him home from time to time. One occasion was the general election of 1887, which Macdonald feared he might lose. *Grip* greeted Tupper's arrival from London with this cartoon.

looked so vulnerable and yet it had been returned to office. Blake told Laurier, "The case against the Government was so overwhelming, it ought to have so absolutely enlisted the more intelligent and independent and moral parts of the community. . . ." Blake had the sulks, so Conservatives said, and flung himself off to Florida, as bitter as Mackenzie had been in 1878. The party wanted to keep Blake; it pleaded with him to stay; but Blake resigned and the leadership of the party passed to Laurier in June 1887.

It was not difficult to be impressed by Laurier. He was designed by nature to impress. Elegant, courteous, intelligent, with a faint pallor of ill-health never far away, he spoke with studied grace, and almost always with a strong sense of theatre. He was rarely informal, and he was rarely effective in Parliament with repartee. He liked set occasions, and rose to them like the great actor he was. He was not a poet or a musician, though he looked like both; his magic was in his speech. Men and events moved him; he was tremendously impressionable, taking the colour of his emotion, chameleon-like, from his surroundings. This splendid man, it was natural to assume, had splendid motives. They were not splendid, or no more so than anyone else's; they were quite commonplace, as commonplace as Macdonald's, that is, power and the love of the use of it. But Laurier always clothed his motives, as he did himself, so beautifully, it was hard to think of him as a tough politician. He did not look like one; but in men, as in women, appearance is the greatest deceit of all.

In Macdonald's hands the party reins became a bit more slack, though he was still careful about appearances after the awful revelations of 1873. In 1882 he told H. H. Smith, the party's Ontario organizer at the time: "It won't do that the slightest suspicion get abroad that timber licenses or govt. lands could be got in return for political support or election subscriptions. The offer to subscribe for the next elections if a timber limit were granted should be pooh-poohed by you as impossible." "I hope you burn my letters," he once wrote under a similar missive.[3]

The truth was, however, that any "fully circumcised" Conservative — Macdonald was clearly amused at Van Horne's phrase — could expect certain favours from the government, timber limits, land grants among them. Why should not M.P.s use their opportunities? Or was their position more akin to that of a public trustee? George Foster, at times a positive monster of probity (at least he looked it), told Parliament that an M.P. had a right to apply for what the law allowed, the same as anyone else. This was debatable and treacherous ground.

The whole question of patronage wears an air of the fantastic about it. Of all the aspects of Macdonald's government — really any government of the time — that the outsider from the 1970s finds most difficult to comprehend, the most vexatious, the most intriguing, is political patronage. Patronage has not vanished of course; it is with us still; it is still annoying to see a good man passed up for a position in favour of someone who has been more loyal politically and is usually less competent. But government now covers such a range compared to what it did in the nineteenth century; civil service acts have taken so many appointments and promotions out of the hands of political officers that relatively few positions are left. In the nineteenth century, party supporters expected much more. What they expected, judging by the correspondence preserved, is surprising. The satire in Leacock's *Sunshine Sketches of a Little Town*, that Erasmus Archer wanted a job for his son Pete because he was absolutely hopeless and good for nothing, was not that far from reality. Nova Scotia, and the Maritime provinces generally, seem to have the sincerest devotion to patronage in all its varieties; the ramifications, for example, of appointing a Collector of Customs at Antigonish, would make even hardened central Canadian politicians wince.

But the Maritime provinces were not alone in their devotion to patronage, though they went after it with an ardour, a sincerity, an unblushing determination that rather makes the flesh crawl. "I think," wrote Sir Alexander Campbell to Macdonald from Halifax, "the fact is that like Quebec their only idea here of progress is to get the Government to do something — " The postmastership of Belleville, Ontario, introduces appropriately the higher world of political patronage. The minister whose responsibility it was to make the recommendation was the Postmaster General, in this case, in 1880, Sir Alexander Campbell. He usually solicited the nominations from the local M.P., provided the local M.P. was a Conservative. If the local M.P. was a Liberal, then it could be the Conservative who

Halifax about 1885, as seen from George Island. The famous Citadel crowns the hill to the left.

had tried for the seat at the most recent general election. Or it could be a Conservative who sat for the same riding in the Provincial Legislature. For example, in Antigonish County, Nova Scotia, the M.P. until 1885 was a Liberal; the member for Antigonish in the Provincial Assembly was a Conservative, John Thompson, and he had the main say in the federal patronage in Antigonish County between 1878 and 1882. In the case of the Belleville postmastership the local M.P. was a Conservative, Mackenzie Bowell, who was also in the cabinet. Macdonald had received a letter from Henry Corby of the distilling family of Belleville, asking about the postmastership. Macdonald referred it to Bowell, who reminded his chief that the situation was really rather complicated. Senator Robert Read, also from Belleville, had asked for that position for his son-in-law, Mr. Campion, who was one of a large family of Conservatives who were residents of Bowell's riding and had always been "as true as steel." Not only that, but the Postmaster General's brother, C. J. Campbell, was also an applicant. There were a number of others, besides. But the best part of this extraordinary story was, as Bowell put it to Macdonald, "In addition to this the position is *not vacant* nor do I know when it will be as the present Postmaster Mr. I. H. Meachem is to all appearances as capable of performing the duties of the office, as he has been for years past, and has no *intention* of *resigning.* . . . "

Patronage also carried with it responsibilities. One of Bowell's old Belleville acquaintances was Lewis Wallbridge. He wanted a job on the bench. Finally he got one; in 1882 Wallbridge was made Chief Justice of Manitoba, a part of the world, it is probably safe to say, he had never laid eyes on. The

trouble was that Lewis Wallbridge had very bad teeth, some missing, and some others looking as if they should be. Macdonald was concerned with the dignity of the Manitoba bench. Bowell found that problem no easier than the postmastership:

> The great question of teeth or no teeth, I find, is somewhat difficult to solve.
>
> Whilst I agree with you that it would add much to the appearance, and perhaps dignity, of the Bench, if the Chief Justice had a mouth of good teeth, still when you consider the extreme egotism of the Chief Justice of Manitoba, and the difficulty of approaching him upon a subject of such *gnashing* importance, you will see the difficulty. . . .
>
> However I set three or four at him,— our friend Dan Murphy among the number — who said that he would induce Wallbridge to consent provided I would "pledge a quarter's salary in *advance*"— which of course I did — still I have very great doubt of his succeeding.
>
> The people, and the Bar, of Belleville gave him [Wallbridge] a very flattering reception last night, presented him with a gold watch and other articles to adorn his western Wigwam; and he was as proud and strutted about the platform like a Peacock with his tail spread.*

Local M.P.s were usually consulted, but Macdonald always resisted any attempt on their part to assert a categorical right to recommend patronage in their ridings. When four Toronto M.P.s tried it in 1880, Macdonald wrote to J. C. Aikens, about to become Minister of Inland Revenue, "My dear

Winnipeg about 1885. The pinnacles and tower of the old City Hall rise in the centre of the painting. Main Street curves away to the left, toward Portage Avenue. The City Market is to the right, across King Street from the City Hall.

*In fairness to Wallbridge it has to be said that he ended up being well liked in Manitoba, and his death in 1889 was much regretted by the bar in Winnipeg.

Aikens — I want to put down all this stupid nonsense of the Toronto M.P.'s"[4]

The overall rule was, as Mackenzie Bowell pointed out to parliament quite explicitly, when anything was to be done you consulted your friends. The whole system of government worked that way, and it was "the merest hypocrisy to preach or lay down any other doctrine as being practiced by any political party in this country." Macdonald, it is fair to say, agreed with this though he would have put it more judiciously. If you did have confidence in a government, you could solicit favours from it; if you didn't, you couldn't. There was literally no other way of making appointments. Gilbert and Sullivan in *Iolanthe* (1882) made delightful fun of members of the House of Lords getting their peerages by competitive examination, instead of by patronage. Canada got a Civil Service Act in 1881 that was an important first stage toward the idea of an impartial civil service; but it was only that and no more. Alexander Mackenzie successfully opposed demands for a wholesale removal of Conservatives from the civil service, when the Nova Scotians and others had wanted a clean sweep. It might have been better if he had followed the Nova Scotian advice. Some of the difficulties of Mackenzie's régime were owing to shamelessly partisan behaviour of some Conservatives in government posts. Cartwright said it was impossible to keep a secret; it was like living in a glass house.

Not all patronage was bad, however. It was through Sir Alexander Campbell, the Postmaster-General, that Archibald Lampman, one of our greatest poets, transferred out of school-teaching (at which he was hopeless) to the Post Office at Ottawa. Wilfred Campbell got a job in the civil service. So did Duncan Campbell Scott. All three turned out to be able, honest civil servants, and the three Ottawa poets formed an agreeable and happy triumvirate. The relation between Scott and Lampman was particularly fruitful, and they began to take canoe trips in the Gatineau country together. From which, perhaps, are these lovely lines about a summer evening on the river:

> . . . the night wind
> Wandering in puffs from off the darkening hill,
> Breathes warm or cool; and now the whip-poor-will,
> Beyond the river margins glassed and thinned,
> Whips the cool hollows with his liquid note.

Lampman's poetry is worth all his post office salaries put in a mailbag together. The work he did not like much, but he did it well and it gave him time and security, two essentials for writers and poets. On one of his civil service holidays, he went to the north shore of the St. Lawrence, to Les Eboulements, some seventy miles below Quebec, west of Murray Bay. There, looking out across the St. Lawrence at sunset, twelve miles across the great river, he set down one of the most splendid sonnets in our literature.

> Broad shadows fall. On all the mountain side
> The scythe-swept fields are silent. Slowly home
> By the long beach the high-piled hay-carts come
> Splashing the pale salt shallows. Over wide
> Fawn-coloured wastes of mud the slipping tide,
> Round the dun rocks and wattled fisheries,
> Creeps murmuring in. And now by twos and threes
> O'er the slow spreading pools with clamorour chide,
> Belated crows from strip to strip take flight.
> Soon will the first star shine; yet ere the night
> Reach onward to the pale-green distances,
> The sun's last shaft beyond the gray sea-floor
> Still dreams upon the Kamouraska shore,
> And the long line of golden villages.

Those golden villages of Kamouraska, Macdonald knew well; they were just thirty miles away from his own summers at St. Patrice, near Rivière du Loup. Macdonald knew Quebec well but he never really campaigned there. He would appear at election meetings in Nova Scotia once in a long while, but Quebec he left in the hands of his cabinet ministers from Quebec. Probably the reason was he never felt at home in French. There is no evidence whatever that he ever attempted to speak it. This in a sense delivered him into the hands of his Quebec ministers, and he depended upon them.

Ever since Cartier died, the mantle had been assumed by Hector Langevin. Langevin was quite unlike Cartier. There were no wild Saturday-night stag parties at Langevin's. He had none of Cartier's pugnacity or spirit. He had other virtues. He was a painstaking administrator, who took trouble to master the details of his department, Public Works. There was later to be evidence that he mastered them only too well. He had finesse, good temper and a decent sense of discretion, all of which Cartier had lacked. But he was not very useful for general parliamentary business; Macdonald had tried to encourage him to master more of the details of business outside of his department, but he never quite made it. And his pedestrian manner in the House, his monotonous voice, gave him the parliamentary style of a loyal lieutenant who might never be anything more.

Then in 1882 Chapleau came along. Langevin never again had real peace. In 1882 Chapleau was forty-two, Langevin fifty-six; Chapleau had been in Quebec cabinets for the past decade, and had been premier of Quebec since 1879. He was a man of tremendous power on the public platform, nearly irresistible, unscrupulous, tough, demagogic, who believed, as he once wrote Macdonald, "qui veut la fin veut les moyens."* Politics was war. Politics was piracy. Money was the sinews of war, piracy and, one might add for Chapleau, of love. His *tendances boulevardières*, that happy and judicious French expression, were notorious. Chapleau was once upon a time destined for the church, where his tremendous magnetism would have won him a great following. French Canadians said, *Que d'âmes il aurait pu sauver, et qu'il a perdues!* (English does not quite render the neatness of this. "What souls he could have been able to save, and what souls he has lost!") Chapleau wanted to come to Ottawa. He wanted to emulate Cartier; keep a useful lieutenant at Quebec City, as Premier of Quebec, and lord it at Ottawa, as Cartier had done, and as Chapleau well knew how.

Macdonald also needed Chapleau to strengthen his Montreal wing. Langevin had the disadvantage of being from Quebec City, whereas Chapleau was born in Ste Therese, just north of Montreal, and had always sat for Terrebonne, the county there. Chapleau was a Montrealer. Madame Quebec seemed not unhappy to be rid of him; a cartoon in Grip suggested Chapleau as Madame Quebec's wild boy.

> MME. QUEBEC — It's so kind of you to take him, Sir John! He's nearly brought me to ruin!
> SIR JOHN — Have no fear Madame; under *my* tuition he shall learn prudence, economy, industry and thrift!

*The English version is, "The end justifies the means."

TWO OFFICIAL LANGUAGES.
"AS USELESS AS TWO TONGUES ON A NORTH-WEST CART."

So Chapleau was made Secretary of State, a post not devoid of reputation, but in effect he was superintendent of the red tape, parchment and sealing wax. It was pretty thin pickings. Chapleau was hoping, indeed expecting, that sooner or later he would be put in charge of one of the big spending departments, like Langevin's Public Works. He was never to get one. Chapleau twisted, turned, manoeuvred, tried to undercut Langevin, struck up acquaintances with Quebec Liberals every once in a while, but as long as Macdonald was alive Chapleau remained Secretary of State. He did *not* like it!

The day the dissolution of 1887 was announced, January 15th, Macdonald sent a hurried note to Langevin. "Chapleau's going to resign, so I must see you tonight. Come in the cab I send this by." No one can entirely sort out the relations between Chapleau and Langevin, but they were bad. Chapleau revelled in intrigue, positively enjoyed factional infighting; Langevin had little taste for it. If Langevin stopped for lunch in Montreal or to see friends, Chapleau was apt to complain that Langevin was invading his territory. Chapleau complained in October 1886 that Langevin's paper in Montreal, *Le Monde*, got all the patronage, and Chapleau's group at *La Minerve* did all the work. Chapleau wanted the J. J. Ross government of Quebec to fight the Riel issue head on; Langevin advised trying to evade it. Langevin won. He won too often for Chapleau. Soft words kept Chapleau from resigning for a time, but a

Some topics of contention stretch far back in Canadian history. This Bengough cartoon on bilingualism was published in *Grip* on February 15, 1890.

193

quarrel blew up over a Quebec legal appointment. Two days later Chapleau's resignation came.

Macdonald persuaded him to stay, but Chapleau's terms were surprisingly harsh. The force comes through in French. "Je veut qu'il soit bien entendu," Chapleau wrote, "et cela devrait être mis par écrit...." The bargain shows the nature of the fighting terrain of these two great barons, Langevin and Chapleau. Chapleau was to have absolute control of party affairs in his barony, the area being from Trois-Rivières to Pontiac, that is, the whole of Quebec from Trois-Rivières westward to the Ontario border, except for the Eastern Townships. He wanted control of election candidates and election funds. He wanted the immediate retirement of the Under-Secretary of State, and replacement by one of Chapleau's nominees. Macdonald agreed to nearly all his terms, almost without condition. But things had not worked out at the provincial level for Chapleau. His successor there had been replaced, though a Conservative régime still continued in power. By 1885 it had become old, fat and too comfortable. There were forces in Quebec making for reform. One was the church's ultramontane wing, the political branch of which was called "Les Castors."* They were super-Conservatives. They did not really mind J. J. Ross, the Conservative Premier, for he was French-Canadian despite his name and not unsympathetic to the ultramontanes; but they did not like Conservative operators like Chapleau. They tended to wrinkle up their noses at the very mention of him or his friends.

Another force making for purity in Quebec politics had, traditionally, been the Liberal party. It was still lean and hungry after many years out of office. Except for the brief Liberal régime of Henri Joly de Lotbinière from March 1878 to October 1879, Quebec had had Conservative governments ever since 1867. Joly symbolized the old-fashioned, pure, economy-minded Liberalism that many English-speaking voters in Quebec liked, not unlike the régime that they sometimes admired, that of Oliver Mowat in Ontario, who had ruled there steadily since 1872. But Joly resigned the leadership of the Liberal opposition in 1883, and it then fell upon Honoré Mercier, nine years younger.

Mercier, like Chapleau, was a born politician. He was

Castor means "beaver," but the translation has no significance here.

194

irresistible before a crowd. He could move a crowd to tears or laughter and he could even — this is harder to do — instruct them. Charles Langelier, who had often watched Mercier, remarked, "I never met anyone in political life like Mercier, (except perhaps Papineau) who has remained etched so sharply in the memory of the public." The real blaze of Mercier's political career was to last only six years, from 1886 to 1892, but that tremendous illumination lit up the whole Quebec landscape.

Mercier's Liberalism was not, however, like Joly's. Mercier wanted power, not reforms, and he was prepared to get power by means that Joly eschewed. Mercier used the traditional base of the Liberal party, but he added support that Joly could not have used and would not have used. Mercier fished for and got support from the Castors. Since Joly had been a French Protestant, that was not possible for him; Mercier, however, had been educated at the Jesuit Collège de Ste Marie at Montreal. Mercier had no background of Liberal anti-clericalism. Moreover Mercier promised, or appeared to promise, to English-speaking voters in Quebec, honest, economical government, associated in their minds with Liberal régimes like Joly's. These English Liberal voters tended to regard the Conservative party in Quebec as a conspiracy of French and Irish Catholics to milk the province. And English-speaking voters were in a majority in eight counties and a significant factor in six others.

None of this support might have been sufficient to bring down the old and well-entrenched Conservative régime in Quebec; but late in 1885 the Riel issue came on stage. There were Quebec Liberals who believed that the Riel issue ought to be left severely alone. After all, the J. J. Ross Conservative government of Quebec had nothing to do with Riel. His execution was not their fault. Joly was bitterly opposed to using Riel, and resigned his Assembly seat over it. But Mercier was always more nationalist-minded than Joly and he was also less scrupulous. When the news came in November 1885 that Riel was to be hanged, Montreal Liberals were alleged to have said, "Well, well! So much the better. That's worth twenty counties in Quebec to us." The Riel issue raised up a tremendous storm in Quebec, and Langevin, Chapleau and Caron all faced it with great courage. Mercier had but to capitalize on it if he could. And he certainly could.

A RIEL UGLY POSITION.

Riel had been sentenced to death a few weeks before this cartoon appeared in *Grip*. In it Bengough neatly portrayed the dilemma in which the violent popular reaction for and against the verdict placed Macdonald.

195

The bitterness of French-Canadian feeling about the execution of Riel was something that could not be blinked away. It would remain for a long time to come part of their attitude to the Dominion government. Perhaps Riel himself was not so important. He had been, after all, at odds with the church; in the West he had been preaching his own peculiar mystical brand of Catholicism. Riel was insane, and Mercier knew it. But French Canadians generally were not well informed about conditions in the West. It was not difficult to persuade them that Riel's trial was prejudiced and vindictive. So strong was Riel's case, so the argument went, that even an English-speaking jury had to recommend mercy. Mercy Riel did not get, and the French-Canadian ministers of the Macdonald government had been unable to get it for him. So the *gibet de Regina* became a powerful symbol. It was a symbol of what French Canadians believed was the insensate hatred of English-speaking Canadians towards the poor Métis whose main wish had been to live as they had always done, and whose grievances had led them blindly to take up arms against a distant, unfeeling and incompetent government.

This made a powerful appeal on the Quebec hustings. Nevertheless, Mercier did not win the provincial election of October 1886 with a clear majority. It was not until the Legislature met in January 1887 that the J. J. Ross government was defeated in the House and then Mercier became Premier. He soon acquired a great following. He was, like Macdonald, a man of immense charm; his followers, the younger ones especially, adored him; his was a temperament of flame and steel. But those who had put Mercier into power hoping for pure, economical government were to be disappointed. The cure for the years of Conservative wickedness was to be about as bad as the disease. There is a delicious cartoon in *Grip*, November 1886:

> MME. QUEBEC — Now, Mr. Mercier, take care that you don't give me too decent a government — for I won't stand it!
> M. MERCIER — Don't worry, Madame; there's not the slightest danger!

Mercier went to the polls in a provincial general election in June 1890. When Chapleau tried to drum up funds to help defeat him, the Montreal businessmen said, "What is the use of throwing money away?" They were right. Mercier won a clear 12-seat majority in a House of 65. But in December 1891 he was forced to resign over the Baie des Chaleurs Railway Scandal, and in March 1892 the Quebec Conservatives (Riel issue and all) swept back into power with 52 out of the 65 seats. Mercier died of diabetes in 1894. He had always wanted to defeat Macdonald but he had never succeeded.

He had made things difficult enough. They were well-matched adversaries, each representing in their very personalities the peculiar geniuses of French and English. One of Mercier's most celebrated coups was the Jesuit Estates Act of 1888.

It was an old, tangled, difficult issue. Successive premiers of Quebec had wrestled with it. Chapleau had tried; J. J. Ross had tried. Mercier succeeded. The general view in Quebec was that an eighty-eighty-year old and prickly question was well out of the way. Mercier put into the Act, however, a long preamble, including correspondence with the Vatican, and giving power to the pope to conciliate the contending ecclesiastical factions of the church in Quebec. This preamble was several things: an attempt to justify the Act to Quebec voters was one; but it was, almost certainly, a deliberate tease at Ontario Protestants who had made such a row against Riel three years before.

The Ontario Protestants rose to the bait like hungry trout. Some Toronto newspapers, who were a bit lacking in interesting news just then, took up the issue in the summer of 1888 with avidity, and before long demands were pouring into Ottawa for the disallowance of the Act. And here one comes fairly up against the lively, tender prejudices of Protestant Ontario on the subject of Roman Catholics, particularly French Roman Catholics.

No other Canadian province enjoyed anything like the prejudices of Ontario Protestants. These existed elsewhere, of course, but nowhere in Canada so luxuriantly as in Ontario. In other provinces one met Roman Catholics more or less every day in most moderate-sized towns. Outside of main cities, the Roman Catholic population of Ontario was rather scattered, and it was possible to live in some parts of Ontario without even knowing what a Roman Catholic looked like.

Xenophobic reactions lived in the traditional fears of Protestants, but old fears had been revived and ramified in the

Montreal, looking down the river, c. 1885.

pontificate of Pius IX (1846-1878). The more sober and careful pontificate of Leo XIII (1878-1903) did nothing to change church doctrine on the very points that alarmed the Protestants; indeed, the encyclical *Immortale Dei*, November 1885, and especially *Libertas*, of June 1888, suggested that Leo XIII was following in the steps of Pius IX, that though popes come and go, the church went on forever.* Thus, Protestants could never rest. If they did, they would be overwhelmed. There was much that was good in the great Catholic revival of the mid-nineteenth century, but there was much also that suggested the church's desire to retake the great domains lost to her in the Reformation. Some famous and learned divines of the Church of England had gone over to Catholicism and had become prelates of the Roman Church, most conspicuously Cardinal Newman and Cardinal Manning. Catholicism thus began to look to Protestants like a sinister engine of great subtlety, in-

*The first signs of change were only to appear in May 1891 with *Rerum novarum*, concerned with the conditions of the working classes.

exhaustible persistence and infinite patience; and what it once caught it never willingly gave up.

It was easy for unprincipled newspapers in Ontario with nothing much to do and with circulations to build, to work contemporary events in ways to appeal to prejudices of this kind, as easy as it had been for French-Canadian newspapers and politicians to exploit Louis Riel as a martyr, and with less justification. There were also politicians in Ontario willing to do the same. Some were looking for power and influence but some were also primitive enough to be genuinely convinced of the rightness of their views; in fact, accurately representing many of their constituents. They tended to come from, and to represent in parliament, back-tier counties of Ontario that had had long traditions of Protestantism, where Roman Catholics were few and where the Catholic Church looked like a miasma of evil looming over the narrow farm horizons. Many of "the noble thirteen" who insisted so passionately upon disallowance of the Jesuit Estates Act in the 1889 session of Parliament came from backgrounds like this: from Wiarton in Bruce County; from Barrie, Bradford, in Simcoe County; Shanty Bay in Muskoka; Newburgh in Lennox and Addington; districts where Protestantism and the Orange Order had been traditions, prejudices if you like, that neither education nor common sense could effectually change.

By far the most sophisticated and intelligent man of this group was D'Alton McCarthy. His position points up the whole debate of what Canada was to become. He had something of the intellectual hardness of the Protestant Irish. Born in Ireland, he came to Canada when he was eleven years old. Elected to Parliament at the age of forty, he was soon close to Macdonald, who at first looked upon him as a favourite son and even as a possible successor. It was no secret that about 1884 McCarthy could have had the portfolio of Minister of Justice if he wanted it. But he said plainly he could not afford to live on a minister's salary, which was indeed thin enough. That portfolio of Justice went, in the ironic way of politics, to a Methodist turned Roman Catholic ("pervert" was the nineteenth-century Canadian expression) from Halifax, John Thompson. So McCarthy remained outside the Conservative cabinet, and by the later 1880s his intellectual and political convictions had begun to take him further away from it than ever.

McCarthy's ruthless and inexorable conclusions were hard to resist. His argument was simple, clear and, for Canada, dangerous. Nations, said McCarthy, live by shared beliefs and experiences. This common national life can only be achieved in countries that have a common language. Language is the cement of nationality. "Was the country to be English or French?" McCarthy would ask. In his view it had to be one or the other, or no country at all. Thus Switzerland, Belgium and the Austrian Empire could not be truly nations. The splintering of Austria in 1919 into its Hungarian, Czech-Slovak, Jugoslav and German components is exactly what McCarthy would have predicted. Thus Canada in the later 1880s had to come to the point of decision about her future. There was no reason why the French language need be extinguished right away. Obviously it couldn't be. But its extension or even its entrenchment ought not to be permitted. Canadians ought to be able to see on the horizon the end of French. McCarthy therefore opposed all concessions on the subject of language rights. If ballots did not do it now, bayonets would have to do it later.

He was equally opposed on political grounds to Roman Catholicism. Here his argument was more subtle. He had no objection to the church as such. He would argue that every religion had an equal right to be a solace for its adherents. What he objected to in the Roman Catholic Church was exactly what the Methodists and Baptists used to object to in the Church of England: a claim to be catholic. It claimed to be universal. It claimed authority, religious and to a degree civil, over its adherents. It would not stay put in what McCarthy believed was its proper role. It moved in a world of politics, men and affairs, not just in religion.

McCarthy's intellectual force was therefore in these bold, splendid, politically inconvenient premises. There was, indeed, something to admire in McCarthy. Ordinary politicians looked like greasy and shop-worn merchants beside this gorgeous knight, armed and accoutred, on a prancing steed. Even his opponents admired his logic and the remorseless rules he drew from it. It was magnificent but it was not politics; at least it was not politics for Canada. In a country composed of two million Roman Catholics, most of them French, and three million Protestants, nearly all English, it was, as sensible people in Parliament remarked, mischievous in the last degree to accept views like McCarthy's. No one doubted his sincerity, but hell is paved with sincerity.

Canada had developed by a series of rather delicate accommodations in difficult questions of language and religion. Without them the country would not work. McCarthy would have replied the country so working was not worth having, but not many agreed with him. Laurier took for answer good English liberal doctrine, the right of men to choose their own religion and to be entitled to a certain minimum of rights in education and language. Macdonald, characteristically, took refuge in humour. To all the tirades from Protestant Ontarians for disallowance of the Jesuit Estates Act, he turned a deaf ear. The Act was constitutional. It solved a peculiarly Quebec problem. What need had Ottawa to interfere? He replied in Parliament with an old story, as he often did; it was about a Jew who had ordered a ham sandwich in a restaurant and was about to eat it when a ferocious thunderstorm broke outside and lightning flashed in the street. The Jew said, "All that fuss about a bit of ham!" The motion for disallowance of the Jesuits Estates Act was defeated overwhelmingly, 1:00 A.M., March 29, 1889, by 188 to 13.

Where was Canada going? What was her national goal? Did anyone have any idea? Could Canada ever be a nation? Part colony, part independent, part French, with no anthem, no collective self, a congeries of this and that, put together by geography, railways, politics, and a great deal of self-interest and corruption: was *this* a country? Yet there were those who aspired to make it so, even if grounded upon hard-won compromises between not altogether tractable countrymen. Charles G. D. Roberts, age thirty, was young enough to be restless and impatient, and old enough to say so:

> O Falterer, let thy past convince
>   Thy future, — all the growth, the gain
> The fame since Cartier knew thee, since
>   Thy shores beheld Champlain!

> But thou, my country, dream not thou!
>   Wake, and behold how night is done,—
> How on thy breast, and o'er thy brow,
>   Bursts the uprising sun!

Roberts' union of French and English in that poem, each bringing their own strengths, traditions and language to a common nation, is closer than most Canadians came to defining an articulate national idea for their country. If we are prone to smile a little at our uncertain ancestors, let it be said that the national question was difficult. Independence from Great Britain was not tantamount to Canadian nationhood. Rather it was the moral equivalent of annexation to the United States. Almost no one in power believed anything else. Youngsters like Roberts had their hopes bruised time and again on that rock. It was difficult for responsible politicians to envisage the day when Canada would have an existence free and independent from Great Britain, and at the same time be free and independent from the United States. And the schizophrenic internal core of Canada, especially visible in the later 1880s, made the conception of a real nation, built rationally, articulated clearly in a constitution, difficult to conceive. So Canada's view of herself was amorphous, floating, wisps of ideas, when something more substantial was needed.

The Liberal party offered another possibility: commercial union with the United States. This had been adopted by the new leader of the Liberal party, Wilfrid Laurier, as something new and different that would appeal to the voters and bring on the kind of low-tariff commercial prosperity that appealed to Liberal leaders. Laurier knew little or nothing about tariffs or trade. Tariffs are complicated, and one emerged from a wrestle with them dishevelled and only somewhat enlightened. Laurier did not like to be dishevelled. He did not approach questions the way Blake did, after hours of hard work in the Parliamentary Library. Laurier was more apt to sit down and think about them. There is lots to be said for thought; it certainly took less work.

Commercial union was a proposal for the obliteration of tariff barriers between Canada and the United States, basically for a common market between the two countries. It was a clear and unequivocal idea. The Liberals adopted it. There were some misgivings from the right wing of the party, and from Blake and Mackenzie, but none at all from the great free trade men, Cartwright and Mills. Laurier did not know or care about details. He wanted a clear policy and he got one.

Whatever advantages Canada might derive from a com-

LAYING OUT THE GRIT CAMPAIGN

mercial union with the United States — and there were some
advantages — the whole issue was soon obscured by political
overtones. The Americans themselves became interested in
commercial union almost from the first, as the major step
toward political union. What was worse for the Canadian
Liberals, they said so. It did not help when a commercial union
bill was introduced into the American Congress in December
1888, inviting the President of the United States to open negotiations, as a leading congressman Benjamin Butterworth put it,
"looking to the assimilating unity of the people of the Dominion
of Canada and the United States under one Government." It
did not get far in Congress but it did not have to. The Canadian
Conservatives were soon branding commercial union as annexa-
tionist. They said that those who wanted commercial union
were tadpoles; they swam now in Canadian water, but when
commercial union was adopted they would turn into frogs and
hop across the border. The Liberal Party and Liberal newspapers struggled manfully, and publicly, with commercial
union. Then they changed the name to "unrestricted reci-

A lithograph published on
the eve of the general election of 1891, which was
fought on the issue of
commercial union or un-
restricted reciprocity with
the United States. The
Conservatives contended
that either would be a first
step towards annexation,
and in the cartoon it will
be noted the Liberal
leaders are shown poring
over a "Map of the Cana-
dian States."

procity." It was a mouthful to start with, difficult to explain and not quite the same thing. It had one great virtue: it sounded nice, thus it appealed to Liberal voters. It had one great defect: the Americans wouldn't touch it. Commercial union interested them, unrestricted reciprocity did not. The very word "reciprocity" in the American Congress was a shout that brought out clouds of the crows and starlings, the lobby, who lived in Capitol Hill to defend the American tariff.

The Conservatives were not so foolish as to reject any possibility of reciprocity with the United States. They could cheerfully (and in outraged tones) denounce Liberal versions of reciprocity as commercial union leading to annexation; but any Canadian government, Liberal or Conservative, would have accepted at any time, from 1867 onward, an American offer of reciprocity in natural products. It was what Canadians had had in the Reciprocity Treaty from 1854 to 1866. The trouble was the Americans would not offer it. Instead, in 1890 they passed the McKinley Tariff, imposing new and higher duties on agricultural products imported into the United States. This was not very promising. At the same time James G. Blaine, the American Secretary of State, negotiated a reciprocity arrangement with Newfoundland, early in 1890. This proposed treaty mightily embarrassed the British, pleased the Newfoundlanders, and much annoyed the Canadians. The Canadians made representations to London, and to the chagrin of New-

Electric light and power came into use in the last decade of Macdonald's life. The first attempt to light a Canadian city with electricity was made in Victoria. Shown in this photograph is one of the three 150-foot masts erected in 1883, each of which carried a cluster of four or five arc lights. These were expected to light the whole centre of the city. Needless to say, this enterprising experiment was a failure.

foundland the treaty was blocked. The Canadians said, in
effect, Newfoundland could not have a reciprocity treaty with
the United States unless it included Canada too. There were
some Canadian negotiations in Washington, but Blaine was not
really interested. His scheme with Newfoundland had political
overtones, and unless Canada was interested in those he was
not going to bother.

Macdonald read American politics realistically. He never
liked bluster much from whatever source. Once in the early
1870s, Colonel John Gray, M.P. for Saint John, made a high-
toned, absurd speech against the United States, in reply to an
equally ridiculous one made by Zachariah Chandler in the U.S.
Senate against Great Britain. After Gray's speech, Macdonald
went into the lobby and said to a group of friends, "This is a
greater country than the United States, a much greater country

than the United States, and we've got a bigger fool than Chandler."[6]

The prognosis for general elections in 1891 or 1892 was perhaps less desperate than for 1887, but not as much preparation had been made, and Macdonald was probably forced to dissolve before he was quite ready to. The Langevin Affair was starting to build up ugly clouds on the eastern horizon. As early as November 29, 1890, *Grip* had a cartoon showing a wild storm coming. Sir Hector Langevin and Sir John were clutching their coats. "It's coming this way, Sir John," said Langevin fearfully, "but if we can manage to reach the General Election before it strikes — that's our only hope!" Macdonald had refused an enquiry about it but he knew it was coming. Then the discovery of the Farrer pamphlet clinched his determination to dissolve.

Edward Farrer was a brilliant, trenchant, if at times irresponsible writer at the Toronto *Globe*. He believed that Canada's destiny was union with the United States but he was sufficiently erratic, said Goldwin Smith, that if he "could get Canada into the United States tomorrow he would start next day to get her out." Farrer wrote a pamphlet for an American political friend, showing how American policies might be devised for driving Canada into annexation. The Conservatives got hold of the proof sheets. It was dynamite. It was nearly as good as a reciprocity treaty.

Macdonald thus met the Liberal position head-on. His position was quite unequivocal. He would not touch commercial union or unrestricted reciprocity. Both meant annexation and he was a Canadian first, last, and all the time. He put this in ringing terms: "a British subject I was born, and a British subject I will die. . . . the sooner the grass was growing over my grave the better rather than that I should see the degradation of the country which I have loved so much and which I have served for so long."[7] His contemporaries understood him perfectly, and cheered him to the echo. But few speeches of his have ever been more misunderstood by posterity. Posterity has been consistently fooled by the adjective "British," which for Macdonald in that context meant clearly "Canadian." He did not use "Canadian subject" because it had no meaning, legal or otherwise at that time. For Macdonald was nearly as critical of the British as he was of the Americans. He had no particular

206

THE OLD FLAG.
THE OLD POLICY,
THE OLD LEADER.

PUBLISHED BY THE INDUSTRIAL LEAGUE, FREDERIC NICHOLLS, HON. SEC.

Toronto Litho Co.

taste for "overwashed Englishmen"; he preferred salty men from Canada with brains and bite like John Henry Pope who came from the Eastern Townships. True, he was more tolerant than Langevin of the interminable delays and *lenteurs* that attended any negotiations in England. Langevin said that people complained sometimes of the Canadian civil servants; but, he added, they were lightning compared to those in London.

Macdonald, of course, had practically invented delay. But he had no patience with high-flown schemes like federation of the Empire, that talked of the greater glory of Empire, that talked big and said little of practical value. In 1884, when Britain got into trouble in the Sudan, he could see no point in helping Gladstone and Company out of the hole they had got into from their own stupidity. His attitude to Britain in Egypt in 1884 was not that far removed from that of Lester Pearson in 1956. He reined Tupper in sharply in 1889 when he made a speech in England on imperial federation, and insisted that Tupper should report it as a private statement, not one coming from the Canadian High Commissioner. Macdonald had two good reasons, French and English: Langevin was nervous about Tupper's position, and Macdonald thought it was nonsense.[8] Macdonald was nearly as much a Canadian nationalist as Thompson, and in 1890 supported Thompson's view that Canada should have exclusive right to deal with the copyright question and, like Thompson, wanted a Canadian judge on the Judicial Committee on the Privy Council to protect Dominion interests against the erosion they had subtained there as a result of decisions since 1883. In Macdonald's mind Britain was not at stake in 1891 or anything essentially British: it was Canada.

The election of 1891 was not an easy battle, and the lines were sharply drawn. Rarely had Canadians to vote on such sharply distinguished policies. Money was brought in. The Liberals got money from the United States; the Attorney-General of Nova Scotia brought in some on his way back from Kentucky, but not enough. The Conservatives got money from the CPR, "the Tory Government on wheels," as the Toronto *Globe* put it. The election was hard on Macdonald. It started in February, with polling day March 5th. He was taken ill in Napanee on February 25th, and then stayed with his brother-in-law in Kingston, who had been a widower for fifteen years and lived in a bare, comfortless house. There Macdonald was besieged by politicians who wanted to extract the last ounce of service from him. "Joe," he told Pope one cheerless February afternoon, "if you would know the depth of meanness of human nature, you have got to be a Prime Minister running a general election!"

The Conservatives polled a bigger percentage of the popular vote than in 1887. They slightly increased their popular support in every province but Ontario. What counted, however, was seats in Parliament and there the Macdonald government lost ground. Liberals picked up seats both in Quebec and Ontario. Macdonald's majority was now only twenty-seven seats.

Parliament met on April 29, 1891. The Liberals were full of ginger knowing that a shift of fourteen seats would put them in power, and with the McGreevy-Langevin Scandal hot and ready. Israel Tarte, that black-haired political genius, officially made his charges in the House on May 11th, and they went to committee to be heard. That might lose the government a few votes; but the early divisions of the House showed little government weakness yet. Macdonald's majority continued to hold.

The Liberals were not as strong as they seemed. Blake was out of Parliament, and there was a bitter quarrel between him and the party leaders over unrestricted reciprocity. Much of the quarrel was public. The party as a whole was uncomfortable over this split. Blake certainly had his crotchets; he was a neurotic, tense, unhappy person; *Grip* portrayed him as Hamlet, decisions trembling in the balance of his tortured mind. But he was widely respected as an honest, if awkward intellectual who faced difficult questions at great personal cost. Blake was never to sit in a Canadian Parliament again.

Parliament was not the same. Something like seventy of the M.P.s were new to the House after the 1891 election. Many of Macdonald's old friends had gone, mostly just too old to run in elections any more. One of Macdonald's greatest losses had occurred in 1888. Thomas White died suddenly on Saturday, April 21st, aged fifty-eight. "He had mastered the N-West and all its questions," Macdonald wrote sadly to Stephen, "and a life of usefulness seemed before him, when he was so suddenly cut down." On the following Monday the House had gathered wordlessly. "One by one the members took their places, the

John Macdonald
may 13, 88

Unfortunately this photograph of Macdonald has faded somewhat, but it is particularly interesting because it is signed and dated and was taken in his study at Earnscliffe. He was 73 in 1888.

little pages clustered with childish seriousness about the foot of the Speaker's Chair, the galleries too, full and quiet, and the purple and gold light poured through the tall windows."[9] Macdonald was too overcome to move the adjournment of the House; Langevin had to do it for him.

A year later John Henry Pope died after a long illness. It was an even more personal loss. No one in cabinet was ever as close to Macdonald as the rough-hewn, tough-minded, able, shrewd old curmudgeon from the Eastern Townships. Macdonald had known him since 1857. Pope once dismissed a long opposition charge in the House by getting up and saying simply, "There ain't nothin' to it." That Macdonald was fond of Pope tells much about Macdonald; he had little use for talk, and a lively appreciation of capacity.

Macdonald himself gradually recovered from his election illness, but it was slow, and at seventy-six years of age he had the right to be tired. The work never let up. Tupper saw him in April, just before going back to England. Macdonald looked wearily up from his papers and said, "I wish to God you were in my place." Tupper replied, "Thank God I am not."[10] When Parliament met, Macdonald appeared to be his jaunty old self, but the jauntiness was partly put on. Macdonald knew how old and tired he was. John Charlton, one of the Liberals who was forever agitating about legislating Sunday into a day of rest, walked across the floor of the Commons early in May, shook hands with Macdonald and asked after his health. Macdonald looked at Charlton with a wan smile. "My dear fellow," he said, "I feel I shall not trouble you long."[11]

The House grew a bit disorderly, as though party discipline had been eased off. "We sit every night now," wrote Thompson on May 22nd, "and have it hot in every sense of the word. Sir John is very well and bright again." The government was actually beaten on an unimportant division for the first time since coming to power in 1878. The old man felt it keenly. The defeat was the result of two ministerial dinners the same night, one at Chapleau's, the other at Dewdney's. Macdonald had even to come in from Earnscliffe to help hold the fort while the juniors were out feasting.

He continued to have his own dinners. Saturday night dinner parties during the session had been a long Earnscliffe tradition. Agnes held Saturday afternoon teas too. Sara Jeannette Duncan went to one of the latter in May 1888. A large good-natured mastiff was sunning himself in front of the door. The hall was large and old-fashioned and at the end was the drawing room, sunlit and comfortable, which looked out on the Ottawa River through pines and birches. At five o'clock tea was brought in, and occasionally Macdonald himself would leave affairs of state and come to chat with Agnes' visitors, "in the jocund fashion that brings, with his name, so ready a smile to the lips of his friends. I am bound to say," Sara Duncan went on, "that not many Liberal foes are to be seen within the portals of Earnscliffe." That would be Agnes' doing, more than Sir

Windsor Castle.

July 2. 1891.

Dear Lady Macdonald,

Though I have not the pleasure of knowing you personally, I am desirous of writing to express that I share most deeply in my deep sympathy with

OPPOSITE, TOP RIGHT Macdonald's body lying in state in the Senate Chamber of the Parliament Buildings. Thousands filed past the coffin when the Chamber was opened to the public.

TOP LEFT First page of the letter of condolence sent by Queen Victoria to Lady Macdonald shortly after Sir John's death. It concluded with a reference to the Barony that Lady Macdonald was about to receive: "It gives me much pleasure to mark my high sense of Sir John Macdonald's distinguished services by conferring on you a public mark of regard for yourself as well as for him."

BELOW The funeral procession leaving the Parliament Buildings on June 10, 1891. Sir John's body was taken by train to Kingston, where it lay in state a second time in the City Hall, after which it was buried in Cataraqui Cemetery beside the graves of his parents, his first wife and their infant son.

John's. In party matters she was more Conservative than the Prime Minister. If there were the usual tea party, Saturday afternoon, May 23, 1891, Macdonald did not come. He had a cabinet meeting, and came home for the dinner party at seven o'clock. He was in tremendous form that night at dinner. When Joseph Pope left Earnscliffe at ten o'clock, he really felt that the vigorous Macdonald of 1887 had been restored to them.

A week later it was a different story. While in bed recovering from a cold and a slight stroke, Macdonald was overtaken on Friday, May 29th, by a devastating stroke that in seconds had paralyzed his right side and bereft him of speech. Up at the House of Commons a lively debate was going on. Langevin suddenly received a message from the doctor, Sir James Grant. "I have just seen Sir John," it read, "haemorrhage into the brain. Condition quite hopeless. As you are next to the Chief, I thought well to send you this private note."[12] Langevin stared at it. He crossed the floor to tell Laurier, and in a voice so low and tremulous he could hardly be heard, announced it to a now silent House. The House at once adjourned. Langevin didn't move. He had worked with Macdonald for thirty-three years. He had served him loyally, had stood by him through thick and thin. Now he sat at his desk beside Macdonald's, the tears streaming down his face.

Macdonald died peacefully on Saturday, June 6, 1891. The extent of public feeling came as a great surprise to many hard-bitten newspapermen. He had acquired a tremendous hold upon the popular imagination. With some, the surprise was a personal sense of tragedy. David Creighton, the editor of the Toronto *Empire*, wrote to the Librarian of Parliament, "I have never realized till this how I have personally loved the old man."[13] The most glowing tribute came from no Conservative at all, but from the editor of a paper that had often vilified Macdonald, the Toronto *Globe*. John Willison had long watched Macdonald from the press gallery and in the fulness of his heart wrote this splendid eulogy:

> The young member was always noticed. The waverer was strengthened, and the wounded were healed. His appeals to party loyalty were always effective. His followers never failed to laugh when he joked. They always cheered his appeals. They always warmed into enthusiasm when he pointed to his majority in the House and in the country, and

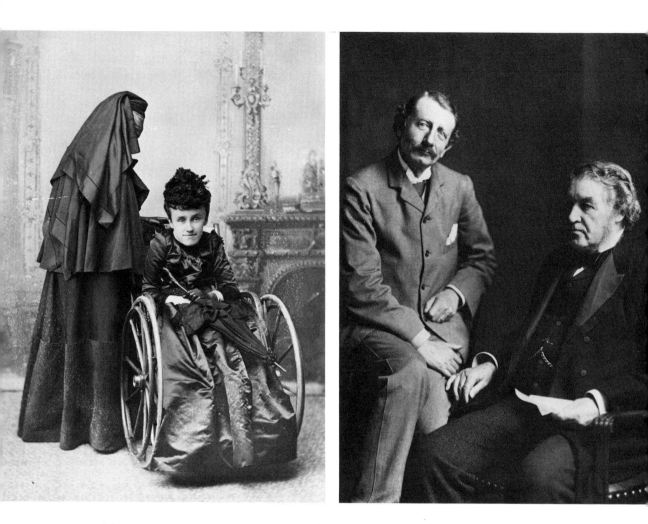

to the record of his achievements. The Conservatives in Parliament and in the constituencies loved Sir John Macdonald, and few men who had ever followed him could withstand his personal appeal. He had won great victories for his party, he had led them to triumph again and again, and they were grateful and loyal to the end, and mourned for him as for one taken out from their very households.[14]

Macdonald was not a saint and it will do no good to make him one. He continued to drink and occasionally would make an ass of himself long after 1873. He loved a good story. He regaled Lord Lansdowne, who had had to leave Canada for less interesting places like India, with George Foster's matrimonial adventures. You know Foster, said Macdonald. Serious, non-drinker, a shy, rather lugubrious schoolmaster, who became Minister of Marine and Fisheries in 1885. He fell in love with his Ottawa landlady, Mrs. Addie Chisholm, whose husband had deserted her some years before. She got an Illinois divorce, one of those where the train stops twenty minutes for refreshments, and fifteen minutes for divorces. Foster married her there. They came back to Ottawa as man and wife but they weren't, not by Canadian law. They will be ignored by Ottawa society, said Macdonald, and Foster has ruined a promising career. "But as Sir Matthew Hale long ago said, 'There is no wisdom below the belt.' "[15]

Macdonald's prognosis was wrong. Foster survived happily. Lady Aberdeen in 1893 decided that the nonsense had gone on long enough and actually admitted Addie Chisholm Foster to Government House. After Addie died in 1918, Foster married again at the age of seventy-three. Perhaps Macdonald's estimate of the fate of Foster was an indication of his own timidity, socially and perhaps even politically. Macdonald could never have done what Foster did. "He was always timid and yielding," T. C. Patteson suggested, "and if he has ever taken a bold stand I think it was because he had a bold man at his elbow at the time."[16]

He was at times wickedly partisan. The outrageous parliamentary redistribution of 1882 was typical of this side of him. So was the Franchise Act of 1885. It was hard for Liberals to forgive. Some of his actions were hard for anyone to forgive. Joseph Rymal, at the time the wit of the House, was driven from Parliament by the gerrymander of 1882. "We meant to make you howl," said Macdonald wickedly. The trouble was that his political success blinded men to what were the real as opposed to the obvious elements in it. He was unabashedly partisan in getting into power and staying there. But the politics he administered were with few exceptions large and generously conceived. G. M. Grant once said of him, "His mind has windows in it all round." He may never have quite understood the West; he left Quebec to Cartier, then Langevin and Chapleau; but he understood men, and many in their turn loved him.

His greatest gifts to Canada were his intelligence and his tolerance, and his remarkable ability to recognize capacity in others. His intelligence was large and refreshing, and he had an extraordinarily well-stocked mind. T. C. Patteson, five years after his comment quoted above, got into a literary argument with some friends in Toronto and naturally turned to the Prime

OPPOSITE RIGHT Hugh John Macdonald, son of Sir John, with Sir Charles Tupper, photographed in 1896, when Hugh John was Minister of the Interior in the short-lived Tupper administration. He was elected to Parliament in 1891 and for a few weeks thus shared membership in the House of Commons with his father. Later he turned to provincial politics and was Premier of Manitoba in 1900. He was knighted in 1913.

Minister of Canada. "What is the next line to, 'Ye gentlemen of England who sit at home at ease'? Please endorse answer." And on the back of the note is written, in Macdonald's neat, flowing hand, "Ah, little do you think upon the dangers of the seas." This was in January 1890. There the letter sits, in the Patteson Papers in Toronto, a curious comment on Macdonald's range of literary knowledge. He once quoted at Martin Griffin, the Parliamentary Librarian, a story about the Duchess of Newcastle (she died about 1673), when asked by a minister to nominate a particular candidate for one of her boroughs. She replied, "I have been bullied by a usurper [Cromwell], oppressed by a King [Charles II], but I won't be ridden by a lackey. Your man shan't stand." Macdonald sent a note a month later to say that he had himself found the source of the story, in the letters of Horace Walpole. One had the impression, as A. W. McLelan of Nova Scotia told him once, that there were wheels in his head that had not even been moved yet.

His was a mind of infinite variety, richly endowed, fertile in expedients; he was impatient of mere words; he distrusted emotion; his cynicism, if that is the word, was but the astringent necessary to clear his mind of cant, to be able to focus it sharply upon the world, and upon men as they really were. His greatness lay not only in his instinct for the time and place for new political departures, an instinct which anyway worked better in opposition than in power; his greatness lay still more in his grasp of the means by which these changes might be realized. Visionaries like Howe or Galt were, perhaps, less rare than a man like Macdonald who, when at last finally and reluctantly convinced that change was necessary, grappled with realities not always very scrupulously, for the means by which it could be achieved. If at times he bullied the provinces, or frequently forgot there was more to Canada than the Dominion government and the Conservative party, or was never too delicate about the use of money at elections or about patronage: if all those things that can be legitimately set against him are set, nevertheless his intelligence, generosity, patience and shrewd common sense were a splendid endowment for a young country and for its expansive future that was already coming into sight. And as Agnes would surely have agreed, he was, and he is, tremendous company.

Notes

Chapter 1

1. Public Archives of Ontario, T. C. Patteson Papers, John A. Macdonald to Patteson, February 16, 1876 (confidential); January 18, 1878.
2. J. K. Johnson has published a most useful paper on this subject, "John A. Macdonald, the young non-politician," in the Canadian Historical Association, *Historical Papers*, 1971. Professor Johnson has also edited three volumes of Macdonald's letters, and very well done they are too: *The letters of Sir John A. Macdonald 1836-1857* (Ottawa: Queen's Printer, 1968); *The letters of Sir John A. Macdonald 1858-1861* (Ottawa: Queen's Printer, 1969); and *Affectionately yours: the letters of Sir John A. Macdonald and his family* (Toronto: Macmillan, 1969).
3. This was published in the Kingston *Herald*, April 23, 1844. See J. K. Johnson (ed.), *The letters of Sir John A. Macdonald 1836-1857*, p. 12.
4. Macdonald to James R. Gowan, March 12, 1861, cited in *The letters of Sir John A. Macdonald 1858-1861*, p. 312.
5. Macdonald to James Strachan, February 9, 1854, cited in *The letters of Sir John A. Macdonald 1836-1857*, p. 202.

Chapter 2

1. Public Archives of Canada, Sir John Thompson Papers, Vol. 288, Thompson to Annie Thompson, November 3, 1885. Whenever Thompson and his wife were away from each other they wrote every day, and their correspondence, by remarkable luck, has been almost completely preserved.
2. Judith Fingard, "A winter's tale: the seasonal contours of colonial poverty," given to the Canadian Historical Association at its 1974 meeting, and, presumably, to be published in the Association's *Historical Papers*, 1974.
3. *Canadian Illustrated News*, February 10, 1872.
4. PAC, Sir John Thompson Papers, Vol. 24, Francis Cunningham to Thompson, January 26, 1882; Vol. 25, March 13, 1882.
5. Maurice Pope (ed.), *Public servant: the memoirs of Sir Joseph Pope* (Toronto: Oxford University Press, 1960), p. 38. Sir Joseph Pope was Macdonald's private secretary from 1882 until 1891, and has written extensively and well about his old chief. See the bibliographical note at the end of the book.
6. University of Western Ontario, James Coyne Papers, Hugh John Macdonald to Coyne, December 15, 1871.

Chapter 3

1. Queen's University, Williamson Papers, Agnes Macdonald to James Williamson, July 15 [1894].

2. Maurice Pope (ed.), *Public servant: the memoirs of Sir Joseph Pope*, pp. 60, 156.
3. D. G. Creighton, *The road to Confederation* (Toronto: Macmillan, 1964), pp. 60-1. Probably the finest biography written in Canada is Professor Creighton's of Sir John A. Macdonald. It is discussed briefly in the bibliography at the back of the book.
4. G. E. Marindin (ed.), *Letters of Frederic, Lord Blachford . . . 1860-1871* (London: John Murray, 1896), pp. 301-2. This letter is also cited in Creighton's *Road to Confederation*, pp. 420-1.
5. Public Archives of British Columbia, Crease Papers, Musgrave to Crease, August 8, 1870. This letter is cited in Margaret Ormsby, *British Columbia: a history* (Toronto: Macmillan, 1958), pp. 247-8.

Chapter 4
1. Macdonald to Alexander Morris, April 21, 1871 (private and confidential), from Washington, in Joseph Pope (ed.), *The correspondence of Sir John Macdonald* (Toronto: Oxford University Press, 1921), pp. 145-6.
2. *Grip*, Toronto, July 14, 1877. I have altered the punctuation in this passage. It was elaborately designed to give "Little Canada" lisping talk.
3. Public Archives of Ontario, Alexander Campbell Papers, Box 3, Macdonald to J. S. McCuaig, August 14, 1872 (private), from Toronto.
4. *Ibid.*, C. J. Campbell to his brother, Alexander Campbell, August 22, 1872, from Toronto.
5. *Canadian Illustrated News*, January 3, 1874.
6. Public Archives of Canada, Sir Joseph Pope Papers, Vol. 2, Andrew Holland to Pope, October 26, 1914.
7. Archives Publiques de Québec, Collection Chapais, Papiers Langevin, Boîte 8, Cartier to Langevin, 20 février 1873, privée. (My own translation of Cartier's French.)
8. There are two interesting and sympathetic articles on French-Canadian life in *The Week*, Toronto, March 31 and April 7, 1887, by "G.C.C.," which draw many contrasts between rural life in Ontario and Quebec.
9. Joseph Schull, *Laurier* (Toronto: Macmillan, 1965), p. 124.
10. J. Barnard, *Mémoires Chapais* (Montréal: Fides, 1961-64), I, 55, Thomas Chapais to his sister Georgette, 16 novembre 1877. This splendid letter should really be read in French, but I have tried to preserve something of its spirit.
11. This fanciful reminiscence comes from S. J. Dawson, M.P. Algoma, Ontario, in Canada, House of Commons, *Debates, 1880-1881*, p. 405 (January 12, 1881).

Chapter 5
1. *Grip*, Toronto, October 7, 1876; November 4, 1876; November 1, 1890.

2. *The Bystander*, Toronto, new series, January, 1883.
3. *Grip*, Toronto, November 4, 1876.
4. J. W. Bengough recounted this after Macdonald's death, in *Grip*, June 13, 1891.
5. Canada, *Sessional Papers, 1895*, No. 21, "Report of the Royal Commission on the Liquor Traffic in Canada," p. 100.
6. See especially the recollection of James H. Gray, who quotes the song in full, *The Boy from Winnipeg* (Toronto: Macmillan, 1970), pp. 28-9.
7. Canada, House of Commons, *Debates, 1880*, 1149 (April 6, 1880).
8. The Armstrong Royal Commission on the relations of Labour and Capital in Canada was established in December, 1886. Its report was published in 1889. The evidence was very extensive, and was published both in the newspapers of the time, and by the government. It is about 5,000 pages long. It has been recently abridged and published by Greg Kealey, *Canada investigates industrialism: the Royal Commission of the relations of labour and capital, 1889* (Toronto, 1973). The reference is to p. 304.

Chapter 6
1. Quoted by T. M. Daly, the Minister of the Interior, Canada House of Commons, *Debates, 1889*, 377 (February 28, 1889).
2. George Grant recounted his 1883 experiences in the West in a series of articles in *The Week*, Toronto, beginning December 18, 1883, entitled, "The C.P.R., by the Kicking Horse Pass and the Selkirks." This argument is taken from his Article II, December 27, 1883. The whole series has been shortened and reprinted with photographs and maps, in *Canada, an Historical Magazine*, over three issues, Vol. 1, No. 1 (Autumn, 1973) to Vol. I, No. 3 (Spring, 1974).
3. Hugh Dempsey, *Crowfoot, Chief of the Blackfeet* (Edmonton: Hurtig, 1972), p. 89. A fine biography of a great chief.
4. *Ibid.*, p. 134.
5. Canada, *Sessional Papers, 1895*, No. 21, "Report of the Royal Commission on the Liquor Traffic in Canada," p. 197; also James H. Gray's book, *Booze; the impact of whisky on the Prairie West* (Toronto: Macmillan, 1972), p. 35.
6. J. H. E. Secretan, *Canada's great highway* (London: John Lane, 1924), pp. 39-40.
7. Public Archives of Canada, Lansdowne Papers, Macdonald to Lansdowne, September 28, 1889. Lord Lansdowne had been Governor-General of Canada 1883-1887, and was now in India.
8. University of King's College, Halifax, Bliss Carman Papers, Carman to his sister Nancy, April 14, 1892, from New York.
9. Public Archives of Canada, Sir Charles Tupper Papers, Vol. 7, Macdonald to Tupper, June 21, 1886, private, from Ottawa.
10. Public Archives of Canada, Sir John Thompson Papers, Vol. 289, Thompson to his wife Annie, June 26, 1886, from Ottawa.

Chapter 7

1. This whole description of Macdonald's campaign in Ontario in the fall of 1886 is given with great verve by John Thompson in a series of letters to his wife, written from trains and hotel rooms over these weeks. See Vol. 289, Thompson Papers, Public Archives of Canada.
2. Public Archives of Ontario, T. C. Patteson Papers, Alexander Campbell to Patteson, August 8, 1885, private and confidential, from Newport, Rhode Island.
3. Public Archives of Canada, H. H. Smith Papers, Macdonald to Smith, September 29, 1882, private; same, October 17, 1882, private and confidential.
4. Public Archives of Canada, Macdonald Papers, Vol. 186, Macdonald's endorsement on the letter of the four Toronto M.P.s of November 1, 1880. For Bowell's correspondence see Vol. 189, Bowell to Macdonald, December 9, 1880, private; same, December 27, 1882, private.
5. Public Archives of Canada, Macdonald Papers, Vol. 205, Chapleau to Macdonald, October 31, 1886, private and confidential; same, January 13, 1887, private; same, January 15, 1887; same, January 20, 1887; Macdonald to Chapleau, January 21, 1887, private and confidential (draft).
6. University of Toronto Library, Charlton Papers, "Reminiscences," p. 639.
7. Toronto *Empire*, February 18, 1891, reporting Macdonald's speech of February 17th.
8. Public Archives of Canada, Sir Charles Tupper Papers, Vol. 8, Macdonald to Tupper, August 14, 1889, private, from Rivière du Loup; Tupper to Charles Hibbert Tupper, September 14, 1889; Macdonald to Tupper, September 28, 1889.
9. *The Week*, Toronto, April 26, 1888, "Ottawa letter," by Sara Jeannette Duncan.
10. Public Archives of Canada, Sir Charles Tupper Papers, Vol. 9, Tupper to C. H. Tupper, June 4, 1891, from Vienna.
11. University of Toronto Library, Charlton Papers, "Reminiscences," p. 636.
12. Archives Publiques du Québec, Collection Chapais, Papiers Langevin, Boîte 17, Grant to Langevin, May 29, 1891, private.
13. Public Archives of Canada, Martin Griffin Papers, Creighton to Griffin, June 2, 1891.
14. Toronto *Globe*, June 8, 1891. This was reprinted almost without change in Sir John Willison's *Sir Wilfrid Laurier and the Liberal party* (Toronto: G. N. Morang, 1903), 2 vols., II, 19.
15. Public Archives of Canada, Lord Lansdowne Papers, Macdonald to Lansdowne, September 28, 1889 (microfilm).
16. Public Archives of Ontario, Sir Alexander Campbell Papers, T. C. Patteson to Campbell, August 11, 1885, private.

Bibliography

ANY FURTHER READING on Macdonald and his times has really to begin with the great biography of Macdonald, D. G. Creighton's two-volume masterpiece *John A. Macdonald, the young politician* and *John A. Macdonald, the old chieftain* (Toronto: Macmillan, 1952, 1955). Sympathetic to Macdonald it is indeed; some have said too much so: but it is written with great style and from a splendid fund of research. At times it is brilliant. Read, for example, the description of Macdonald at the Stone Mills tavern in 1851 (I, 172-3) or Macdonald as a good two-bottle man (II, 249-52).

A younger Macdonald scholar, and newer to the scene, is J. K. Johnson who has skilfully edited three books of Macdonald letters and has contributed greatly to our knowledge of the legal and business side to Macdonald's career. Professor Johnson's works are cited in full in the notes to Chapter 1.

Macdonald's private secretary from 1882 to 1891 was Joseph Pope (1854-1926) who was afterwards Under-Secretary of State, and who published in 1894 the first substantial study of Macdonald under the title *The Memoirs of the Right Honourable Sir John Alexander Macdonald*. Although Pope believed that it was too early, in 1894 to write the definitive biography (one reason for the title he chose), nevertheless the Pope biography remained the standard work on Macdonald until Donald Creighton's in the 1950s. Sir Joseph Pope also published in 1915 a short, attractive and rather neglected little biography *The Day of Sir John Macdonald*, as Volume 29 in the "Chronicles of Canada" series. Even more important, and still good reading, is *The Correspondence of Sir John Macdonald* (Toronto: Oxford University Press, 1921). Sir Joseph Pope's own memoirs are most interesting and were published by his son Maurice Pope, *Public Servant: the Memoirs of Sir Joseph Pope* (Toronto: Oxford University Press, 1960).

The late nineteenth century is rich in other reminiscences. Sir Richard Cartwright's *Reminiscences* (Toronto: Wm. Briggs, 1912) is at times almost apoplectic in dislike of Macdonald, but Cartwright should not be dismissed merely as a sorehead. Any fair account of Macdonald has to take account of him. More judicious and attractive are Sir John Willison's *Reminiscences, political and personal* (Toronto: McClelland & Stewart, 1919); G. H. Ham's *Reminiscences of a Raconteur* ... (Toronto: Musson, 1921); and Hector Charlesworth's attractive series beginning with his *Candid Chronicles* (Toronto: Macmillan, 1925). Those who read French will like J. Barnard's *Mémoires Chapais*, 3 vols. (Montréal: Fides, 1961-64) and, from the Liberal side, Charles Langelier's *Souvenirs politiques, 1878-1900*, 2 vols. (Québec: Dussault et Proulx, 1909). Other books appear in the notes.

There are, of course, a number of good biographies of other famous figures of the period, of George Brown, Alexander Mackenzie and Wilfrid Laurier. All are mentioned in a large critical bibliography for this period in my *Arduous Destiny: Canada, 1874-1896* (Toronto: McClelland & Stewart, 1971). I have also cited a number of articles there, as well as theses; these take the reader out to the frontiers of the most recent research. One attractive article that should be mentioned here is not new, but old, and well worth anyone's time, Norman Ward's "The formative years of the House of Commons, 1867-1891" in the *Canadian Journal of Economics and Political Science*, Vol. 18, No. 4 (November, 1952). Hugh Stevenson presents an illustrated and entertaining article on Hugh John Macdonald, Macdonald's son, in "The Prime Minister's son goes west" in the *Beaver*, Winter 1963, pp. 32-43.

As for the periodicals in Macdonald's time, the notes and comments in this book will surely suggest the fun to be had in *Grip*; but there are also *The Week*, the *Canadian Monthly*, the *Canadian Illustrated News*, the *Bystander*, to say nothing of 250 or more newspapers that provide a quite inexhaustible source for the times of Sir John Macdonald.

Index